THE NATIONAL MALL

THE JOHNS HOPKINS UNIVERSITY PRESS *Baltimore*

The NATIONAL

RETHINKING WASHINGTON'S MONUMENTAL CORE

MALL

Edited by Nathan Glazer and Cynthia R. Field

FOREWORD BY JAMES F. COOPER

This volume was organized at the Newington-Cropsey Cultural Studies Center by
Programs Director: Sandra L. Sanderson
Project Editor: James Leggio
Photography Consultant: Maggie Berkvist
Research Assistant: Karen Mulder

The Johns Hopkins University Press
2715 North Charles Street
Baltimore, Maryland 21218-4363
www.press.jhu.edu

Library of Congress Cataloging-in-Publication Data

The National Mall : rethinking Washington's
monumental core / edited by Nathan Glazer and
Cynthia R. Field, foreword by James F. Cooper.
p. cm.
Includes bibliographical references and index.
ISBN-13: 978-0-8018-8805-2 (hardcover : alk. paper)
ISBN-10: 0-8018-8805-0 (hardcover : alk. paper)
1. Mall, The (Washington, D.C.) 2. Washington
(D.C.)—Buildings, structures, etc. 3. Landscape
protection—Washington (D.C.) 4. City planning—
Washington (D.C.) 5. Memorials—Social aspects—
United States. 6. Monuments—Social aspects—
United States. 7. Public spaces—Social aspects—
United States. 8. Landscape protection—United
States—Case studies. 9. Aesthetics, American—
Case studies. 10. City planning—United States—
Case studies. I. Glazer, Nathan. II. Field,
Cynthia R.
  F203.5.M2M35   2008
    975.3—dc22   2007034001

An earlier version of the essay by Richard Kurin was
previously published in different form in his *Smithsonian Folklife Festival: Culture of, by, and for the People*
(Washington, D.C.: Smithsonian Institution, 1998).

"A Simple Space of Turf" copyright © Witold
Rybczynski

*Special discounts are available for bulk purchases of this
book. For more information, please contact Special Sales at
410-516-6936 or specialsales@press.jhu.edu.*

The Johns Hopkins University Press uses environmen-
tally friendly book materials, including recycled text
paper that is composed of at least 30 percent post-
consumer waste, whenever possible. All of our book
papers are acid-free, and our jackets and covers are
printed on paper with recycled content.

Contents

THE SYMBIOTIC RELATIONSHIP between a civilization and its culture is most fervently displayed at the center of a national sacred place. Over the last two centuries, the National Mall in Washington has become a locus of memory and meaning, a center of our collective history and art. *The National Mall and the Nation: Rethinking Washington's Monumental Core* explores the significance of this venerable space, past, present, and future, and considers how we can best guide the sometimes conflicting demands of preservation and growth. In sponsoring this collection of essays, the Newington-Cropsey Cultural Studies Center continues to fulfill its mission to preserve the best of the past as the essential foundation of future achievement. Through a variety of multidisciplinary projects over the last two decades, the Center has explored the idea that the arts are a perennial resource in sustaining and advancing civilization.

The authors we invited to contribute to this book bring varied perspectives as historians and art historians, architects and anthropologists. Over the years, the Mall has become a place of national pilgrimage, and some of our writers consider the civic rituals and public celebrations, the protests, marches, rallies, and festivals that bring the space to life. Others focus on the Mall as built environment. Buildings and monuments, landscapes and public gatherings— all bear witness to how intimately this space is linked to the nation's spiritual roots and history. The image of the Mall that emerges from this book honors, we believe, the richness and complexity of its history and its promise for the future.

The Mall is both a living monument and a work in progress. From the beginning, the design of Washington was a project with both aesthetic and civic imperatives. George Washington and Pierre L'Enfant envisioned a capital city that would embody the fledgling Republic's ideals. In 1902, on the crest of the city beautiful movement, the McMillan Commission laid out an ambitious new plan that acknowledged the growth of the nation and established a framework for the development of its public space. The beginning of the twenty-first century marks an auspicious moment in the history of the Mall. Its importance to a wide range of Americans has been dramatized by controversies over recent projects such as the World War II Memorial and the National Museum of the American Indian, perhaps the last component of the Smithsonian Institution to be built on the Mall itself.

Foreword

The Capital Planning Commission and the National Coalition to Save Our Mall are two organizations that play essential roles in considering the future direction of our most important civic space. The Mall is physically finite, and its artistic integrity is precious. New architecture and memorial projects over the last decade have prompted concerns about stylistic purity and overcrowding. While much of the debate has focused on the relative merits of one style or another, there is a more fundamental issue: How can we respect the past yet serve the coming generations?

Taken in its entirety, the Mall can be viewed as a work of art. Though it is subject to several different disciplines and constituencies, it nonetheless constitutes an artistic whole, not simply a conglomerate of parts responding to special interests. Like the Forum in ancient Rome, it is a place of public gathering as well as a political and sacred space. The way the Mall evolves to meet this unique mixture of public needs will reflect how we see ourselves as a people, giving shape to our national goals and individual aspirations. If the twenty-first-century stewards of the Mall approach their responsibilities with scholarship, respect, and imagination, we can ensure the vitality of Washington's monumental core.

I thank our coeditors, Nathan Glazer and Cynthia Field, and all the scholars who contributed to this exciting project. This book would not have been possible without the tireless efforts of the Center's programs director, Sandra Sanderson, who deftly brought together all the disparate elements of historical scholarship, photography research, and prepress production. Last, I express my gratitude to James Leggio and Maggie Berkvist, who guided us through the intricacies of this project with professionalism, wisdom, and wit.

JAMES F. COOPER
Director
The Newington-Cropsey Cultural Studies Center, New York

THE NATIONAL MALL

Introduction
Nathan Glazer

❦ THE MALL IN WASHINGTON is the most cherished tract of urban public land in the United States. Stretching from the Capitol to the Lincoln Memorial, it is the defining center of ceremonial and public Washington. The major sights and museums and memorials are clustered there, every visitor goes there, and many do not venture far from it. It is a remarkable and uniquely American creation, but it took a hundred years of aborted efforts and misguided interventions before the plan that defines it as it is today emerged and a good part of another hundred years before most of the plan was realized.

The guiding plan was the work of the Senate Park Commission, also known as the McMillan Commission, after the senator from Michigan who chaired the Committee on the District of Columbia and who, with a Senate resolution in March 1901, created the commission to prepare a park improvement plan for the district, rethinking and greatly expanding the general plan devised by Pierre Charles L'Enfant a century before. Daniel Burnham, the Chicago architect and city planner who had been the chief organizer of the very successful World's Columbian Exposition in Chicago in 1893, was asked to serve on the commission along with the young landscape architect Frederick Law Olmsted Jr. Burnham and Olmsted asked two other members of the Chicago fair group to join them, the architect Charles Follen McKim, of the leading architectural firm McKim, Mead & White, and the sculptor Augustus Saint-Gaudens. These four men were the commission.

In less than a year, the plan that was to shape the future of the Mall in Washington sprang forth whole, in models, drawings, perspectives, and a written report, all presented in Washington at the beginning of 1902. In terms of influence, this was to be one of the most successful large planning proposals in history, certainly in American history. That the plan was produced in less than a year by three busy men located in different cities (Saint-Gaudens was not able to participate fully in the work of the group), who had to use railroads to meet each other, who communicated by letter, telegraph, and early telephone, and who were able to take seven weeks off to travel in Europe to review its major cities and parks, is itself a remarkable achievement. Those of us who live in an age dependent on e-mail and airplanes can only wonder at their energy and decisiveness.

The work of the McMillan Commission forms the subject of part 1 of this book. As a prelude to that, Michael J. Lewis describes, as best it can be discerned, the original intent for the Mall of Pierre L'Enfant, the planner of Washington, D.C. L'Enfant had been appointed by George Washington during his first presidential term, and his conception for the axis that forms the Mall may have been inspired by a sketch by Thomas Jefferson. The Mall is thus linked at its origins with two of the giant figures of the American founding. Its realization differed from L'Enfant's conception, however, and Lewis sketches

the misadventures of the proposed Mall during the nineteenth century, describes how the original plan, extended, reworked, reconceived, became the model for the building and shaping of the Mall for the next hundred years.

Charles Follen McKim is the major subject of the essay by Richard Guy Wilson, the authority on the "American Renaissance" of the turn of the century. This period has left behind many of the monumental buildings that shaped the American city. The dominantly Roman forms of the sketches and models of the McMillan Plan can be traced to McKim's taste, and they controlled what was built on the Mall for the next forty years. In her essay, Cynthia Field examines the role of Daniel Burnham, that odd but remarkably influential figure who was inspired by the vision of bringing beauty, form, and dignity to the American city. He has recently been brought to the attention of a much larger audience by Erik Larson's widely read novel on the 1893 Chicago world's fair, *The Devil in the White City*.

For the most distinctive feature of the Mall, the wide strip of turf, neither avenue nor park, that runs down its center, we must go to the third figure of the commission, the landscape architect Frederick Law Olmsted Jr., the subject of the essay by Witold Rybczynski. Olmsted was the son of and successor to the maker of Central Park, the founding figure in the history of American landscape architecture, who has left his stamp on the American landscape from Stanford to Boston and many places between. The younger Olmsted was himself a major figure in the development and institutionalization of an American landscape architecture and was the creator of the first professional program in the field, at Harvard University. The connection to his father's plan for New York's Central Park, Rybczynski shows, is more than biographical. The Mall thus picks up and joins numerous threads of the American founding and history, political and aesthetic.

Whatever the inspiration Burnham, McKim, and Olmsted gained from their seven-week trip to the great cities of Europe in 1901 and whatever their commitment to the classical ideal (there were hardly any alternatives at the time), the Mall they proposed and designed on their return bore a strong and distinctive American stamp. Their model was sober Rome rather than the extravagant elaborations of classical forms they had seen in Paris. They did not propose a great avenue or boulevard or a presidential park or a huge ceremonial square: the vistas in their plan featured no palaces, churches, or men on horseback. The Mall the commissioners designed may have been imperial in its intentions: America was in an imperial mood in the wake of the Spanish-American War, with new colonial possessions, and with Theodore Roosevelt as president. But the Mall could not be anything but democratic, with its origin in the Capitol of the world's greatest democracy, its midpoint in the giant, unadorned obelisk to Washington, and its conclusion in a memorial to Abraham Lincoln that the commissioners proposed and that was built in remarkably short order, as these things go in America. The most distinctive characteristic of the Mall, as Burnham, McKim, and Olmsted designed it, was that it be a "broad and simple space of turf," with all its potential associations

with the great, wide-open spaces of America, as Michael Lewis notes.

While no part of the original design, or indeed of the redesign and reconception at the beginning of the twentieth century, the Mall has become, as part 2 demonstrates, "the nation's gathering place," for purposes grand and solemn, as well as popular and political and, yes, populist. Edith Turner, an anthropologist, brings to our attention the various ways, in different cultures and societies, by which places become sacred and solemn, inspiring awe and respect. Clearly, the Mall is our American version of such a place. Frederick Turner reminds us of the various meanings and markings of places of pilgrimage; a visit to the Mall, with its inspiring monuments to the founders and savior of the American Republic, certainly qualifies as such a place of pilgrimage. Turner ponders how we should take account of this distinctive role in our thinking about the Mall and its future by bringing to our attention the various functions of places of pilgrimage and how they shape a space. Richard Kurin describes more popular uses of the Mall, illustrating how it is regularly transformed into a fairground celebrating the cultures of the world and the various regions of the United States, which in itself holds almost a world of different cultures.

But this use as a fairground and as a gathering place for protest and celebration threatens some central features of the Mall. In part 3 we describe the problems that we face in preserving what has become our central ceremonial space at the beginning of its third century.

The building of the World War II Memorial and the conflicts around its placement and design, the recent decision to site the National Museum of African American History and Culture on the last bit of available museum space on the Mall, the plan to build a monument to President Eisenhower adjacent to the Mall, and the lineup of proposals for other more-than-worthy monuments and museums that will certainly have advocates demanding a presence on the Mall—these developments will continue to challenge the preservation of the Mall in the coming decades. But along with the controversies over presence and siting is the further issue of design. In an age when all certainties in art and building have been overthrown and when advanced and admired art takes forms never dreamed of when the Mall was designed, what can our future museums and memorials be, and how can we determine what they should be? This is the theme of my essay, which takes up the challenge posed by the "shootout on the Mall" in the 1930s over the monument to Thomas Jefferson. Of course it was going to be Roman, as Burnham and McKim and Olmsted would certainly have expected, but then the arts establishment exploded in protest, and classicism was banned from the Mall, it was thought, forever.

The people's meeting ground, the place of pilgrimage, where we honor our monumental efforts in war and the great men who have shaped our country—but how? With what emblems and symbols do we move and reach the people who want to erect these memorials? What means are available to us? What traditions, if any?

And then, why on the Mall? Can we consider it completed, indeed more than completed as monuments never intended or foreseen by its designers now crowd in on it, as more extensions and visitor centers are proposed for every memorial, and ever more monuments and memorials that will require their own array of service buildings are proposed. The requirements for security that have become so urgent since the disaster of September 11, 2001, raise new problems of design and crowding. What kind of protection must we have, of what design, with what effect on the pilgrims coming to the monuments and memorials, as they are squeezed perhaps into underground tunnels, distanced by new protective structures?

These are the problems brought up by Judy Scott Feldman and Patricia E. Gallagher. There are excellent plans to hold up further building on the Mall, but how can they be made to prevail in a democracy where the people, and the people's representatives, rule?

The creation of the present-day Mall was and is a remarkable demonstration of how a pluralist democracy can plan and build, even without an imperial president or other decisive authority. The plan was not enshrined in legislation; no Congress or president decreed that the McMillan Plan should be implemented; no money was appropriated for the plan as such. The money came piecemeal and slowly, for one project after another, much of it from individuals and the public, but the projects remained more or less in line with the plan as the decades proceeded. A hundred years later, the plan was for the most part realized.

The great question following the centenary of the presentation of the McMillan Plan is, what now? As the last places for major museums are filled; as monuments begin to intrude on the great swath of turf that distinguishes the Mall; as new projects for museums, memorials, and monuments are urgently proposed and demanded; as new challenges never dreamed of one hundred years ago have to be met—what will become of the plan's cogent and compelling design?

Much of this book looks ahead to these new issues and new problems facing the Mall. Such questions also require us to look backward, however, to see what we can learn from the revolution in architecture, in design and public imagery, and in national self-understanding that has taken place over the decades that the McMillan Plan was being implemented.

Halfway through the course of the plan's realization, something very radical happened in how we think about architecture and design. The classical tradition, which had pretty much defined what great public building should be for two thousand years, and certainly defined what was thought should be the character of America's major public buildings, was suddenly upended by the rise of modernism. Over the course of the twentieth century, our sense of our own history also changed shape, and we had to think not only of Washington, Lincoln, and Jefferson but also of the legacy of slavery, the fate of the American Indian, the role of women in American history, and even— though it is not strictly within our nation's own history—of the Holocaust.

In the period after the presentation of the McMillan Plan, Washington saw the construction of numerous buildings in an urbane but generalized classicizing style. The building project proposed by the plan began self-confidently with the grand

Union Station, went on to the domed Museum of Natural History, and climaxed with the domed National Gallery of Art. But then John Russell Pope, who had designed the sublime National Gallery of Art, was given the commission to design the Jefferson Memorial, one of the major defining elements of the McMillan Plan. It is the southern anchor, matching the White House to the north, of a north-south axis, crossing the main east-west axis defined by the Capitol and the Lincoln Memorial. Pope came up of course with another domed structure, another of the numerous progeny of the Pantheon in Rome. The world of modernism, architects and critics, erupted in protest: this was not the way Jefferson should be memorialized in the 1930s, they claimed. Pope's design was built in the end, but it was the last classical building to grace the Mall and its environs. Afterward came the flat-roofed Museum of American History, the flat-roofed National Air and Space Museum, the donut of the Hirshhorn Museum, the riot of triangles that is the East Building of the National Gallery of Art. But in our new century, does one detect some spirit of classicism raising its battered head again in the newly built World War II Memorial? It only adds to our confusion as to what should be built.

The transformation in how we view our national history has had an equally important effect on how we view the Mall and on how we think of its future as a commemorative site. Considerations of shrinking available space become difficult to balance. The last space possible on the original plan for major buildings has become the large museum devoted to the story of the American Indian. But now a somewhat more constrained space, still on the Mall, and the only one left, is to become the museum of African American history.[1] It will have to be shoehorned in. And can one doubt that there will be an urgent and politically powerful demand for a museum devoted to the Latino or Hispanic American experience?[2] Nor can this possibly be the end. There is to be a monument to Presidents John and John Quincy Adams. How can the second and sixth presidents, the only presidents among the first seven who were not slaveholders, be denied a prominent location? That prominence must only be greater if Abigail Adams is included, for it will help moderate the patriarchal aura of the Mall.

The pressure on the Mall to make room for ever more museums, memorials, and monuments is enormous. The federal planning agency for the District of Columbia (the district has its own planning agency) has done yeoman's work, as Patricia Gallagher tells us, in proposing the spreading out of new museums and memorials to locations away from the Mall precinct, to protect the city's monumental core from overdevelopment. But whatever the good sense of their plans, what can they do in the face of a Congress determined to ignore their valuable and necessary cautions?

It is not only physical structures that press upon and crowd the Mall but people, too, whose numbers increase as the number of noteworthy attractions rises. This is true of every great tourist destination, but the Mall also attracts demonstrators and spectators to various events scheduled on its grounds. And the Mall is not paved with stone or some other hard material that can accommodate great numbers;

underfoot is tender grass and soil whose compaction can damage the all-important rows of trees. "The people's home ground" is also a place of popular performances and celebrations, which in recent years have drawn great numbers but also raise serious environmental problems, as Richard Kurin describes. Yet how can the Mall be denied as a place for demonstration, festival, gathering, and pilgrimage? The original designers of the Mall did not have these functions in mind, but they must be accommodated.

As the uses to which the Mall is put continue to grow, they raise questions about which are legitimate and which should be limited. A recent controversy was sparked by a huge celebration of the opening of the season of the National Football League and the introduction of a new soft drink by Pepsi-Cola, who, along with other corporate sponsors, were given the right to obstruct much of the Mall for a stretch of days, to stage huge concerts, and to cover the area with large banners touting the event's sponsors. Many responded to this with outrage. Popular artists had often performed on the Mall but generally to mark the Fourth of July or Memorial Day or similar days of national celebration or to celebrate great public events. Was this a proper use of the Mall? "Last week," a correspondent for the *Washington Post* wrote, "the National Football League partied its way into Washington lore with a crassly commercial enterprise on the National Mall." The writer went on to characterize the NFL as "the perpetrator of the most extravagant misuse of the nation's front lawn in history."[3] Members of Congress were also incensed. Senator Jeff Bingaman offered a measure that would ban the use of structures and signs on the Mall bearing commercial advertisements, and it passed ninety-two to four, perhaps the first time since the creation of the McMillan Commission that the Senate had taken policy action specifically related to the Mall.[4] One would think that at least this kind of use could be banned.

But the matter was not so simple: the Mall, as so many other public institutions and functions, had become dependent on corporate sponsorship. Corporate sponsors were not happy about the limitations of the Bingaman resolution. Events from the National Cherry Blossom Festival to the summer movies screened on the Mall would be endangered if corporate sponsors withdrew their support. The National Park Service was left in a not very happy position, and future policy toward sponsored events remains a matter of debate.[5]

Perhaps the most serious challenge to the Mall today is posed by the need for increased security after the terrorist attacks of September 11, 2001. The Capitol, the Washington Monument, and many other structures on or adjacent to the Mall may become targets of terrorist attacks. How are they to be protected? Unsightly and intrusive obstacles have been placed all around Washington, and are especially noticeable at the Washington Monument, which has never had an attractive and suitable landscape surround. The National Park Service has proposed an expensive five-hundred-foot tunnel underneath the Mall as the way visitors will approach the monument.[6] A huge underground approach to the Capitol—not for security reasons alone—is now being constructed, and a large part of the Capitol grounds have been torn up for this construction.

These must change the experience of a visit to the Capitol, or the Washington Monument, and not necessarily for the better.

How to deal with security problems requires more thought and certainly better design solutions. The Mall as an open and accessible space for the celebration of our national experience may be much altered by how we deal with this challenge.

On a happier note, yet another new development will also shape the Mall in the future, and this is the growth of residential developments to the north of Pennsylvania Avenue. Urban diversity, in the form of residents, shops, and restaurants, is moving closer to the Mall, which has long been cut off from the city by the rows of museums along its northern and southern edges. If there was any hope that it might become more like the Champs-Elysées or the Tuileries in Paris— a desire that might have influenced L'Enfant in his original plan for Washington and has appeared to many observers to be something the Mall needs—that hope was undermined by the absence of nearby residents. That is now changing. The area around the Mall will never have the density of the residential areas around Central Park in New York or the great ceremonial axis of Paris, but even a relatively few residents may begin to change the way the Mall is used and developed. We may yet see more in the way of places to eat and drink and socialize starting to infiltrate the Mall, as nearby residents make more use of it and as entrepreneurs see possibilities. There is still space for such uses between the museums, but much will depend on the good sense of the agencies that control the Mall and development upon it.

The Mall, as Burnham, McKim, and Olmsted conceived it, is now complete—indeed, more than complete as new uses press upon it. Inevitably, the Mall must change in the future, as it has changed in the past. Yet we hope that these changes will remain faithful to the overarching ideas of design and of commemorative purpose that have guided it for so long and given it shape. Perhaps the Mall should change the way the U.S. Constitution changes—slowly, in small increments, with any necessary amendments carefully crafted to sustain its original, defining principles. As Richard Longstreth has written, "[A] sense of continuity in the whole is the overriding theme. This sense of continuity is indeed rare in our culture, and is perhaps one reason so many people have long considered the Mall so remarkable a place."[7] This is well put. Change, yes, but also continuity with a two-hundred-year effort to make a great ceremonial center for the nation.

PART 1

The DESIGN *of the* MALL

The Idea of the American Mall
Michael J. Lewis

❋ ONE OF THE HALLMARKS of a great work of art is its sense of inevitability: the way in which it defies all correction or improvement. Even when confronted with the evidence of alternative proposals and earlier incarnations, we find it impossible to imagine it taking any other form. So it is with that noble array of axial vistas, monuments, and stately public buildings, the National Mall in Washington. It is the physical setting of American democracy even as it is a monumental allegory of that democracy. Like those other great spaces of political theater, the agora of ancient Athens and the Forum of imperial Rome, it is in some sense both the thing itself and a symbol of the thing.

As created by the plan of the Senate Park Commission, also known as the McMillan Plan, published in 1902, the Washington Mall is an elegant diagram of political equilibrium: its two formal axes cross at a right angle, each of the resulting four cardinal points bearing a monumental classical structure.[1] Each structure addresses its counterpart with splendid dynamic reciprocity: the domed Capitol complements the rectangular Lincoln Memorial, just as the rectangular White House complements the domed Jefferson Memorial. And where the two axes meet, the fulcrum of these two mighty levers, a heroic obelisk rises. Here formal geometry achieves the stature of tragic poetry. Jefferson and Lincoln, the authors of the Bill of Rights and the Emancipation Proclamation,

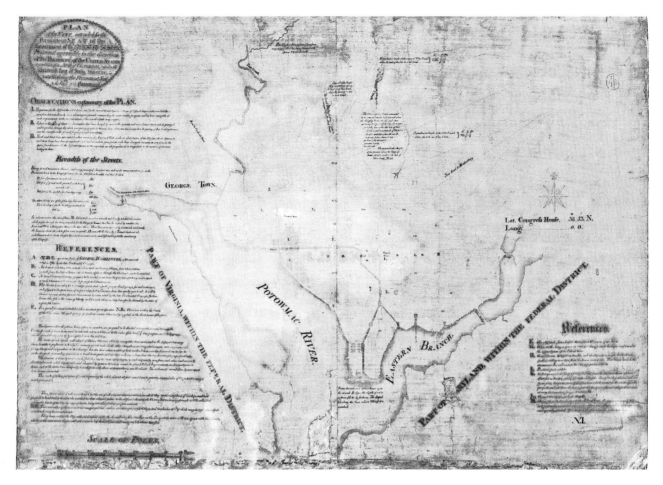

FIG. 1
The L'Enfant Plan, 1791
*Library of Congress, Geography
and Map Division*

are visibly juxtaposed against the executive and legislative branches, America's freedom makers ever admonishing America's freedom takers.

So flawless and transcendent—and so inevitable—is this alignment of form and function that we assume it was there from the start. And yet the Mall is not an artifact of the waning eighteenth century but rather the waning nineteenth. It dates to that swaggering decade after the Spanish-American War, when an irresistible tide of cultural confidence and energy acted upon a national infatuation with French classicism. It is the product of that great historical coincidence, and in no other era could

it have come about. Had a similar combination of civic energy and financial means existed in another era (during the early American Republic, for example, or the Victorian era) the Mall would look radically different today.

Even the function of the Mall is rooted in the late nineteenth century. While it is the public stage of our representative democracy—the physical point of contact between the people, their elected representatives, and their political memory— it came to this role late in its life.[2] During its first century it served no active political function whatsoever. Not until 1894, when Jacob Coxey marched his scruffy army of the unemployed on Washington, was it the site of formal and organized public demonstration. The Mall, far from being inevitable, is the distinctive product of the Progressive Era, embodying its florid rhetoric, its thrusting civic activism, even its social discontents.

Now, under the pressure of new construction and increasing concerns about security, the Mall is about to experience its most sweeping changes in a century. It is likely to lose some of its essential character, that fragile alliance of Progressive Era politics and classical revival fashionability. The McMillan Plan was above all an aesthetic creation, in which formal properties predominated. In the coming Mall, aesthetic concerns will be subordinated to didactic considerations and to issues of crowd control, handicapped access, and—inevitably—security. Its essential character will come to reflect the early twenty-first century just as precisely as it once mirrored the early twentieth. But in serving a bundle of competing clients, without a heroic and overriding aesthetic unity, the Mall will revert to what it was for its first century, a great experimental landscape for exploring the most searching questions of American identity.

From Jefferson to L'Enfant

Pierre Charles L'Enfant, unhappy and mercurial genius, is justly celebrated as the planner of Washington. Between March 1791 and March 1792, when he was removed from office, he devised the startlingly original plan that has guided the city's growth and development ever since. Of all the elements of L'Enfant's complex plan (fig. 1), the Mall is perhaps the oldest. It has its origins in Thomas Jefferson's own clever sketch plan for the city, which he made the last week of March 1791, at the very moment L'Enfant was beginning his preliminary survey of the city's site.[3]

Jefferson's highly rational sketch of the city was as unlike L'Enfant's plan as can be imagined. It proposed a rigorous checkerboard of building lots, whose monumental core was to be a grand east-west axis, anchored by the Capitol and President's House at either end. This grand axis was the germ of the present Mall. Even as L'Enfant devised his own sweeping Baroque geometry, he kept Jefferson's idea of the grand axis, which terminated at one end with the Capitol. He even kept Jefferson's hilltop site for the Capitol, although he banished the President's House to the north. As he did so, he adapted one more of Jefferson's ideas: Jefferson's plan had shown an informal park, designated as "public walks," which occupied the residual space between his grand axis and the Tiber Creek to the south. L'Enfant took this park function and moved it directly atop Jefferson's grand axis, where it assumed more formal geometric character. He even retained Jefferson's very term for the park, not Mall but "public walks."[4]

Thus the Mall originated not as a civic forum evoking Roman splendor but as a public garden. In its informal character, it was clearly distinguished from the monumental axiality with which Jefferson sited the principal civic buildings. It is fitting that Jefferson, who created two of the most sublime landscapes in American history—those of Monticello and the University of Virginia—should also have been the original visionary of the Mall.

By shifting the public walks to the location of Jefferson's grand axis, L'Enfant heightened their importance. He proposed to treat them as a landscaped park, organized around a central tree-lined path that proceeded from the Capitol to the Potomac, terminating in an equestrian statue of Washington. The statue was to sit directly to the south of the President's House, giving a cross axis to the main axis of the Mall. But while this pair of intersecting axes connected the Mall visually and geometrically to Washington's two great public buildings, they were not joined together in a continuous public ensemble. On the contrary, L'Enfant carefully separated these buildings from the public walks by the insertion of his Tiber Canal, scrupulously segregating the recreational area from the working machinery of the Republic. Instead of government buildings, his Mall was to be lined by theaters and cultural institutions. These elements were already envisioned by June 21, 1791, when L'Enfant reported to President Washington in his characteristically mangled English: "the publicque walk . . . will be agreable and convenient to the whole city which . . . will have an easy access to this place of general resort and all long side of which may be placed play house—room of assembly—academmies and all such sort of places as may be attractive to the larned and afford diversion to the idle."[5] (Just such a *room of assembly* may be the odd bow-fronted building on the north side of the Mall, between Tenth and Twelfth streets, shown on the Thackara and Vallance map of 1792.)

Blessed with such facilities, the Mall—as L'Enfant saw it—would be the principal social amenity of his city. Two months later, he assured President Washington that "the publick walk . . . will give to the city from the very beginning a superior charm over most of those in the world."[6] Here landscape rather than architecture should predominate. Even the Capitol was to be softened by a landscape feature: an artificial waterfall at the base of the building, which would flow into the Tiber Canal. There it would form "a cascade of forty feet high, or more than one hundred wide, which would produce the most happy effect in rolling down to fill up the canal and discharge itself in the Potomac."[7] Thus the Mall terminated at either end in a vignette of nature and art in harmony: the Capitol on its cascade to the east, and to the west the statue of George Washington in its wooded park above the Potomac.

L'Enfant's Mall was to have no lofty monumental role. That was reserved for Pennsylvania Avenue, "the grand avenue connecting the [presidential] palace and the Federal House."[8] This distinction was as much political as artistic. After all, no one had devoted more thought than L'Enfant to the problem of representing the new Republic in artistic terms. In 1789, he redesigned Federal Hall in New York for Washington's inauguration, creating an extensive iconographic program, and in 1791 he was asked by Alexander Hamilton, the first Secretary of the Treasury, to design an American coin.[9] His treatment of the Mall as public walk likewise reflected his understanding of the peculiar nature of American democracy.

L'Enfant's design is permeated with the concept of federalism. He seems to have believed that for a federation of independent states, an imposing memorial site of Roman magnificence was inappropriate. Instead of the single national forum that the Mall became in the twentieth century, L'Enfant dispersed throughout the city fifteen separate squares to represent the individual states. These, in distinction to the public walk, were indeed envisioned as civic *fora*, as solemn public spaces in which republican virtue was to be instilled through didactic monuments: "The center of each Square will admit of Statues, Columns, Obelisks, or any other ornament such as the different states may choose to erect: to perpetuate not only the memory of such individuals whose counsels or Military achievements were conspicuous in giving liberty and independence to this Country; but also those whose usefulness hath rendered them worthy of general imitation, to invite the youth of succeeding generations to tread in the paths of those sages, or heroes whom their country has thought proper to celebrate."[10] Thus even as L'Enfant's Baroque plan refused to culminate in an absolutist climax at some central point of power, so too its monuments were dispersed and decentralized, like the diffuse power of the early American Republic.

So L'Enfant imagined the Mall not as the didactic stage of American political memory but as a congenial park, offering "diversion to the idle." Of course, between 1792 and 1902, when the McMillan Plan was instituted, the nature of American political power had been thoroughly transformed. After the Civil War, the centralization of power in the national government would proceed implacably. While Roman imperial associations were inappropriate to the decentralized government of Washington's day, they would be fitting and appropriate for the United States of the early twentieth century.

The Mall in the Nineteenth Century

The slow pace of Washington's development prevented the Mall from being the attractive public walk that L'Enfant envisioned. Developing the Mall required a harnessing of political and financial power not possible with the decentralized government of the United States. And like many of the ingenious but costly inventions of the L'Enfant plan, it was not taken seriously. There was no shortage of bright ideas. In 1796, the commissioners of the new city wrote to George Washington suggesting that an "elegant building" on the Mall might help speed its development.[11] Perhaps they had in mind the president's oft-cited demand for a national university. But during that strapped decade there was no time for such luxuries. Like the plan for an equestrian monument to George Washington, decades would pass before any action was taken. Not until 1816 were plans drawn up for a national university for the Mall.

This was the work of the architect Benjamin Henry Latrobe (fig. 2), who was appointed by President Jefferson in 1803 to complete the Capitol and White House. During his long and troubled tenure in Washington, Latrobe made several proposals for landscaping the periphery of the Mall, including plans for the Tiber Canal (1804) and the Capitol grounds

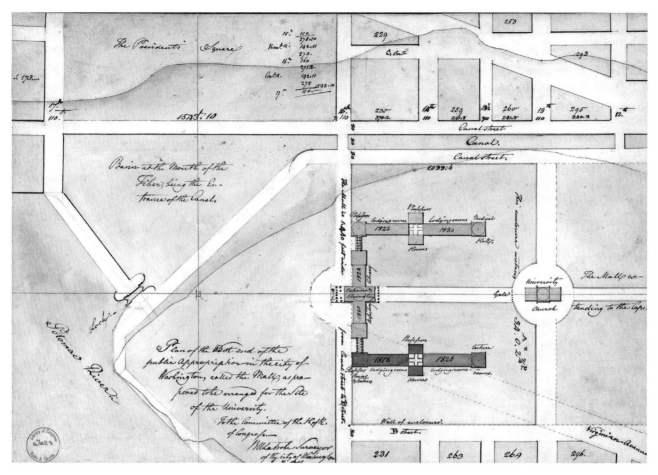

FIG. 2
Benjamin Latrobe, design for
the National University (pen,
ink, and watercolor, 1816)
*Library of Congress, Geography
and Map Division*

Opposite
FIG. 3
Thomas Jefferson's University
of Virginia, Charlottesville
Dan Grogan

(1815). In January 1816, he made an audacious proposal for a national university on
the Mall. L'Enfant himself had proposed
such a university, although on a different
site; nothing came of it. But Latrobe felt a
national university required a nationally
conspicuous site, and the Mall provided a
spectacular one. His university would sit
where Fourteenth Street intersected Virginia Avenue, at the extreme western end
of the Mall (which Latrobe now already
called by that name).[12]

Latrobe proposed a U-shaped complex,
open to the east, its arms directed toward
the Capitol. Its architecture echoed the
form of the Capitol with its dominant

dome: Latrobe placed a domed observatory at the center of the U-shape and
across from this, in the university's open
courtyard, its university chapel, which
also was capped by a dome. Both domes
would fall along the imaginary line connecting the Capitol dome with the future
Washington Monument, immeasurably
strengthening the force of the Mall's
main axis. Of course, while this cascade
of domes would have strengthened that
axis visually, it would also have guaranteed that it could no longer be traversed
in a straight line.

Latrobe's brilliant design integrated
all aspects of a university into a compact

and interlocking unity. Lecture halls and professors' apartments alternated with lodging rooms for students and were connected with colonnades. Eight separate pavilions in all were proposed and made subordinate to the central observatory dome, whose importance was further marked by a grand portico at either end. This separation of the complex into eight independent units made it possible to build it in separate, phased campaigns. Latrobe's long experience with the fickle budgets of the Capitol had taught him a shrewd realism.

While Latrobe's brave scheme came to naught, it has the most distinguished architectural progeny. It is easy to recognize in it the scheme of Jefferson's University of Virginia (fig. 3), which was founded the following year and to which Latrobe contributed designs and advice. Both share the same colonnaded dome, presiding over an interlocking organism of pavilions, apartments, and colonnades; both open onto a broad vista of landscape. It is again fitting that these two quintessential American landscapes are linked by the person of Jefferson, all of whose projects are marked by a conflation of Enlightenment rationalism and an informed love of landscape that only a surveyor-planter could muster.

In its axial formality and didactic purpose, Latrobe's university anticipated the McMillan Plan, but such an arrangement was not yet to be; the Mall remained the casual public walk that L'Enfant had envisioned. Three striking attempts were made to complete the landscaping of the Mall (strangely, in ten year intervals: in 1831, 1841, and 1851). None was fully realized, and they show how ambivalent about the Mall the city of Washington remained in the nineteenth century, unable to decide whether it was to be formal or informal, or what purpose it should serve.[13]

The first two attempts were made by the architect and engineer Robert Mills, the protégé of both Latrobe and Jefferson. (The third attempt, in 1851, would be made by Andrew Jackson Downing.) In 1831, Mills was charged with regularizing the Tiber Canal, which he took as the chance to regularize the form of the Mall. This he did in the bleakest, most utilitarian way possible—simply marching the street grid of Washington blithely over the Mall. A circular road would have encircled the Washington Monument site, the only grace note in the otherwise heartless scheme. Mercifully, it was not carried out, although Mills continued to think about the Mall, as he came to enjoy something of a monopoly on federal buildings during the 1830s.

Mills's great chance came in 1841. In that year, the slow-moving machinery of the great Smithsonian bequest (the benefactor, James Smithson, had died in 1829) at last had progressed to the point where deliberation began on the site and nature of the Smithsonian Institution. Mills was a logical choice as architect, for he was then designing the nation's three most important public-building projects: the Patent Office, Treasury, and Post Office. Mills was appointed by Secretary of War Joel R. Poinsett to make designs for the Smithsonian building and also for a botanical garden on the Mall, which would extend from Seventh to Twelfth Street.

Mills was out of his depth. Once again he interrupted the Mall with cross streets, carving it up into separate vignettes of landscape, each of which was subordi-

DESIGN
OF THE NATIONAL
WASHINGTON MONUMENT

FIG. 5
Robert Mills, design for the Washington Monument
(lithograph, ca. 1846)
Library of Congress, Prints and Photographs Division

nated to the monument it fronted. These landscapes were episodic and additive, and the whole was a crazy quilt, lacking continuity and managing to turn the heroic sweep of the Mall into a set of discrete units.[14] A second proposal in the same year for landscaping the grounds of the Smithsonian Institution would have been even more disruptive, extending Seventh and Twelfth Streets across the Mall and severing its epic axis. Gratefully, neither of these was realized—nor was Mills's awkward scheme for a battlemented Gothic Smithsonian Institution (although it paved the way for the medieval essay that was eventually built).

Mills tended to think in parts, a weakness not shared by Andrew Jackson Downing, America's foremost landscape planner and theorist. In his plan of 1851, a virtuoso achievement of American planning, Downing stressed the sublime axial continuity of the Mall's landscape. Although he accepted the necessary evil of the compulsory cross streets, he refused to let them interrupt the spatial flow from east to west. Athwart the cross streets, he placed long, looping carriage paths, great swinging arms that ran the length of the entire Mall. In good picturesque practice, he varied the types of landscape, providing an "Evergreen Garden," a "Fountain Park," and drives that followed the "pleasing natural undulations of surface." To maintain the picturesque character, Downing screened the periphery of the Mall from the city beyond by a continuous line of trees. Loosely connected to the Mall was the "President's Park" or "Parade," immediately south of the White House. This was a formal circular lawn that was entered by a triumphal arch, recalling

those of modern Paris. The arch was designed by Downing's assistant, Calvert Vaux, who inherited Downing's practice upon his death in 1852.[15]

Downing's proposal was the first to reconcile the three different roles that the Mall had been asked to perform: the recreational, the didactic, and the symbolic. He firmly believed that landscape itself was a moral and didactic instrument, and in an extraordinary document accompanying his plan, he explained how his Mall would serve as a kind of teaching institution: "The Public Grounds at Washington, treated in the manner I have here suggested, would undoubtedly become a Public School of Instruction in everything that relates to the tasteful arrangement of parks, and grounds, and the growth and culture of trees, while they would serve, more than anything else that could be devised, to embellish and give interest to the Capital. The straight lines and broad Avenues of the streets of Washington would be pleasantly relieved and contrasted by the beauty of curved lines and natural groups of trees in the various parks."[16] In Downing's scheme, scientific motives mixed with patriotic ones, as he proposed to plant the "Monument Park" at the west end of the Mall "wholly with *American* trees, of large growth."[17] Civic virtue was to be inculcated, but with vistas and trees, rather than by Latrobe's national university.

Some fragments of this visionary scheme were realized, but without Downing's executive ability to carry them out, the project languished and was forgotten in the storms of the Civil War. However, as an idea it lived on in the work of Calvert Vaux, who together with Frederick Law

Olmsted won the competition for New York's Central Park five years later. There he preserved Downing's cardinal principles: the division of the park into formal parade ground, pastoral landscape, and wilderness; the use of a surrounding mantle of trees to shut out the city; and maintaining the all-important continuity of landscape, requiring the suppression of cross streets. To some extent, Central Park may be looked at as Downing's greatest—albeit posthumous—achievement, devised in his project for the Mall and then transferred vicariously to New York by Vaux, where it remains America's finest man-made landscape.

And so the origins of both the University of Virginia and Central Park, those two didactic landscape creations, pass through the Mall in Washington. That they did so was not simply fortuitous, but was in the nature of the Mall. Nowhere in America was there a more prestigious swath of landscape, the front yard of American democracy; nowhere such an opportunity to propose major institutions on such a large scale.

But not all of the structures that came to clutter the Mall were of clear national merit. Beginning in 1846 with the Smithsonian Institution (fig. 4)—that meandering Romanesque essay in red sandstone by James Renwick—the Mall now became the site of piecemeal and additive development. This tended to reinforce the picturesque and informal character that L'Enfant had envisioned and which Downing had sought to strengthen. But at the precise moment that the Smithsonian threatened to define the Mall as a Romantic landscape, another structure emphasized its fundamentally classical character.

This was the Washington Monument, Robert Mills's mighty marble obelisk, whose design was selected in 1845 (fig. 5). Placed near where L'Enfant had proposed his equestrian statue of President Washington, it would eventually rise to a height of 555 feet 5 5/8 inches, giving the Mall its only truly epic monument, the only one sufficiently colossal to govern its sublime scale. With the building of the Smithsonian Institution and the Washington Monument, the fundamental paradox inherent in the Mall—torn from the beginning between being a forum and being a park—now assumed tangible form.

The piecemeal development of the Mall that ensued suited the Victorian appetite for picturesque irregularity. The Smithsonian was followed by the stately Department of Agriculture Building (built in 1867 and destroyed in 1930) and the festive National Museum Building—now the Arts and Industries Building (1881). And in good American fashion, no sooner was a garden established than a railway was chopped through it: in 1873 the Pennsylvania Railroad built its station on Sixth Street at the head of the Mall. This was a vibrantly colored High Victorian colossus, designed by the Philadelphia architect-engineer Joseph M. Wilson. It made the Mall a fragmented set of objects—useful, commemorative, or didactic—loosely held together by the general axial order. The hearty Victorian generation could appreciate this vital disorder; their successors, a more fastidious lot, could not.

The McMillan Plan and Beyond

Nothing so separates the Victorian world from its successors as its quaint conviction that art must be useful and must serve a moral function. This is the doctrine decisively swept away by the aesthetic movement, which held that the role of art was not to teach or persuade but to please: art for art's sake. The great redesign of the 1902 McMillan Plan is to some extent simply the application of aesthetic movement principles to the Mall, on the largest possible scale. In place of the disjointed Victorian Mall, with its episodic buildings and didactic vignettes, the McMillan Plan sought to subordinate the entire Mall to an aesthetic unity—to make it the country's single largest work of art. Its principles were formal and visual: continuity of vistas and space, harmony in architectural character and materials, and a sensitive and exquisitely refined relationship of part to whole.

It is appropriate that two of the authors of the McMillan Plan were themselves leading lights of the aesthetic movement: the sculptor Augustus Saint-Gaudens and the architect Charles Follen McKim. But it is also fitting that the committee included Frederick Law Olmsted Jr., the son of the man who had had preserved the kernel of Downing's Romantic landscape for the Mall in his Central Park plan, nearly a half century before. Here the great century of thought about this most American of landscapes—thought carried out successively by Jefferson and L'Enfant, Downing, and the two Olmsteds—at last reached its fulfillment. And without question the Mall, as created by the McMillan Plan, is among the grandest and most sublime monuments in the history of urban planning.

This is precisely the problem it now faces. Unlike the permissive Mall of the nineteenth century, which could tolerate a considerable amount of experimentation and change, the McMillan Plan brought with it the frosty and unforgiving nature of a complete work of art. Once its aesthetic character was refined in each minute detail, and once its mighty program was carried out (which cannot really be said to have been completed until the 1960s), it offered little scope for emendation or improvement. The new monuments of the past two decades—the Vietnam Veterans Memorial, the Korean Veterans Memorial, and the Franklin Delano Roosevelt Memorial—have been discreetly tucked at the periphery of the main axis. But this additive approach will only work for so long, even given the immense increase in the size of the Mall with the filling in of the shallows of the Potomac (which created the Tidal Basin).

The enormous controversy that erupted over the building of Friedrich St. Florian's design for the World War II Memorial shows just how difficult it is to tamper with a fully realized work of art. But even this is by no means the most serious change being undertaken at the Mall. Several projects are now under way that promise to completely transform its spatial character. The eastern side of the Capitol is currently being excavated to build an immense subterranean undercroft (its footprint larger than the Capitol itself), whose centerpiece will be a glass-roofed great hall that will function as a visitor center. A similar underground visitor center has been proposed for the Washington

FIG. 6
Reflecting Pool, Lincoln Memorial
in background (photograph,
1920s)
*Library of Congress, Prints and
Photographs Division*

Monument. Instead of entering through its portal, visitors will descend into the earth at some distance and approach it along a kind of sky-lighted trough. In these projects, and in similar ones elsewhere, security and crowd control are the leitmotifs. Long on the drawing board, they may well have been become unstoppable in the aftermath of September 11, 2001. It is clear that they will make the Mall more secure; it is less clear that it will still be the Mall. Its fundamental character may change, perhaps beyond recognition.

One of the central accomplishments of Western culture is the development of public life and its happy derivative, the public building. Instead of the ziggurats or palaces that embodied authority in earlier civilizations, the public building's hallmark was openness, the sheltered enclosure under which citizen met citizen and negotiated the transactions of life, the exchange of goods and of ideas. At a minimum it consisted of the Greek stoa, that

most humane of architectural creations, which comprised little more than an open colonnade, a roof without walls. By making it possible to enclose space without creating an impermeable barrier, the column has been an accessory of democracy from its birth.

Nowhere was this ideology of openness realized more sweepingly than in the public buildings and spaces of the United States. Other societies have been equally rich in land, or equally free from outside threat, so that they did not need to encase their cities with ramparts and bind them in defensive cinctures. But it is a peculiarly American notion to conflate political freedom with open space. Frederick Law Olmsted, the subtle visionary of Central Park, believed that parks had a far loftier goal than mere recreation. Instead, a spacious urban park "produces a feeling which to the poor is a relief from the sense of the restriction, which they generally experience elsewhere in comparing their limits of activity with the apparent freedom of those whose cares and duties have a wider scope."[18] In other words, the idea of mental freedom can be conveyed by the possibility of physical freedom in space. The proposed changes at the Mall will not affect its architecture, but they are likely to destroy one of its essential symbolic traits—one central to the Mall as imagined both by L'Enfant (see fig. 1) and by the McMillan Commission (see fig. 15): its sense of spatial freedom and openness (fig. 6).

This is why some of the changes under way are so radical. Making visitor centers for the Mall's key buildings and monuments—including the Vietnam Veterans Memorial, the Washington Monument, the World War II Memorial, and even the Capitol itself—alters their open, accessible character, especially in the case of the Washington Monument and Capitol, where a center is explicitly to be built as part of a new security perimeter. Not surprisingly, there have been protests against this cluttering of the monuments with such centers.[19]

It may well be that the long afternoon of the Mall as a modern Roman Forum has passed. The attacks on the World War II Memorial for its uncomplicated monumentality and its "triumphalism" suggest as much. That memorial aspires to embody ideal qualities in shimmering white marble—and to do so without hint of irony or self-consciousness—and nothing could be further removed from contemporary sensibility. But then the impulse to raise monuments and let them speak for themselves has always been weak in this country. Historically, Americans have not shown deep feeling for allegory, especially not abstract visual allegory; instead, we have a tremendous capacity for literary exegesis. This habit is deeply rooted in American culture. After all, Protestant America sat down Sunday after Sunday to hear a short scriptural reading that was then subjected to prolonged formal analysis and from which a moral lesson was extracted. This habit of literary exegesis remains the fundamental American literary experience. If the Mall of the twenty-first century is to be a less artistically resolved place—more fragmented, less spatially unified, and dominated more by visitor centers than abstract symbols—it is only returning to its ultimate roots, in that informal and relaxed gathering of academies, playhouses, and diversions that prophetic L'Enfant once envisioned.

American Renaissance

CHARLES FOLLEN MCKIM AND THE AESTHETIC IDEAL
Richard Guy Wilson

❧ AN ARTIST'S PERSONAL AESTHETIC and his or her conception of beauty and significance are fundamental to understanding a work of art, whether it be a painting, a sculpture, a building, or even a city. For the plan created by the individuals appointed to the Senate Park Commission (also known as the McMillan Commission) for Washington, aesthetics are crucial; a clear ruling taste runs through the scheme as presented in models and renderings at the Corcoran Gallery on January 15, 1902, and in the commission's published report.

Each of the commissioners brought different talents to the undertaking. The architect and urban planner Daniel H. Burnham, who was chair of the group, excelled in personal contacts, and much of the later success of the plan can be laid to his persuasive and expansive nature. Burnham believed in thinking big, and he convinced the railway executive Alexander Cassatt (assisted by a handsome subsidy from the government) to move the large B&O Railroad station from the Mall and to construct the new Union Station.[1] The landscape designer Frederick Law Olmsted Jr. brought to the table prior knowledge of Washington, and his influence can be seen in the large park network that was part of the scheme and certainly in some of the landscaping features.[2] The sculptor Augustus Saint-Gaudens, because of ill health, contributed the least, yet the role of stat-

FIG. 7
Lincoln Memorial, West Potomac Park
Jack Boudier, 1992; Library of Congress, Prints and Photographs Division

FIG. 8
Union Square (rendering by
Charles Graham, ca. 1904)
*Library of Congress, Prints and
Photographs Division*

uary and memorials in the plan confirms his legacy. And finally there was the architect Charles Follen McKim, who took primary responsibility for the design of the Mall, which became the major feature by which the Senate Park Commission plan is largely known.

What McKim and his colleagues created with their 1902 Mall plan was a design almost without precedent in American architecture and city planning. In its civic scale, the Mall plan surpassed all previous American attempts, and its audacity in revising what had happened to the Mall since 1800 would set the course for the next one hundred years in Washington. Although McKim, his compatriots, and later scholars cited Pierre Charles L'Enfant's 1791–92 plans for the Mall as instrumental, McKim went far

beyond what L'Enfant had envisioned. On the level of scale and control, McKim asserted a new vision for not just the nation's capital, but also for the country as a whole.

McKim reconfigured the Mall and framed more clearly the major terminal points. He reasserted the primacy of a central axis but extended it another mile beyond the original cross axis near the Washington Monument and terminated it with a *rond-point* and a memorial. At this *rond-point*, the commission's report explained, "as the Arc de Triomphe crowns the Place de l'Étoile at Paris, should stand a memorial erected to the memory of that one man in our history as a nation who is worthy to be named with George Washington—Abraham Lincoln."[3] Across the Potomac River, linking the Lincoln

Memorial (fig. 7), with the National Cemetery at Arlington (and indicating their connection with the Civil War), McKim placed a memorial bridge symbolically connecting the North and the South. He extended the cross axis from the White House and projected on it, to the south, another memorial group that in the late 1930s became the site of the Jefferson Memorial. He designed an elaborate sunken garden with architectural features recalling the château of Vaux-le-Vicomte and the Villa Madama in Rome, along with public recreation areas and a stadium. Between the new sunken garden and the Lincoln Memorial, a great canal with cross-axial arms "similar in character and general treatment to the canals at Versailles and Fontainebleau, in France, and Hampton Court in England" was planned (only a portion of it was built).[4] In front of the Capitol, a Union Square was designed with statuary and fountains that, he claimed, "would compare favorably, in both extent and treatment, with the Place de la Concorde in Paris."[5]

In McKim's proposal the broad, central grass carpet measuring three hundred feet across was lined on each side by four rows of American elms that acted as the coordinating element. This treatment of rows of trees was explained as having precedent in England and the Continent and also in American colonial towns in the North and South. Also cited in the commission's report as a source was the Tuileries Garden, which performed as a uniting element with the Louvre and the Arc de Triomphe (fig. 9).[6] Behind the Mall and also surrounding the White House and the Capitol would be a row (and, in the area of the current Federal Triangle, several rows)

of low-rising, white, classically inspired buildings. With its broad scale and density of detail, the design of the Mall projected an audacious new concept of what the civic heart of America might be.

Uncovering the motives that lay behind the Senate Parks Commission's plan and especially the Mall design reveals a great complexity. All designs are to some degree products of their time, place, context, and interplay of personalities. The local political situation in Washington influenced the design, as did the national goals of the Theodore Roosevelt administration and the political ambitions and business connections of Senator James McMillan of Michigan, chairman of the Senate committee that set up the commission. The idea of a bridge spanning the Potomac had been projected as early as 1851 and debated in Congress starting in the mid-1880s. The reclamation of the Potomac Flats west of the Washington Monument carried out since 1882 provided the land for the western extension of the Mall. The Mall area had received attention at the 1900 American Institute of Architects national meeting in Washington, and several proposals had been put forward that, while vastly different from McKim's design, provided some inspiration.

While there is general agreement that the commission's Mall design came from "his direct personal supervision" over a period of nine months, McKim had a large cadre of architects working for him, among them William T. Partridge, who acted as his primary assistant on the project.[7] There were the various renderers, such as Jules Guerin, who did many drawings, and Francis L. V. Hoppin, who produced the magnificent bird's-eye view

FIG. 9
Arc de Triomphe and Champs-
Elysées, Paris
Yann Arthus Bertrant / Corbis

from Arlington. Certainly, each collaborator contributed some elements but exactly what probably never will be known. Also, the Park Commission's three other distinguished members—Burnham, Olmsted, and Saint-Gaudens—certainly made suggestions.

Nonetheless, the Mall design came primarily from McKim himself, and it is his aesthetic sense, or values of beauty, that need to be understood. The many European and American sources that McKim very specifically cited as precedents for his design indicate his artistic tastes and influences. But even more, it is McKim's own background and work within the cultural milieu of the American Renaissance,

illustrated in his own few pronouncements on architecture, that reveal his aesthetic values, and those embodied in the Mall design.

An Architect in Context

Charles Follen McKim was born in Pennsylvania in 1847. His father was a former Presbyterian minister who became a radical abolitionist and his mother a Quaker. McKim's upbringing, in which personal responsibility and devotion to a larger purpose were emphasized, nurtured his sense of public duty; in his adult life he insisted that architecture existed not as personal whim but as a responsibility. For him, the architect had a duty in the public sphere as a creator of spaces and buildings but also as an ennobler of life.[8]

McKim recognized architecture as a carrier of cultural values, as his development suggests. He spent 1866–67 at Harvard studying engineering, a summer in the office of the Ruskin-infatuated architect and writer Russell Sturgis, and then 1867–70 at the École des Beaux-Arts in the atelier of Honoré Daumet. He returned to the United States and, after a period in the New York office of Henry Hobson Richardson, he worked on his own, forming a partnership with William R. Mead and William Bigelow in 1877, and adding Stanford White in 1879 in place of the departing Bigelow. The early work of McKim, Mead & White through the early 1880s explored the reigning Queen Anne and Gothic idioms imported from England, along with other exotic styles, such as the Japanese and the Moorish. McKim and his partners helped create an American idiom based on elements of the American colonial vernacular, as in the great shingled buildings he designed in Newport, Rhode Island. By the mid-1880s, McKim realized that the wood vernacular could be expanded only so far and that urban, public buildings required a more substantial and evocative architecture. The Henry Villard houses (1882–86), on Madison Avenue in New York between Fiftieth and Fifty-first Streets, and the Boston Public Library (1887–95), on Copley Square, amply demonstrate McKim and his partners' discovery of the Italian Renaissance as the new American image. Both structures contained elaborate decorative programs of sculpture, paintings, and furniture that stressed the connections of contemporary America to the Renaissance. The size and scale of the projects increased, as exemplified by McKim's design for the new campus of Columbia University on Morningside Heights in New York (1892–1901). Even the scope of his output increased, as McKim's firm designed nearly a thousand buildings during his lifetime.[9]

The cultural milieu of McKim and his partners and their discovery and employment of the various classical styles received many titles but perhaps the most popular, and one they would agree with, is the term "American Renaissance."[10] They did not mean it as a style but rather as a state of mind or a mood and spirit of identification. Many of the artists of the period not only studied, copied, and adopted the motifs of the Italian past but also modeled themselves on Renaissance figures. Charles Follen McKim had the nickname "Bramante" in his office while his more flamboyant partner Stanford White was "Cellini."[11] These references to the Italian Renaissance architect Donato Bramante and the sixteenth-century ornamentalist Benvenuto Cellini catch the character of each partner: McKim the monumental formalist and White the decorative genius. The patrons of these American Renaissance architects frequently reminded some observers of Italian princes; one architect claimed that "our merchant princes, our large manufacturers, our money coining miners . . . are more disposed to emulate the expenditures of the Medici . . . than to conform to the habits of their thrifty forefathers."[12] Henry Adams observed, "[T]here is always an odor of spice and brown sugar about the Medicis. They patronized art as Mr. Rockefeller or Mr. Havemeyer does."[13] Sometimes the analogy was suggested by events, as when Augustus Saint-Gaudens exclaimed to Daniel Burnham of Chicago after an initial planning meeting for the "White City" of the World's Columbian Exposition, "Look here old fellow, do you realize that this is the greatest meeting of artists since the fifteenth century!"[14] One critic wrote about Biltmore, the vast château Richard Morris Hunt created for George Washington Vanderbilt in North Carolina, "We call Biltmore French Renaissance now; it will be American Renaissance later on."[15]

Elements of the American Renaissance started to appear in the 1870s, when the country, emerging from the gloom of the Civil War and experiencing great industrial expansion, began to reconsider its origins with the approach of the centennial of 1876. Some of those who had amassed new wealth sought to secure their status by buying or copying European art, furniture, sculpture, and architecture. The term "American Renaissance" first appeared in 1880 and it was in frequent use from the late 1880s through the 1910s and coincided with the nation's imperialistic exploits and the great cultural expansion at home that witnessed the founding of libraries, museums, and other institutions of culture, along with great houses for the wealthy. From the mid-1910s well into the 1930s, one can find elements of the American Renaissance, such as in the Federal Triangle and the National Gallery of Art in Washington. The term continued to be used even as a new mythology and self-identification began to appear—modernism and the

Machine Age in the 1920s and 1930s— and the concept of identification with the Renaissance past disappeared.[16]

The essence of the American Renaissance lay in the belief that a high, or a noble, culture should provide the basis for an American art. This sacralization of high culture created a canon of great art in which classicism and its derivatives came to be venerated.[17] Architecturally, the American Renaissance opposed the thoughtless appropriation of motifs and styles that, it was claimed, had dominated the spirit of American architecture from the 1840s to the 1880s. It was anti-Victorian and part of the general "cleanup" and simplification of the arts during the turn-of-the-century period. Beginning as a reform to existing art, the American Renaissance mentality became the status quo and created new institutions such as the American Academy in Rome, the American Federation of Arts, and many societies of painters, sculptors, and artists. These groups charged themselves with the institution and preservation of cultural standards. Frank Millet, a leading painter, explained the need to go abroad to study at the École des Beaux-Arts in Paris or at the American Academy in Rome: "Our artists are only half educated . . . they have not had the traditions of art as a birthright . . . what we want in our artists is cultivation."[18] This view eventually became a conservative defense, and although artists associated with the American Renaissance claimed that they were being modern in bringing the classics up to date, they were avowedly antimodernist.

This conservative position held that the past provided the source for art and that the operative methodology, or aesthetic, for new work lay with eclecticism. Eclecticism—the selection and usage of styles, motifs, and images drawn from a variety of sources—came to mean, for the American Renaissance, reliance on various classical styles or their derivatives. In terms of architecture, this meant Greek, Roman, Italian, French, English, and other classical Renaissance stylistic offspring such as the American colonial and federal. Classicism provided the basis, or mainstream, of the American Renaissance, though in appropriate cases, such as religious institutions and colleges, medieval and other styles could be employed. In the other arts—sculpture, painting, and furniture design—classicism was the touchstone. The underlying ethos of much of the art was summed up by Kenyon Cox, a leading painter who collaborated with McKim on several projects and became a polemicist for this renewed classicism, when he explained: "The Classic Spirit is the disinterested search for perfection; it is the love of clearness and reasonableness and self-control; it is, above all, the love of permanence and of continuity. It asks of a work of art, not that it shall be novel or effective, but that it shall be fine and noble. . . . It wishes to add link by link to the chain of tradition, but it does not wish to break the chain."[19] Art provided an index to civilization, or as John Ruskin, the popular English critic explained: "It has been my endeavor to show . . . how every form of noble architecture is in some sort the embodiment of the Polity, Life, History, and the Religious faith of Nations."[20] According to the American Renaissance ideology, great nations produced great architecture (and associated arts) while debased peoples produced degenerate architecture. Where would the United States rank?

To answer this question, many Americans increasingly looked abroad and sought to import not just European artifacts and styles but culture and other intangibles. Although Americans had a long history of looking to Europe for cultural standards, after the Civil War an increasing number of American artists and architects, such as McKim, studied at the École des Beaux-Arts or other foreign academies. Before the 1870s, many Americans viewed Europeans with suspicion and felt them to be lacking in morals, but as Edith Wharton's novels show, by the turn of the century they were actively courted, and American millionaires even sought European husbands for their daughters.[21] Wealthy Americans purchased foreign estates and titles, and they imported paintings, tapestries, furniture, entire rooms, and parts of buildings, which became the basis of many American museums.

The concept of the Renaissance as a high point of Western civilization and the beginning of the modern age provided the link Americans needed. The word renaissance—meaning not simply "rebirth" but, more specifically, the revival in Italy of classical antiquity in art, architecture, and letters during the fourteenth through the sixteenth centuries—first came into English usage in the 1840s.[22] Initially, commentators such as John Ruskin or, in the United States, Charles Eliot Norton and James Jackson Jarves deplored the Renaissance. They saw the medieval period as the high point and the Renaissance as the downfall. But starting in the 1870s, the Renaissance began to receive a more positive interpretation in several books. Studies by the Swiss historian Jacob Burckhardt (first published in Germany in the 1850s and 1860s) and Englishmen Walter Pater and John Addington Symonds viewed the Italian Renaissance as the foundation of modern art. A New York reviewer claimed: "We are children of the Renaissance. And not only are we children of the Renaissance, but as Burckhardt truly says the influence of that mother age is still at work among us."[23] One reviewer of Symonds observed a Hegelian force, the Renaissance spirit "traveling onwards with ever-increasing vigor."[24] This identification of the Italian Renaissance with modern America became endemic; indeed, it was felt that America would surpass the Renaissance. Bernard Berenson, a Boston and Cambridge protégé who became the world authority on Italian Renaissance painting, prefaced his first book, *The Venetian Painters* (1894), with the observation: "We ourselves, because of our faith in science and the power of work, are instinctively in sympathy with the Renaissance. . . . [T]he spirit, which animates us, was anticipated by the spirit of the Renaissance, and more than anticipated. That spirit seems like the small rough model after which ours is being fashioned."[25]

McKim's Words and Works

McKim's aesthetic views coincide with this American Renaissance mentality and illuminate his work for the Senate Park Commission. As an architect, he felt that his designs explained his aesthetic and spoke for themselves; he therefore wrote very little and disliked public speaking. However, from a few writings, from public addresses he was forced to give as president of the American Institute of Architects (AIA) in 1902 and on receiving the Royal Institute of British Architects (RIBA) King's Gold Medal in 1903, and from memories of those who knew him, some textual documentation of his aesthetic can be gained. These sources give verbal form to what his architecture appears to demonstrate: the idea that classicism provided the basis of architectural beauty.

Most important to McKim were the lineage and heritage of classicism and the precedent of European sources. Perhaps the most succinct expression of this can be found in his AIA talk given in Washington, shortly after the initial presentation of the Senate Park Commission Plan. McKim said: "Architecture is the oldest of the Arts. Its principles were developed early in the history of the race; its laws were formulated long before the Christian era; and its most exquisite flowers bloomed under skies that fostered the production of beauty. Succeeding ages have had their special problems calling for special adaptations. New occasions have taught the architect new duties. Periods of prosperity or of permanence in social conditions have offered new opportunities, until there has grown up a vast universal language of architecture." McKim concluded that architects who sought to transcend their time and build for posterity must know the past.[26]

The origins of McKim's aesthetic lay in the cultural context of his day, such as the American Renaissance of which he was a prime creator. However, they did not emerge all at once. Although he attended the École des Beaux-Arts, the work he did on returning to the United States reflected very little of what could be assumed to be his École training. McKim's period in Paris was during the aftermath of the student uprising over Gothic revivalist Eugène-Emmanuel Viollet-le-Duc, when many design currents were active. Unfortunately, none of McKim's École projects remain. Nonetheless, elements of the École's methodology regarding classicism as the basis of design and the primacy of the plan in the design of buildings would certainly come into play later in McKim's work.

Another source for McKim's aesthetic beliefs was his discovery of early American architecture. Much later in life, in his 1903 RIBA speech, he recalled the "thrill of surprise and pleasure I experienced on my first visit to England, more than thirty years ago." McKim's visit came in the summer of 1869, when he explored English architecture with young men from Richard Norman Shaw's office. Shaw and other architects were in the midst of creating the Queen Anne and Olde English styles based on English prototypes of the sixteenth to eighteenth centuries. McKim discovered a "strange familiarity" in the buildings.[27] Back in the United States, he began to investigate early American architecture. The initial focus was Newport, where in 1874 he commissioned a book of photographs of early buildings.[28] Some of these he published in his role as associate editor of *The New York Sketch Book of Architecture* (1874–76), wherein he called for a recording of the "the early architecture of our country."[29]

Initially, McKim and his future partners incorporated the more vernacular elements into their designs; however, his photographer did record more formal Georgian houses, and in 1876 he published a photograph of New York's City Hall (fig. 10), a grand neoclassical design by John McComb and Joseph Mangin, with the comment that it was by far the greatest public building in the city.[30] By the mid-1880s, and concurrent with the Villard and Boston Public Library commissions, McKim and his partners had abandoned the shingled vernacular for the more formal Georgian for their country and resort houses. Certainly on one level McKim played to his audience in London at the RIBA talk as he stressed the links between the United States and England, yet he also displayed his convictions about the classical basis of American design. He cited Sir Christopher Wren for his contributions and said the U.S. Capitol, the White House, and Washington's City Hall were "animated by a pure taste and devoted love of beauty." Although the basis of McKim's architecture certainly had French elements, still, English classicism played a role. For instance, McKim claimed, "Our obligations . . . to Sir Christopher Wren are very imperfectly understood"; and earlier, while in Europe with the McMillan Commission, he had praised Saint Paul's (fig. 11), as the finest of Protestant cathedrals—"the finest dome building since Saint Peter's and even superior to the latter in external ensemble."[31]

Although by the mid-1880s McKim and his partners were exploring American Georgian, Italian, Spanish, and other Renaissance prototypes for their work, alternatives nonetheless existed, as can been seen in the firm's Gothic Revival designs for churches (St Peter's Episcopal, Morristown, New Jersey, 1892) and other buildings. The big shift came with the World's Columbian Exposition (fig. 12) in Chicago and the decision to rely on a generic classicism as the ruling idiom for

FIG. 10
City Hall, New York (photome-
chanical print, ca. 1900)
*Library of Congress, Prints and
Photographs Division*

the Court of Honor. To Richard Morris
Hunt he described it as "the Classic policy," and he observed that the role of his
Agricultural Building should be to serve
as "one of the walls of the court." He cited
as important the "girding around by a single order of architecture 60 feet high" and
"symmetry."[32] In other letters, McKim
argued for reproductions of important
European sculptures such as the Farnese
Bull group (Naples Archaeological Museum),
which he had recently had cast, and that a

carver should follow "Greek character . . .
and shun all approach to romance as he
would the devil."[33]

Central to McKim's aesthetic lay the
belief that the past offered clues and
that the American architect should go
abroad to study. Samuel A. B. Abbott, who
chaired the Boston Public Library's Board
of Trustees, wrote to McKim in 1889 after
a trip abroad: "I paid particular attention
to the Chancelleria [*sic*], the Farnese, and
the Strozzi palaces, because you have

FIG. 11
Saint Paul's Cathedral, London
(drawing, ca. 1719)
Hulton Archive / Getty Images

talked so much of them."[34] Hence he founded in 1894, in the wake of the success of the World's Columbian Exposition, the American School of Architecture in Rome, which in 1896 became the American Academy in Rome. To McKim, the importance of Rome was self-evident: "The advantages Rome has to offer to students of architecture and the allied arts need not be urged. What with the architectural and sculptural monuments and mural paintings, its galleries filled with the chef d'oeuvres of every epoch, no other city offers such a field for study or an atmosphere so replete with the best precedents." McKim went on to evoke the names of "Brunelleschi, Alberti and Bramante" along with "Raphael" as "among those who head the list of enthusiastic students of the antique, which has continued down to our own day." After reviewing the establishment of other foreign academies in Rome, McKim concluded with "the value of constant and long-continued

study, and proximity with the best examples of architecture, cannot be over estimated."[35] A memoir by H. Siddons Mowbray, a muralist, who decorated a number of McKim's buildings, including the University Club and Morgan Library in New York, quotes McKim as saying: "As Rome went to Greece, and later France, Spain and other countries had gone to Rome, for their own reactions to the splendid standards of Classic and Renaissance Art, so must we become students, and delve, bring back and adapt to conditions here, a ground work on which to build."[36]

Later in his life, McKim liked to quote Thomas Jefferson's pronouncement that the reproduction of European buildings in the United States was a means of educating American public taste in architecture.[37] He argued that the question of an original American style was a misnomer, that classicism and European models pro-

vided the basis for development. In his AIA president's speech he claimed: "It is no derogation of the originality or the versatility of our young men to urge them to study the world's models; never do two exactly similar problems present themselves to the architect. Purpose and location change with each problem; and happy is he who can satisfy those two requirements without being called upon also to invent the language in which he speaks."[38]

McKim sought what he called a "universal style" for architecture based on classical principles. Charles Moore, who acted as secretary of the Senate Park Commission and accompanied McKim, Burnham, and Olmsted on their European research trip, records McKim discoursing on Gothic cathedrals and how much he admired the builders, but McKim invoked a Hegelian argument: "These men had their day and the world has the history—the splendid history; but we shall never go back to the Gothic, because it neither satisfies the manifold needs of to-day nor does it represent present moods of thought. . . . It must give place to a universal style."[39] McKim's universal style was not without reference to specific periods of the past, for as he explained in a letter to Edith Wharton: "The designer should not be too slavish, whether in the composition of a building or a room, in his adherence to the letter of tradition. By conscientious study of the best examples of classic periods, including those of antiquity, it is possible to conceive a perfect result suggestive of a particular period . . . but inspired by the study of them all."[40] This accords with a sentiment expressed during the European trip: "[T]he problems in Washington must be

FIG. 13
Saint Peter's Basilica, Rome
(print, ca. 1700)
Hulton Archive / Getty Images

worked out along Roman rather than Parisian lines; that simplicity, directness and the subordination of ornament to structural uses should prevail; and that modern French work should not be allowed."[41] The final sentiment in this odd passage, which seems to contradict the many positive remarks he made about Paris, disallows only "modern" French work. The grand French classicism of the seventeenth to the early nineteenth centuries was not rejected, but only the current, very frilly classicism of the 1900 Exposition and also art nouveau. Paris exemplified by the Place de la Concorde illuminated "the glories of a city designed as a work of art."[42]

The seven-week trip to Europe during the summer of 1901 offers additional insights into McKim's aesthetic preferences. Shortly before, the Commission had visited Annapolis, Williamsburg, and large colonial river estates to try to better understand the milieu of Washington, Jefferson, and L'Enfant.[43] For the European trip, Olmsted took along a tripod camera with a special lens, and in several of his on-site pictures McKim appears. Some of these photographs are included in the Senate report, supplemented with other photographs purchased abroad and undoubtedly with photographs supplied by McKim and Olmsted's office.

Although Moore claimed that the itinerary came from Olmsted and "was based upon the work of André Le Nôtre," it seems obvious that McKim (and Burnham) played a major role in what was seen and especially in how it was interpreted.[44] Burnham had first visited Europe in 1896 and met McKim in Rome, while McKim had since 1867 visited Europe on at least a biannual, if not yearly, basis. Olmsted had also visited Europe frequently, and Moore notes: "Olmsted, being younger and possessing a brain fertile in expedients, offered many variations on the themes."[45] But as Moore then goes on to note about McKim, "His command of spoken French made him the natural leader."[46] The group visited England, France, Italy, Hungary, Austria, and major cities including London, Paris, and Rome.

Moore's record of the journey notes elements of what might be called McKim's aesthetic that came to play a role on the Mall. For instance McKim liked to view cities from high up and always took the group to top floors of hotels, as in Paris, or climbed towers, as at the Villa Aurora in Rome. In Paris, particular note was made of long vistas, the use of trees, public buildings, squares, arches, and the interweaving of elements: "an overpoweringly elaborate, intricate, and ornamented pattern."[47] The great scale of Saint Peter's Square (fig. 13), was admired both for refinement and strength. McKim and his compatriots admired gardens with strong axial central spaces and dense parallel rows of trees on the sides. Long vistas and *tapis vert* crossed by cross-axial elements were cited in Moore's report. Sculptural groups were frequently commented upon for the silhouettes they created. Fountains also were admired, and it was determined that they were more appropriate to Washington than a sculpture of a man on horseback. The quays in Vienna and Budapest became the source for the Watergate treatment near the Lincoln Memorial. McKim and company were seeking classical architectural solutions for the city. Olmsted acted as the recorder, taking photographs of details and measuring risers, treads, and balusters.

The European trip provided many of the motifs for the Mall, but the real importance lay not with identifying sources but the overall aesthetic demonstrated. In a sense, it was McKim's vision—a scientific eclecticism in which accuracy and fidelity to original sources played a role—but drawn from the best of the classical past.

McKim's aesthetic was the result of both cultural and personal factors: the American Renaissance mentality and his own craving for standards worthy of emulation. In opposition to other voices, such as the young Frank Lloyd Wright, who argued for an original American expression, McKim's aesthetic was based on what he saw as the American birthright, the classical tradition; and for the Mall, McKim's aesthetic preferences lay with European models in cities, gardens, landscaping, fountain, and buildings. Many modifications occurred to McKim's scheme, but its underlying premise still held true. Or, as McKim said, "The architect who would build for the ages to come must have the timing of the ages that are past."[48]

When Dignity and Beauty Were the Order of the Day

THE CONTRIBUTION OF DANIEL H. BURNHAM

Cynthia R. Field

❧ FOR THE ARTISTS of the American Renaissance, the concepts of dignity and beauty were the very touchstones of their art. As Richard Guy Wilson argues in his essay, they were also the concepts inherent in the Senate Park Commission Plan, also known as the McMillan Plan, designed by three of the major figures of the American Renaissance: Daniel H. Burnham, Charles Follen McKim, and Augustus Saint-Gaudens. Wilson has identified McKim's contributions to the plan. What, then, of Burnham's?

As with McKim, the clues to decoding Burnham's contribution to the commission lay in his past works and in the hints given in his speeches and letters but also in contemporaneous descriptions, especially in Burnham's biography by the historian Charles Moore, who had been especially close to the Washington work as secretary to the commission. All the sources acknowledge that Burnham contributed skilled and passionate leadership, which produced a collegial decision-making process. His, also, was the large-scale, comprehensive planning context of the new Mall. The Senate Park Plan is widely considered to be the first comprehensive plan for any city in the United States precisely because it looked at the whole area and knitted together disparate elements.[1] This all-encompassing approach grew out of Burnham's personal concepts of the beauty of a coherent plan and the dignity of order. Finally, Burnham contributed his own ideal-

ism, optimism, and vision to this roadmap to the future.

The Senate Committee on the District of Columbia, which created the Senate Park Commission, frequently used the words *dignity* and *beauty*. In making the charge to the commission, the committee said that "the absence of a well-considered comprehensive plan . . . resulted in compromises that have marred the beauty and dignity of the national capital."[2] What does a word like dignity mean in planning a city? In this context, dignity does not mean bearing or comportment, as it does when we speak about human beings. For a city, dignity means order (fig. 14). The Senate Park Commission Plan therefore sought to realize dignity, and thus beauty, through the form of a comprehensive plan (fig. 15). On that assumption, Burnham declared, "The beauty of the whole composition is superior to that of any individual building."[3] Burnham contributed his own infusion of dignity and beauty, along with idealism, patriotism, organizational leadership, and advocacy.

Urban Planning

The American Renaissance mentality of the period strove to capture not the style of the Renaissance but its spirit. In this connection, it is not surprising that Burnham's concept of planning the city as a whole, as a complex of interrelated systems, revived a similar approach by the great Renaissance writer on city planning Leon Battista Alberti. Both men advocated a broad vision of a whole city, and both gave order to the parts. In his work *On the Art of Building,* Alberti described a city developed not according to a predetermined outline but as a series of interlocking parts grouped according to their function and their appearance. In the heart of his city was a handsome square, the site of a civic grouping of temple, sen-

FIG. 15
Planning drawing for the Senate Park Commission (rendering by F. L. V. Hoppin, ca. 1902)
Library of Congress, Prints and Photographs Division

ate house, and basilica. In scattered locations deemed most proper for their uses were to be buildings for public entertainment, places for exercise, and places for commerce. In Burnham's plans we find similar elements: the civic grouping, the public buildings in scattered locations suitable to their function, and the identified commercial areas that figure in his later plans for San Francisco and Chicago. Through this organization, both men defined the city as a system of parts to be fitted together in the most logical fashion.

The World's Columbian Exposition of 1893 in Chicago (fig. 16) was not a city, nor was it designed according to a plan by Burnham, but he was its director, responsible for turning plan into reality. He successfully developed skills and procedures that he would use in his work as a city planner. Elements from the Chicago exposition's Court of Honor, such as the regular layout, the uniform cornice line, the roughly uniform classicizing style, and the controlled lines of sight, were employed in all Burnham's later planning. In his work on the Senate Park Plan for Washington, he would add the benefits of a firsthand

knowledge of European landscape design and city planning. It would be his first opportunity to enlarge his planning to the scale of an entire city.

Burnham's unique contribution to these efforts was his ability to deal with the city as a single unit composed of interrelated service systems; nonetheless, he would also use his planning skills on smaller projects. His plan for Cleveland, done at roughly the same time as the Senate Park Plan (1902–3), was another showcase for transforming the Court of Honor of the World's Columbian Exposition into a civic center as a tool of city planning. In the Philippines, Burnham's plan for the improvement and development of Manila (1904–5) was composed of those elements that were constant in all his major work: a street system based on a combination of the grid with diagonal and circuit boulevards; a continuous and citywide park system integrated with this street system; and centers for specialized activities such as government and recreation. The geometrically formal plan for Baguio (1904–5), the planned summer capital of the Philippines, revealed once more his

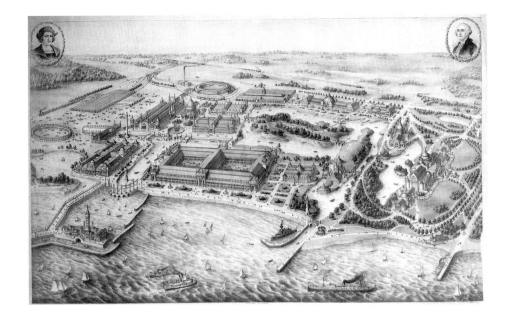

predisposition to stress formal and ceremonial interrelationships in determining
his design principles. Using these now-
familiar elements, Burnham also designed
a plan for San Francisco (1904–6) that
emphasized improving commercial interaction within the city by means of a civic
center, boulevards, and parks and recreation integrated into the overall plan. In
the plan for Chicago (1907–9; fig. 17), all
the elements tested and refined in the earlier plans took on their most developed
forms. Full integration of park and circu-
lation systems with public buildings and
civic centers was achieved and extended
onto a regional scale.

In all cases, the grouping of public
buildings with parklike landscape was
used as an ordering principle. In the Senate Park Plan, structures of a generalized
classical style were grouped together in
several key areas of the plan: around the
White House, around the Capitol, and
along the Mall. One of its proposals was
the grouping of public buildings framing
the Capitol, designed so that the individual buildings were subordinate to the
effect of the whole ensemble. The buildings for executive agencies at Lafayette
Square repeated the interrelated grouping
of the Capitol grounds buildings. Orderly
groupings of matched buildings would, in
the commission's words, "result in a composition of the greatest possible dignity
and impressiveness."[4] Burnham rational-
ized these characteristic clusters saying of
the plan that "There are two sorts of
architectural beauty, first that of an individual building; and second, that of an
orderly and fitting arrangement of many
buildings."[5]

Working with the century-old plan for
the city by Pierre Charles L'Enfant taught
him a lesson he would expound at the
Town Planning Conference held in London in October 1910: that the planner
must look to more than a short-term goal.
He proposed that the planner seek to
inspire a giant leap of the imagination in
order to set in motion the patient steps to

a completed goal. "Such is humanity!" as he analyzed it: "You may expect support for a great cause, whereas men will yawn and slip quietly away from the merely obvious."[6] Burnham's friend Willis Polk synthesized Burnham's message into the well-known, pithy phrase "Make no little plans."[7]

For Burnham, who was a Swedenborgian, order was not merely a sense of organization. The personal expression of the concept of order in his planning grew from Burnham's upbringing in the Transcendental-like Church of the New Jerusalem, founded on the principles of Emanuel Swedenborg (1688–1772). Swedenborg taught that an orderly, consonant relationship between the whole and the parts was the revealed plan of the Supreme Being. As Swedenborg declared, "God is order itself."[8] For Burnham, the order of an overarching plan and the grouping of public buildings within it would have been expressions of Swedenborg's "wholeness of creation," imparting to the city beautiful movement the idea of order as a spiritual good. Burnham reflected this thinking in his own planning advice: "Let your watchword be order and your beacon, beauty."[9] In applying this designed order, as he did with all his city planning work, Burnham stamped his personal signature on the Senate Park Plan.

Burnham's approach to planning was a spiritual one, embodied in urban form. His younger partner Edward Bennett noticed that Burnham referred to Swedenborgian theory in a planning context. Bennett reported that Burnham, while working on the San Francisco plan, thought often of Swedenborg's explanation of the spiritual correspondences in nature and "interested himself in tracing the correspondence of spiritual powers and the municipal powers as indicated in the physical layout of the center of the city."[10] Burnham brought to his work on the Senate Park Plan that same spiritual analysis of the functional interaction among its carefully organized individual elements.

In addition to the orderly groupings and arrangements of buildings, another characteristic of Burnham's city plans was their provision for grand public space. Of them all, the Mall was the grandest vision. McKim made the most significant contributions to the design's architecture and Frederick Law Olmsted Jr. to its landscape, but the symbolic analysis was Burnham's. His vision was that great public space would uplift and enlighten the citizens. Burnham said that an enlightened public "will demand orderly arrangements," which his plans would supply. "And when the public mind is aroused to a strong sense of this need, it will build to the plans we are making, if they are good enough."[11]

Yet Burnham's imaginative development of his ideals and his faith in the capacity of man to achieve them were decidedly of the nineteenth century and already out of step with many of his peers. McKim, who clearly shared his dedication to beauty and his high standards, expressed no such faith in his fellow man to create the ideal future. Burnham's vision of the future was more akin to the hero of Alfred Lord Tennyson's poem "Locksley Hall" (1842), who "dipt into the future far as human eye could see; / Saw the Vision of the world and all the wonder that would be." Tennyson pub-

FIG. 17
Daniel H. Burnham's plan for the
city of Chicago, 1907–9
The Granger Collection, New York

lished his "Locksley Hall Sixty Years After"
with the altered vision expressed in the line
"Cold upon the dead volcano sleeps the
gleam of dying day." Burnham, however,
never lost the optimism of the earlier era.

Like the mid-nineteenth-century historian Thomas Macaulay, Burnham interpreted history as a progressive march
toward a better future.[12] In his lifetime,
there had been rapid improvements in
urban life: sewage systems, water-delivery
systems, gas and electric power, street-
cars, railroad lines connecting cities and
towns, and the invention and production
of the automobile. He imagined even
greater strides forward in the future.[13]
At the Town Planning Conference in London in 1910, Burnham urged listeners to
"remember that the greatest and noblest
that man can do is yet to come, and that
this will ever be so, else evolution is a
myth."[14]

Organizational Leadership

Burnham's ordered comprehensiveness
was so strongly apparent in the Washington work because he was the chairman of
the Senate Park Commission. His role was

self-defined from the beginning as that of organizer and leader. He was no doubt invited because his success as director of the World's Columbian Exposition was well known. According to Charles Moore, Burnham's election as president of the American Institute of Architects eight years earlier was founded on "a recognition of the organizing and administrative abilities of Mr. Burnham."[15] Although the question of who was to be chairman of the commission had not come up during his initial discussion with Senator McMillan, Burnham assumed that he was intended to head the group.[16] He and Olmsted were the two that McMillan invited initially, and Olmsted was considerably his junior. Burnham was applying a lesson he had learned from the Chicago exposition work, that any large planning effort required a centralized organization with a single command.

At the exposition Burnham had imposed a cooperative value structure, putting the goal of the group above that of any individual. This value resonated with the leading members of the architectural establishment, namely Richard Morris Hunt and McKim, Mead & White, who participated as architects of individual buildings at the fair. Burnham wasted no time in forging a similar bond among the McMillan Commission members—Olmsted, McKim, and sculptor Augustus Saint-Gaudens.

After the initial meeting of the commission in Washington, Burnham immediately began to identify and lay out the parts of the project. Within days, he wrote to Olmsted suggesting that he begin laying out the Mall area on a large scale.[17] Burnham also proposed the commission's trip to Europe to study landscape design

and park integration in and near major cities. Burnham's idea was that the group would travel together to see and react to these designs and then discuss their experiences in relation to the Washington work.[18] This itinerary re-created in compressed time the evenings Burnham met with his staff at the famous "shed" on the island in the exposition grounds in Chicago in 1893. Burnham's natural gifts for leadership and his experience at the exposition guaranteed that this commission would be collegial and well directed. In his execution of his responsibility he wisely put his confidence in McKim for the design elements, especially of the Mall, and Olmsted for the landscape design. He enlisted Charles Moore to revise the text to comply with the presentation appropriate for a Senate report.

In Chicago, Burnham's cooperative design process had produced the Court of Honor, which most observers interpreted as an expression of unity. Henry Adams observed that the exposition "was the first expression of American thought as a unity: one must start there."[19] Much the same thought was expressed by the former president of Wellesley College and Dean for Women's Studies at the University of Chicago, Alice Freeman Palmer. In "Some Lasting Results of the World's Fair," she singled out the subordination of individual interests to the interest of the whole as a paramount lesson learned. As she read the Court of Honor, the message was that as a nation we had learned to subordinate the self to the group.[20] For Burnham, the Court first demonstrated how unity might be embodied in an architectural composition. Believing in the Court of Honor arrangement (fig. 18) as both the physical

and the symbolic embodiment of a civilized society, the commission would have been particularly concerned that the Mall site be reimagined, as their report urged, as an expression of unity in a democratic country. This vision of the whole being greater than the parts would have driven their transformation of the urban boulevard of L'Enfant's mall to the greensward framed with rows of trees and harmonious classical buildings of their report.

Evidence of Burnham's organizing contribution is inherent in the Senate Park Commission Plan itself. The broad network envisioned by the plan, the first complete city beautiful plan, bears the stamp of Burnham, the father of the city beautiful approach to planning. The breadth of the plan, with its inclusion of the entire system of parks, many roads, and infrastructure, is firmly given to Burnham, as his other work in city planning demonstrates. Burnham was frequently the chief of large architectural and urban planning efforts. Charles Moore, the shadow member of the commission, wrote in his unpublished "Washington: Past and Present" that the comprehensive overview of the Senate Park Commission Plan was Burnham's contribution.[21]

As with the Chicago exposition, the coordinated breadth of the Senate plan is perhaps its most remarkable feature. In 1893, the World's Columbian Exposition had seemed to its creators and its visitors the ideal urban model. Industrialization and commercial growth had burgeoned quickly in nineteenth-century America. Much of the new wealth had gone into public and private buildings and even parks, yet the cities themselves were not improved. Individual projects remained isolated in the urban jumble caused by rapid growth. While coordinated park systems in Boston and New York were the first efforts at reform in the post–Civil War period, the exposition seemed to offer a new vision. A writer of the time summed up the concept thus: "The White City . . . is an apotheosis, it is a hope. It is not an end, it is a commencement. It is not a result, it is a promise."[22]

The promise for Burnham was that good general plans created beauty by ordering all elements into a logical system because "what is logical is also beautiful."[23] By including parks and open areas, boulevards, streets, and integrated traffic patterns, sculpture and public buildings, the Senate Park Commission created functional links and scenic contrasts of the natural and the formal. The effort of the architectural and landscape planning was to establish an order that was at once real and symbolic. The World's Columbian Exposition had taught Burnham the virtue of creating not just a single beautiful building but also an environment that was aesthetically ordered and well integrated with the architecture. The experience made it apparent that a beautiful city was best produced by the organizational and planning skills for which Burnham was so regarded. Speaking at a gala dinner in his honor in 1893, Burnham drew from the exposition two goals for city design and beautification: the creation of a well-considered plan and an emphasis on the conformity of the parts to the whole.[24] These goals were fully met in the Senate Park Commission Plan.

Advocacy

Burnham's career as a planner was marked by his success in winning acceptance for his plans. Not only were his plans well received, but a great many of them were actually translated into action. In addition to Washington, the cities of Cleveland, Manila, Baguio, and Chicago all retain parts of their Burnham plans.[25] His flair for marketing ideas and his careful cultivation of supporters contributed to this success. Other factors were built into the plans: Romantic imagery, a positive vision of the future, and an element of scope and vision to carry the imagination of future generations. These were not so much conscious elements inserted into the plans as they were personal characteristics.

In presenting his plans to the public, Burnham generally used a florid personal literary style and beautiful verbal imagery. He had a poetic imagination. In his

private correspondence he expressed without restraint the emotional impact of a work of art or the beauty of nature. Beauty as harmony and nature as harmony were featured in Burnham's interpretation. He wrote to the sculptor Lorado Taft about the Black Hawk Monument in Oregon, Illinois: "[T]he noble valley beneath your camp seems to me to have crooned to you and to have rocked you until you have sung its own song straight from the heart of nature—the superb simplicity of the thing and the mystery!"[26]

In the text of the Senate Park Commission report, Charles Moore carefully edited Burnham's highly colored language. In later work, such as the Chicago plan of 1909, he was accustomed to write of "the glow of the evening sky," "the sweet breath of plant life," and of the spirit of man and the nobility of beauty.

He was happiest making word-paintings, figurative pictures that uplifted and inspired. His language seemed to fit the Romantic classicism of the art he favored. The illustrations produced by the artists give form to the halcyon image Burnham's words always evoked, when not sternly edited as they were for the Senate Park Commission report. Carlton Chapman's illustration of the improved riverside and the proposed Lincoln Memorial for that report, for instance, creates the image of the arcadian Golden Age so popular in Renaissance literature and in American Renaissance paintings. In the Boston Public Library, that American Renaissance monument designed by McKim, Mead & White, the prominent paintings of Pierre-Cécile Puvis de Chavannes established the relevance of the Golden Age to the American Renaissance. In the Senate Park Commission illustrations, the Golden Age has been transposed to an urban setting, as it always was in Burnham's speeches.

Burnham was interested in the public visibility of the plan. In addition to the beautiful illustrations produced for the report and publicly exhibited at the Corcoran, Burnham had a small drawing of the proposed Mall lithographed at his own expense for distribution to hundreds of newspapers and the Associated Press.[27] Burnham gave lectures and wrote articles for publication despite his consciousness of his literary limitations. Burnham took up the pen to make the point that he felt would sell the plan—that the beauty created by the planning would have commercial value. In his paper "The Commercial Value of Beauty," he anticipated the draw of the renewed capital city both as tourist destination and place of residence for the numerous wealthy Americans who spent whole seasons in Europe.[28] In order to publicize the plan further, Burnham wrote another article, "White City and Capital City," for the prestigious *Century Illustrated Monthly Magazine.* The thrust of this piece was to identify the two with the emergence of comprehensive city planning. Burnham's argument was that Americans understood the World's Columbian Exposition as a forceful positive model of the value of comprehensive planning and were eager to see it at the nation's capital. He tied the realization of the value of planning to the Progressive reform movement through his observation of a growing desire for lawfulness and order at the municipal level. The lesson of the exposition and of the McMillan Commission work was that there existed

a "need for design and Plan for whole cities."[29]

It was Burnham who led the active opposition to deviation from the plan. In 1904, in a hearing before the Senate Committee on the District of Columbia, Burnham began his testimony by identifying himself as the champion of the concept of beauty in public building. He further claimed that, for the public, beauty in public planning was defined by the visual characteristics of uniformity and coherence as demonstrated at the World's Columbian Exposition.[30] Burnham's political influence was especially strong within the executive branch of government, where he had close ties to President William McKinley's administration. Yet he realized the power of Congress to determine the fate of the plan. He cajoled the weary McKim to lobby for the plan. He logged many miles traveling to Washington and New York to oppose the placement of the new Department of Agriculture building without observing the distance across the Mall called for in the plan.[31]

Beyond the public speaking, beautiful illustrations, and exhaustive lobbying, Burnham contributed to the commission the belief that a well-conceived plan would persist on its own and come to be accomplished. This belief he held from the beginning of his planning career. In his speech at the dinner given in his honor in 1893 celebrating his work on the Columbian Exposition, he said, "If one has capital and a well conceived plan, the thing does itself."[32] He was well prepared by his belief when the Senate Park Commission Plan was challenged. He wrote to McKim at the time of the controversy over the

width of the Mall and the Department of
Agriculture building to assure him that
the plan would persist despite the powerful political opposition of Speaker of the
House Joseph Canon.[33] He was confident
that "a noble, logical diagram once recorded
will never die; long after we are gone, it
will be a living thing, asserting itself with
ever growing insistency."[34]

Vision

The 1910 London Town Planning Conference was a unique moment in architectural history. Following on the heels of
the Berlin and Düsseldorf Universal City
Building Exhibition of May and June 1910,
the conference had the air of a worldwide
seminar. The Royal Institute of British

Architects, sponsor of the event, planned it to be "one of the most comprehensive exhibitions dealing with the subject of town planning and city development ever held."[35]

Burnham had a prominent part in the conference. At the banquet, he was called on to deliver a toast representing the American contingent. He chaired a session devoted to "City Development and Extension" at which Raymond Unwin, H. J. Stübben, and others presented papers.[36] Finally, he delivered an address during the last morning session, devoted to "Cities of the Future." His speech was titled "A City of the Future under a Democratic Government."[37] In this summation, Burnham characterized the breadth and meaning of the Washington work (fig. 19).

Burnham's invocation to the audience was to supply the city with long-range goals and shorter-range methodology. The city plan was meant first and foremost to lift the vision of the city to an ideal level, laying out a challenging project, broad in scope and stretching far into the future. His admiration for the farsighted plan of L'Enfant, which he had studied carefully, inspired Burnham in his planning for the future expansion of Washington. However, the primary factor was his own vision of an ever-expanding future. He infused the plan with this vision: "[T]hink what the country was a hundred years ago, realize what it is today, and think what it will be a hundred years hence;

you cannot plan for the future on too large a scale."[38]

Burnham, who had innate qualities for master planning, had both contributed to and learned from the Senate Park Plan work. He had come to identify the beautiful city with the fabric of democracy. In a democracy, when the majority of people of any town came to believe that dignity, efficiency, and beauty were essential to living, they would cause their wishes to be accomplished, "for a democracy has full power over men, land, and goods, and it can always make its laws fit its purpose."[39] In a democracy, the creation of a great city plan would always be a patriotic act designed to awaken the citizenry to action.[40] Guided by this belief, he raised the vision of the Senate Park Plan to the level of the symbolic, ideal City Beautiful.

Jon Peterson in his authoritative work *The Birth of City Planning in the United States* avers that the decision to present the plan as an ideal originated with Burnham.[41] Benefiting from Burnham's leadership and organizational management, the design of the Mall at the same time encapsulated his visionary idealism in its unity and order (fig. 20). In common with the greatest figures of the American Renaissance, Burnham found beauty as necessary to living as breath.[42] The commission's innovative Mall design, with its ordered space and privileging of nature, made this breath of life available to all citizens.

FIG. 21
Rajpath leading to India Gate,
New Delhi, India
Jeremy Horner / Corbis

"A Simple Space of Turf"

FREDERICK LAW OLMSTED JR.'S IDEA FOR THE MALL
Witold Rybczynski

❧ SYMBOLIC GATHERING SPACES of national importance are common features of established capital cities. They are usually either processional ways, such as the Avenue des Champs-Elysées and the Unter der Linden, or squares, such as Trafalgar Square and Red Square. New capitals have likewise generally followed this pattern: New Delhi has the vast axis of the King's Way (fig. 21); Brasília, the monumental Praça dos Tres Poderas. What is remarkable about the National Mall in Washington is that it is neither an avenue nor a square but a large expanse of grass.

It was not originally meant to be that way. The space between the Capitol and the Washington Monument in the 1791 plan by Pierre Charles L'Enfant (see fig. 1) is described as a "Grand Avenue, 400 feet in breadth, and about a mile in length, bordered with gardens, ending in a slope from the houses on each side."[1] Elsewhere L'Enfant wrote that the buildings would be theaters, music halls, academies, and "all such sort of places as may be attractive to the learned and afford diversion to the idle."[2] It was to be, in his words, a place of "general resort." Coming from an eighteenth-century Parisian, this description meant only one thing: a boulevard. Boulevards were a relatively recent urban form. When the defenses of Paris were decommissioned in 1670, some of the leftover bulwarks (or *bollevarts*) were planted with trees and became favored sites for leisurely promenading. Later, the bulwarks were demolished but the habit of promenading continued and, according to Spiro Kostof, "By the late eighteenth century the west end boulevards of Paris were lined with luxury stores, cafés, and theaters."[3] That was probably what L'Enfant had in mind.

Although the general outline of L'Enfant's design for Washington was followed, an 1804 engraved plan of the "District of Columbia and Vicinity" identifies the long open space not as Grand Avenue but as "Mall."[4] It is unclear how and why this change of names occurred. A mall was the British version of a boulevard. The first mall—simply called "The Mall"—was in Saint James's Park, London (fig. 22). It was laid out in 1660 as a playing field for a French croquet-like game called pall-mall. By the end of the eighteenth century the game was out of favor, but the broad avenue with four lines of trees survived as a fashionable promenade. Washington's Mall was merely an engraver's conceit, however, for despite the growth of the surrounding city, the long, open space remained untouched. There were several proposals to remedy the situation. In the 1790s William Thornton, the first Architect of the Capitol, ignored L'Enfant's plan and suggested a picturesque British park with meadows, clumps of trees, and a lake. In 1815 his successor, Benjamin Henry Latrobe, drew a plan along the same lines. Seven years later Charles Bulfinch, while also working on the Capitol, proposed a similar informal landscape treatment. Neither project was implemented. Nor was Robert Mills's rather clumsy design, which divided the Mall into a series of gardens.

In 1850 President Millard Fillmore commissioned Andrew Jackson Downing, the leading garden designer of the day, to prepare a "plan of improvement" for the Mall. Downing, a vocal advocate of urban parks, proposed neither an avenue nor a mall but a "National Park." His plan divided the long strip of land into six distinct parts. At the foot of Capitol Hill, he placed a botanical garden and three glass conservatories. Next was a British park with a fountain, serpentine paths, and carriage drives around a manmade lake. He surrounded the recently built Smithsonian with a large "Pleasure Garden" that was heavily treed and included a meadow. This was followed by an arboretum in the form of an evergreen garden with concentric footpaths. The unfinished obelisk of the Washington Monument (which Robert Mills had started building in 1848) was the focus of a "Monument Park," which was planted with clumps of trees threaded through with meandering carriage drives. The sixth section, which corresponds roughly to the present-day Ellipse, was a circular parade ground circumscribed by a row of elms and a carriage drive. The entrance to this gathering space was from Pennsylvania Avenue, through a Roman triumphal arch.

Less than a decade later, similar elements—meadows, naturalistic planting, lakes, carriage drives, walks—would be used in Central Park to great effect, but the two designs could not be more different. In New York City, Calvert Vaux (who assisted Downing in Washington) and Frederick Law Olmsted created a unified plan, but Downing divided the long Washington site into discrete, self-contained

FIG. 22
Procession of the gold state coach along the Mall from Buckingham Palace to Saint Paul's Cathedral to celebrate the Golden Jubilee of Queen Elizabeth II, London, June 4, 2002
AP Images / Wide World Photos / David Sandison

parcels. He called these parcels "scenes," and since he was by temperament a pedagogue, walking through his park would have been like walking from classroom to classroom: here are the botanical specimens, here is the pretty lake, here we learn about trees, and so on. The chief fault of the design was not Downing's rather prosaic conception, however, but rather its relation to the urban context. Central Park's naturalistic landscape was meant to provide a foil to—and a respite from—the relentless grid of Manhattan; central Washington didn't have a grid but instead a varied plan of diagonal avenues and carefully sited public buildings. It didn't need a foil.

Downing's sudden death in 1852, only a year after work began, effectively put a stop to the "National Park." Only the eastern portion was built. The design was further compromised when Congress permitted the Washington & Alexandria Railroad to build tracks and a terminal roughly on the site of the projected lake. The rest of the ground remained bare (fig. 23). Here is an 1870 description: "A large common . . . presenting a surface of yellow or white clay, cut into by deep gullies, and without trees except one or two scraggy and dying sycamores. The streets were mud roads, along which an omnibus scrambled once a day, to the steamboat wharf, and foot travel paced its muddy or dusty way over the bleak, inhospitable common in zigzag meanderings."[5]

There was a chance to make something of the Mall in 1874, when Frederick Law Olmsted was commissioned to prepare a landscape plan for fifty acres around Capitol Hill. Recognizing that any attempt to beautify the grounds of the Capitol would

FIG. 23
Cattle grazing in front of the
Treasury Building (photograph,
1865)
Hulton Archive / Getty Images

be compromised by the unfinished Mall, he suggested broadening the scope of his work to include the entire area up to the Washington Monument. He proposed to collaborate with two other prominent landscape architects: Horace Cleveland, who had worked for Olmsted on Brooklyn's Prospect Park, and William Hammond Hall, who was then building Golden Gate Park in San Francisco. Congress balked at the added expense, however, and instructed Olmsted to confine his efforts to the Capitol grounds. He did so, adding a monumental terrace and broad steps on the west side of the Capitol building (fig. 24). These changes firmly reoriented the Capitol toward the Mall, so that "what has been considered the rear will be rec-

ognized as its more dignified and stately front," he wrote.[6] What exactly would unfold beyond the stately front remained to be seen.

The Mall as a Landscape Idea

The centenary of Washington, D.C., was celebrated in 1900. To mark the occasion, Senator James McMillan of Michigan, who chaired the Senate committee on the District of Columbia, proposed a Centennial Avenue to start at the Capitol, run obliquely across the still unfinished Mall, and extend to the Potomac, which it would cross on a proposed bridge. The plan met with strong opposition from the Army

FIG. 24
Frederick Law Olmsted Sr., plan
for the U.S. Capitol grounds (rendering, 1874)
Architect of the Capitol

Corps of Engineers, which was responsible for federal buildings in the capital city
and saw the senator's plan as an encroachment on their bailiwick.

The American Institute of Architects,
too, was critical of the gauche proposal;
in addition, it wanted to make sure that
architects—not engineers—were in
charge of future replanning of Washington. The dynamic AIA secretary, Glenn
Brown, set things in motion by holding
the institute's annual convention in Washington and setting the improvement of the
national capital as the theme. He invited a
number of individuals to present papers.
Among the speakers was the landscape

FIG. 25
Jardin des Tuileries, Paris (photograph, ca. 1890–1900)
*Library of Congress, Prints and Pho-
tographs Division*

architect Frederick Law Olmsted Jr., who
was asked to talk about "landscaping in
relation to public buildings in Washington."[7] Olmsted, only thirty years old, had
inherited his famous father's firm with his
half-brother John. He illustrated his talk
with lantern slides of celebrated classical
European precedents such as the Tuileries
Gardens (fig. 25) and the Champs-Elysées.
He spoke with authority, for these were
places that he had personally visited and
studied. While emphasizing the need for
formality, he warned against fussy land-

scape effects. "Where the scale of the
general scheme is large," he said, "there
should be a corresponding simplicity."[8]

The junior Olmsted was critical of the
condition of the Mall at that time, finding
that "a great opportunity was thrown
away through disregard of the large meaning of the original plan," which, he argued,
was to provide an appropriate setting for
the Capitol.[9] But he added: "When I speak
of the importance of treating the Mall in
such a way as to relate strongly and visibly
to the Capitol, I do not mean merely, or

necessarily, that a straight road should be slashed down the middle of it."[10] He showed the Long Walk at Windsor Castle (fig. 26), a broad, tree-lined vista, and the so-called *tapis vert* at Versailles, a green carpet of grass enclosed on each side by *bosques*, or dense plantings of trees. It was something like this that he had in mind for the new Mall: "The axis of the Capitol should neither be ignored by the use of a wiggling road and confused informal planning, nor should it be marked by a mere commonplace boulevard, but by an impressively broad and simple space of turf, with strong flanking masses of foliage and architecture and shaded driveways."[11]

An impressively broad and simple space of turf. Olmsted's bold proposal, which seems obvious today, was distinctly original. Almost every speaker at the convention—the architects Cass Gilbert, Edgar V. Seeler, and George Oakley Totten Jr., the sculptor H. K. Bush-Brown, as well as Glenn Brown himself—proposed that the focus of the Mall should be a grand boulevard. Olmsted suggested something quite different: a greensward bordered by trees. The latter were particularly important. In L'Enfant's plan, buildings formed a hard edge to the Mall; in Olmsted's version, the buildings disappeared behind a dense screen of trees. This gave the greensward an almost rural appearance, which remains a distinctive feature of the Mall today.

Even before the convention was over, Brown and delegates of the AIA approached Senator McMillan, who was in the process of being pushed out of the picture by the Corps of Engineers. The complicated story of what happened next has been well told by Jon A. Peterson, who describes the machinations that led to "a behind-the-scenes bargain among McMillan, the AIA, and the Washington Board of Trade intended to advance each other's cause."[12] The result was the formation of a commission of experts (called the Senate Park Commission or the McMillan Commission) under the auspices of McMillan's committee, ostensibly to advise the Senate on the improvement of parks in the district but in reality to prepare a comprehensive plan for the entire monumental core. The AIA suggested that the commission consist of an architect, a landscape architect, and another architect to be nominated by the first two.[13] Asked for names, they proposed the noted Chicago architect and planner Daniel H. Burnham (see Cynthia R. Field's essay) and Frederick Law Olmsted Jr. Two decades earlier, McMillan had hired the senior Olmsted to design a park for Detroit. "I guess the son is as good as the father," the senator is quoted as saying.[14] Burnham and Olmsted picked Charles Follen McKim, the country's leading architect, to be the third member, and added the celebrated sculptor Augustus Saint-Gaudens.

In June 1901 Burnham, Olmsted, and McKim (Saint-Gaudens was ill) embarked on an intensive seven-week tour of European parks and civic spaces. This was chiefly a fact-finding trip, but toward the end the trio also discussed their plans for the nation's capital. According to Olmsted, the "decisions dealing with the width and character of the main mall Vista and its enclosing rows of elms; the framing of the Washington Monument by an orderly expansion of the frame of elms flanking the Mall, [were] first devised in a

FIG. 26
The Long Walk leading to Wind-
sor Castle
Tim Graham / Corbis

plan by McKim and me on a piece of qua-
drille paper in a train en route from Budapest to Paris in 1901."[15] Thus was the design
of the Mall finalized on the Orient Express.

It has often been suggested that credit
for the conception of the Mall belongs
chiefly to McKim (see the essay by Richard Guy Wilson).[16] He was definitely the
most accomplished designer on the commission and a forceful personality whose
New York firm was responsible for the
detailed plans of the Mall. Yet there are
several plausible reasons, in addition to
the statements quoted above, to believe
that it was young Olmsted who played

the pivotal role. To begin with, the Mall
is a landscape idea. Olmsted was in the
vanguard of his profession, having been a
founder of the American Society of Landscape Architects, and was in the process of
establishing a formal university course in
landscape architecture—America's first—
at Harvard.[17] The Mall is also essentially
a planning idea, and Olmsted was interested in city planning (he would go on to
serve as president of the American Institute of Planners). Moreover, he was familiar with the site, having prepared several
reports on Washington's zoo and parks in
the late 1890s and earlier having accompa-

nied his father on visits to the Capitol grounds.[18] It is Olmsted's steady hand that we see in the subsequent realization of the Mall. He outlived his colleagues: Saint-Gaudens died in 1907, McKim in 1909, Burnham in 1912. Olmsted continued to make his presence felt, serving on the Commission of Fine Arts (1910–18), the National Capital Park and Planning Commission (1924–26), and its successor, the National Capital Planning Commission, until 1932, by which time the Mall was largely complete.[19]

A Place of General Resort

Where did Olmsted derive his idea for the Mall? He had a solid background in landscape design, having served an apprenticeship under his father that included a study-tour of the major English and French parks. He was thus intimately familiar with not only the Tuileries Gardens but also the Mall in Saint James's Park and the Long Walk at Windsor. These formal designs do not appear particularly "Olmstedian," but in fact the work of the Olmsted firm had frequently incorporated axial elements. After all, the most famous mall in the United States in 1900 was the one in Central Park (fig. 27), and Olmsted *père* had also designed a half-mile-long mall with parallel rows of American elms for Boston's Franklin Park. He was a great admirer of the seventeenth-century gardener André Lenôtre, who had laid out the great axial lawn at Versailles, and at the Biltmore Estate near Asheville, North Carolina, his last project, he had created a vast, sloping *tapis vert* in front of Richard Morris Hunt's magnificent

façade. It is noteworthy that Frederick Law Olmsted Jr. spent many months at Biltmore overseeing this work.

The senior Olmsted is often credited with founding the landscape architecture profession in the United States. A constant theme of his writing was that while the art of landscape architecture had its roots in Europe, it needed to be adapted to American conditions. His son knew the United States exceptionally well. He accompanied his father by train to California, visiting Yosemite, the Napa Valley, and the Mojave Desert, and he served part of his apprenticeship as a surveyor with the U.S. Coast and Geodetic Survey in the Rocky Mountains. The sense of spaciousness of the western landscape, which so influenced the father, likewise appeared in the work of the son. Unlike Downing's crabbed vision of an enlarged garden, the broad sweep of the Mall recalls the expansiveness of the western plains. The Mall has sometimes been criticized for not being sufficiently integrated into the surrounding city.[20] Lewis Mumford considered it much too wide and sarcastically called it a "green belt, at best a fire barrier."[21] But such criticisms miss the point. The Mall happens to be in a city, but it is not intended to be an urban space; it belongs to the entire continent.

The young Olmsted inherited several character traits from his father: he was a quick study who grasped the "big picture," yet he was practical. His incisive early description of the Mall succinctly establishes its salient feature: respect for L'Enfant's intention but not slavish imitation of his design. The greensward was a classic *tapis vert*, but its pastoral simplicity was more English than French, and its vast

FIG. 27
The Mall in Central Park, New York (photograph, ca. 1905)
Library of Congress, Prints and Photographs Division

dimensions were more American than either. And the Mall was practical: the two dense *bosques* on either side of the greensward—thinned out today by Dutch elm disease—recognized that comfortable strolling in the grueling Washington summers benefited from deep shade. The gravel carriageways (today footpaths) were without curbs or fussy details. The pastoral atmosphere was further accentuated by the general absence of the sort of amenities that characterized Parisian urban gardens: kiosks, cafés, chairs.

One of the most moving of the beautiful watercolor renderings that Burnham's favorite artist, Jules Guerin, made of the future Mall for the Senate Park Commission is a view looking east from Sixth Street.[22] Although the Capitol is faintly visible in the distance, Guerin makes the focus of his picture the flat and featureless space of turf. There are a few pedestrians

among the elms and a single horse-drawn carriage on the drive, but the grass itself is as empty as a stretch of western prairie. And as awe inspiring. Olmsted had spoken of this in his AIA lecture: "The purpose to which the land was first set apart, and the purpose which it can serve with more complete artistic success than any other, is not primarily to rest the weary and give relief from the strain of modern life . . . it is to form a contributing part of the effect of grandeur, power, and dignified magnificence which should mark the seat of government of a great and intensely active people."[23]

This makes the Mall sound like a purely formal space. Yet, walking across the central green today, one is struck by the variety of activities it contains. It has been adopted by touch-football players and Frisbee throwers, by joggers and picnickers, and by tired tourists. It belongs—for once the cliché is apt—to the people. Their plebeian pursuits undermine the urbane sophistication that its designers sought to impart, but they do so in a pleasant way. Nor did Olmsted and McKim foresee the marked political degree to which an "intensely active people" would make use of the Mall. Mass gatherings have provided a sometimes raucous, and not always dignified, counterbalance to "grandeur and magnificence." Over the last century, the Mall has been thronged by Depression-era demonstrators, civil rights activists, anti-war protestors, and Million Man Marchers. (Some of these varied uses of the Mall are discussed in part 2, "The Nation's Gathering Place.")

On a recent June Sunday afternoon, almost the entire area between the Washington Monument and the Capitol was taken over by the Smithsonian Institution for its Folklife Festival. The odd mix included Appalachian fiddlers and young African men building a structure out of adobe bricks next to a cluster of Tuareg tents. Another section, devoted to Scotland, housed a temporary golf green, presumably for the use of kilted duffers. The rest of the grass area was taken up by canvas shelters, picnic tables, and parked trailer trucks. The atmosphere resembled a carnival midway rather than a national monument. Yet it underlined the distinctly American nature of the Mall: somewhat pompous, yet down to earth; of a scale that, while as large as the continent, managed to be not intimidating; and, above all, pragmatically accommodating. A place of general resort, indeed.

PART 2

The NATION'S
GATHERING PLACE

The People's Home Ground

Edith L. B. Turner

❋ I HAVE THE ROAD MAP of downtown Washington open on my table, and there it is, the city colored in yellow to mark the residential streets and in stone purple for the federal buildings and museums. The big buildings can be seen in a huge, spreading, oblong mass crisscrossed by bars of black and red that represent the Metro and the Interstate, while within, seeming to flood in from the tidal river and the sea, I notice a great cut, a ray of green, a swath, a long pod, an opening, a gap in the curtain—it is like looking down from an airplane through a gap in the clouds and seeing the green earth below, light, light green.

This is the National Mall. I call it, as others do, the people's home ground. My aim here is to divine something of the special meaning and special needs of that stretch of land.

I am an anthropologist, and I find myself searching in my memory for equivalent bits of space at the heart of other, quite different cultures. I remember gatherings in Africa for the purpose of making prayer to the spirit of a tree; in that tree resides an ancestor spirit. It is the spirit in the tree that commanded the gathering to take place because the spirit would then make itself known. That is to say, listening people are given the idea to make a shrine and pray there; then they find that the place becomes holy. Why do the spirits want the gatherings? For the power connection that is possible when humans take the step of living in universal, mystical participation. I have seen the power of a praying crowd. I have seen an Inuit crowd change the weather, an African crowd heal a sick person, and a Christian crowd connect with the spirit, as happened long ago in the Christian event of Pentecost.

There are similar big gatherings in other cultures. At the city of Puri in Orissa, India, the god Jagannath visits his people in his giant palanquin, and two other huge floats follow him down the road, accompanied by an enormous crowd. It is a highly spiritual moment.[1] Hasidim and Sephardim meet at the tomb of the Rabbi Shimon Bar Yohai in the city of Meron in northern Israel on Lag B'Omer, a very holy time. And in Christianity, about 10 million pilgrims a year visit the Shrine of Our Lady of Lourdes. In Islam, millions of worshippers travel to Mecca to be in the presence of Allah. They bow their heads to the ground and say humbly, "Labaika Allahumma" (Here I am, O Lord).

Washington, D.C., with 20 million people visiting and sightseeing each year, and with the chief attractions concentrated on and around the Mall, has become a distinctive American gathering place and, yes, pilgrimage site. One can trace the curious evolution of the Mall from "nature preserve" to "the center of a grand capital" to "the people's gathering place." The Mall seems to have established itself as a carrier of the American vision, against all opposition, a two-mile swath of green that has ensured its continuance. We note certain significant emphases in the geography and history of the Mall: the exact measurement of miles and the alignment of sacred memorials and the importance of anniversaries and repetitions or returns to the people's home ground. We witness here the development of root paradigms—tradition in the making, space and time in the process of being sacralized, becoming interresonant, with harmonics. The phenomenon is true material for a symbologist.

Movements and Meaning

The Mall as envisioned by the McMillan Commission in 1901–2 was to forever symbolize the pageant of American history. Frederick Law Olmsted Jr. and Daniel Burnham called for a city where citizens would receive instruction from noble monuments, museums, and sculpture, and within that scheme the plan gave particular emphasis to a memorial to Abraham Lincoln.[2] What the commission might not have anticipated was the development of additional symbolic values over time, as certain sites accumulated increased significance through sequences of key events that would take place there. The development of the symbolic or sacralized space of the Mall might be discussed as a series of anniversaries or periodic returns to the same home ground, each time with greater resonance.

This is especially true in the history of the civil rights movement—for which the Lincoln Memorial became a lodestone in the years after its completion in 1922. Here can be seen the people's tradition forming. On Easter Sunday in 1939, Marian Anderson (fig. 28), the distinguished African American opera singer, performed at the

Lincoln Memorial for a crowd of seventy-five thousand. She sang there because she had been denied the use of Constitution Hall by the Daughters of the American Revolution on account of her race; Eleanor Roosevelt, in protest, resigned from the DAR. Marian Anderson's performance helped to change the Lincoln Memorial from a monument to the president who signed the Emancipation Proclamation to a future platform for others to address civil rights causes afresh.

The site of the memorial became just such a forum for the nascent civil rights movement with Dr. Martin Luther King Jr.'s prayer pilgrimage in May 1957 calling, in essence, for a second emancipation act, with thirty thousand people attending. (A Civil Rights Commission was set up by Congress later the same year.) Then, most remarkably, as the climax of the March on Washington for Jobs and Equality, Dr.

King gave his famous "I Have a Dream" speech on August 28, 1963 (fig. 29), on the steps of the Lincoln Memorial and, with equally powerful symbolism, in the centennial year of Lincoln's Emancipation Proclamation. This was also the centennial year of the Gettysburg Address, the text of which is engraved inside the memorial, and Dr. King revisited some of the "unfinished work" to which Lincoln had then referred. Dr. King's historic speech marked a milestone in the nation's movement toward equal rights for all Americans. In 1986, Dr. King's birthday became a national holiday; a wreath has since been laid on the steps of the memorial each year. In 2003, to mark the fortieth anniversary of his speech, the same granite step, the same stone, on which he stood and spoke was engraved with his name and the words I HAVE A DREAM; thus the space has again been sacralized.

At the ceremony unveiling the engraved stone, Coretta Scott King, his widow, said: "This inscription adds a sense of wholeness to this site. [It] opens a new chapter in America's long journey toward freedom and equality."[3]

The link between the idea of equality and the consecrated site of the Lincoln Memorial was marked in a different way just after Dr. King's assassination. A little more than a month following his death in 1968, the Poor People's Campaign, which he had helped plan, brought more than two thousand people to Washington to live for a time in "Resurrection City," a shantytown spread across fifteen acres of West Potomac Park from the Reflecting Pool to the base of the Lincoln Memorial.

And the Mall's connection with the quest for equal rights continues into more recent times. In 1995, the Million Man March was held here; its speakers cited the Constitution and called for "a more perfect union," so that the many minorities of America might develop into one people: E PLURIBUS UNUM, as engraved on the penny.

The Mall has also been closely associated with rallies against war, most famously the hundreds of protests held here against the Vietnam War in the late 1960s and early 1970s. Perhaps the largest, organized by Vietnam Veterans against the War in April 1971, brought half a mil-

FIG. 30
Vietnam veterans during the dedication of the Vietnam Veterans Memorial, November 13, 1982
Bettmann / Corbis

lion demonstrators into the city. After a succession of such rallies, however, the Mall additionally came to be linked to the nation's post-Vietnam process of healing; fourteen months after the fall of Saigon, the United States marked the bicentennial of its independence on July 4, 1976, with grand displays of fireworks and enormous crowds celebrating on the Mall.

Against this historical backdrop, in another compelling evocation of the people's home ground, on Veterans Day in 1982 the Vietnam Veterans Memorial was dedicated (fig. 30), starting a custom among the bereaved of touching the letters on the wall commemorating the fallen soldier and laying flowers and letters at the foot of the particular inscription. The "wall" itself is exactly oriented so that the first angle that descends into the ground points to the Washington Monument, and the second angle ascending from below points to the Lincoln Memorial. The Vietnam Veterans Memorial was criticized at the time because large rallies were impossible at the site (in any case, none were permitted). But rituals evolved later. To pick a perhaps surprising example, in 1989 a group of bikers started an annual "Run for the Wall," a collective motorcycle parade across America from California ending in Washington with rites at the Vietnam Memorial.[4] The people have thus found a way to honor the memorial in spite of the ban on rallies there; the bikers have sacralized this monument as a group.

Over the years, hundreds of other rallies for scores of different causes have taken place, seeking to validate a particular cause by taking it onto a plot of ground so intimately involved with the nation's core values. These events have included not only antiwar and civil rights rallies but also antinuclear rallies, rallies against unfair housing practices, against President Nixon, in support of missing soldiers, in support of embassy hostages in Iran, for the victims of drunk drivers, gay rights rallies, foreign policy rallies, women's rallies, Native American rallies, environmentalist rallies, rallies for abortion rights, for the rights of the fetus, the right to smoke marijuana, for an end to intervention in El Salvador, freedom for Cuba, for Taiwan, Thailand, Pakistan, South Africa, and China, rallies for the world's hungry, the Hands Across America rally, the Promise Keepers rally, the AIDS Quilt, the Million Mom March, rallies for debt relief . . . the list goes on.

Among the most affecting of these gatherings have been the displays of the AIDS Quilt (fig. 31), the vast and growing assemblage of thousands of panels, measuring six feet by three feet apiece, each dedicated to an individual who has died in the epidemic and considered a "gift" to that person. The quilt was first displayed in Washington in 1987, then again in 1988, 1989, and 1992, and most recently in 1996. The first display numbered two thousand panels; in 1988 there were eight thousand, and then finally twenty-one thousand panels, the area of twelve football fields—making the quilt, it was said, the largest community art project in history. Indeed,

at its last showing in Washington, the quilt had grown so huge that it had to be transported in ten train cars and unfolded by almost a thousand people. Of that 1996 presentation, a spokesman for the Names Project said, "We're running out of spaces in urban America that can accommodate the quilt."[5] But there was still the National Mall. Put on view there, the quilt stretched from the grounds of the Washington Monument to the foot of Capitol Hill—a memorial not so much on the Mall as almost *becoming* the Mall.

The quilt project was nominated for the Nobel Peace Prize in 1989. Historically, the quilt helped to break down the walls between gays and heterosexuals. In part, perhaps, it was able to do this because the AIDS Quilt experience unfolded on a monumental scale—a scale comparable to that of the National Mall on which it was displayed—and thereby provoked a genuine awe that enhanced the quilt's emotional power.

The Space at the Capital's Center

These and many, many other examples of the symbolic character of the people's home ground have been built up over time. Great edifices of government history, science, and culture—gray stone flanking green space. That open green space is a true "lacuna," a negation of substance and detail in the middle of a capital city. At the beginning of this article, I hinted at the simplicities at the heart of religions, and now we see that a connection exists between the great power of an empty space and a reversion to simplicity,

FIG. 31
The AIDS Quilt, October 1996
AP Images / Wide World Photos

the simply human. Strong forms of this movement back to the unnamable truth are found in other cultures. Among the African Ndembu, where I first studied, the people remain silent about the name of their deity, the God of Rain. He is too powerful to name. When they open up his shrine, it is empty. In the Old Testament, the Ark of the Covenant has nothing inside it but the scrolls of the law. God is in the Ark, but God is ungraspable. Jesus said the Kingdom of Heaven is within you, not in a building made by hands. Mosques are empty of images, because in Islam it is

believed that God cannot be depicted in images. The much-ornamented and complex Muslim prayer rug, the rug on which Muslims kneel to pray and prostrate themselves, reveals in the middle of the weaving an undecorated oval space. That blank is God. Similar examples appear in Indonesia, New Guinea, among Native Americans, among Aborigines, and in many other indigenous symbolic systems.[6]

The function of the Mall is indeed like that of a lung; there needs to be an empty space inside. What occurs on the Mall is the oxygenation of the people, their freedom. Somehow the people recognize the Mall as belonging to them, never mind the efforts of the old planners who decided to turn the place into a Versailles. It somehow got turned into what we see now. The people had to retain that wide, accessible home, a space between the two freedom makers, Lincoln and Jefferson, and the two seats of power, the Capitol and the White House. The scenes on any Fourth of July (fig. 32) show how it happens. The inhabitants of the Mall are just—the people. Mark the way they come in vast companies, threading through the streets of Washington and flooding into the Mall to the heart of their democracy. I see a gentle, liberated, slightly wild people in picnic clothes moving easily, so different from the British public (I am a U.S. citizen now). The Americans come to the Mall in families. The children go to the Air and Space Museum and say "Coo-ool" to Apollo 11. We all want to hear that word of praise from our children.

The Mall is not a place where one worships some spiritual figure as they do at Lourdes or Jerusalem. It is for democracy,

the hidden secret of the place. Neither is it a place for hero worship, because the people create their own politicians. The politicians are theirs. The people do not "belong" to their rulers. The politicians belong to *them*. The people created the Mall the way it is. The people know, if they are made to feel powerless, that this is not the way it should be, and they act. Compare France, where they have experienced revolutionary moments of madness—strings of such moments for over two hundred years—all enacted in those closed streets of Paris. Here we have the Mall. It is our "Tidal Basin," a safety area. It changes the country without harming it; and there is power there.

The Scottish anthropologist Victor Turner, at the Lincoln Memorial and on the Mall, July 4, 1982, was pondering in front of Lincoln's statue. He said: "When you look at one side of Lincoln's face you see a stern face, against all forms of hypocrisy and untruth; when you look at the other side you see a mild man, all for peace. So he somehow combines these two attributes, sweetness and force, like few other men have ever done."

Turner walked to the left and read from the inscription of the Gettysburg Address on the wall: "The world will little note nor long remember what we say here."

He said, "Of course we did note it greatly and long, long remembered it."

He went on reading: "a new nation, conceived in liberty, and dedicated to the proposition that all men are created equal."

Turner responded, "And remember the words of the Scottish poet Robbie Burns,

'A man's a man for a' that'—we find those words actually *attested*, actually *embodied* in a nation, in a constitution"—the United States of America.

Sitting later that day on a large picnic cooler in the middle of the Mall surrounded by picnickers and baseball players, with the Capitol behind him, Turner commented, "I would say that all of them have 'gathered themselves to a greatness,' as Shakespeare said. They are trying to express something of the two hundred years of American culture, with all its faults, with its mistakes of foreign policy. Nevertheless they are trying to communicate something special to humankind.

Looking around here I see all these people, drinking colas, sitting in family groups, from Arkansas, Virginia, Georgia, wherever. They're happy. They're clapping their hands at a baseball win. I love this. If we were only able to cleave to the ordinariness, to the decency, to the humanism of this, we would wipe out all the fears, the nonnecessities, the barbarities that the great world powers are trying to inflict on one. Let's be what we are in our picnicking selves! That is love, that is humanism, that is what from the very beginning America was all about. And as a Scotsman I endorse it!"

Washington as a Pilgrimage Site
Frederick Turner

❧ IN LOOKING AT the past and future design of the National Mall, we might well ask ourselves, what is the Mall *for?* Clearly, the answer would include several parts. The Mall is the center of the District of Columbia, which is in turn the center of the federal government, housing the chief bureaucratic offices. The Mall cannot be thought about or planned for in isolation from the city that it serves, and its architecture and landscape design should reflect the meaning of that city. Washington, D.C., is the showpiece of American sovereignty and the symbol of our *demos*—that "We the People" in whom, we claim, the fundamental governing authority of our country is vested.

Equally as important, however, Washington is the paramount pilgrimage center of the American nation. Travelers from across the country and around the world make the pilgrimage to its richly symbolic sites, notably the monuments, museums, and government buildings on the Mall. Yet more than simply a journey, pilgrimage, we should remember, is a deep-seated human activity, one that recovers some archaic unity of experience and brings communities together in ways that remind us of the purpose of our lives. It is, among other things, a curative, ritual act. At major pilgrimage sites in Washington, the nation seeks to heal itself of wounds both old and new.

Yet all cities continually change and rebuild, even as they try to remain faithful to their founding principles. Given the special nature of Washington, what should guide its change in the future? And in particular, what should guide our architectural and landscape designs so as to make Washington a more effective pilgrimage site, a place of curative ritual?

To understand Washington's, and the Mall's, role in the ritual of pilgrimage, we must first investigate the underlying role of such rituals in our national life and, indeed, consider the nature of ritual itself.

The Liminal State of Ritual

Let us take as a model the analysis of society proposed by my father and mother, the anthropologists Victor W. and Edith L. B. Turner, since it fits itself very well to the understanding of pilgrimage. They proposed that society was made up of not only the powers of the strong but also what they termed the "powers of the weak." Except you become as a little child, Jesus said, you shall not enter the kingdom of heaven; whatever you do unto the least of these, my brethren, you do also unto me. Or, in the pagan Roman belief, if you entertained a wandering beggar, that beggar could turn out to be Jove himself in disguise. Across all human cultures, the weak—the mentally disabled, children, pregnant women, the very old, outsiders, beggars, and so on—represent the fundamental humanity on which the whole superstructure of society exists and embody the mysterious powers of the whole.

Thus there are always two regimes in society: a regime of structure (of power, rank, official position, gender roles, status); and a regime of *anti*-structure (of charisma, love, person-to-person relationships, sexual expression, magical influence, spontaneous affect). In our great popular rituals, we turn society upside down in misrule and carnival: in the Mardi Gras of New Orleans, the Carnaval of Rio de Janeiro, and the Fasching festival of the Rhineland, for example, sexual mores are temporarily relaxed. At New Year's Eve parties, we put on false noses and funny hats or dance in masked balls, covering up our ordinary faces and social positions, the better to express our common humanity and our personal uniqueness as opposed to our public role. Life-crisis rituals—birthday celebrations, wakes, marriages (with their strange rites of charivari)—likewise allow an eruption of the powers of the weak.

The Turners called this topsy-turvy, betwixt-and-between condition the "liminal," or threshold, state of ritual, and identified the fellow feeling that it enshrines as "communitas." Rites of passage, for example, involve a three-step movement: they take us into, and through, and then back out of a realm of mystery and experience. The structure of ritual demands barriers at either side, beginning and end, to keep the ordinary world out and the sacred world in—barriers that are marked by rites of separation and rejoining. ("Experience" is itself a key word, cognate with such terms as "per," Latin for "through"; experience is a "going through.") The liminal period is the period during which we cross the threshold and go through a transformation, metamorphosing from one life-stage (or one social mode or one relationship to nature and the gods) to another. The liminal period is not ordinary time but sacred time, or "holiday"—holy day—often assigned in the past to those extra days in the year that did not fit into the ancient calendars. Such rituals provide some safety and control over the passage into this dangerous, sacred place and out of it again, back into ordinary life. But they also leave open the possibility of novel events and insights that, carried back into the ordinary world, can beneficially change the social order—or, more disturbingly, damage it.

Pilgrimage is one of the chief of those rituals, and pilgrimage centers often contain a full range of the liminal characteristics I have described. This can be clearly seen by identifying the special qualities of certain sites in Washington, D.C., seen within the context of pilgrimage sites worldwide.

In considering the design of a city, we must address the purpose of that city. Obviously, Washington, D.C., embodies a splendid architectural and city-planning expression of the powers of the strong, of structure, status roles, ordinary time. As the center of the federal government and the showpiece of sovereignty, it physically represents itself well. But perhaps as a symbol of the *demos*, and especially as a pilgrimage center, it has but partially been thought out, and much perhaps remains to be envisioned and done in its design. Millions of people come to Washington every year; it is the Mecca, so to speak, of our Republic, and we feel that we have not done our duty as parents if we do not bring our children to it at least once. We feel that there is some mysterious experience that we need to go through there, though we are not entirely clear what it

is; sometimes a significant experience happens there, and sometimes, perhaps, it does not, and it should. Are there ways we can help it happen by the way the place is designed? To begin to answer this question, we must ask another: what is pilgrimage?

Human beings are a walking species, and we have over the past two million years walked our way all over the planet, and even on the moon. But what this means, simply, is that nobody is "home," nobody is "at home." We are all exiles. The greatest stories of the world—Genesis, the *Odyssey*, the *Mahabharata*—are about people who have lost their home and are trying to get back. In short, pilgrimage is our ritual of going home. It is the human answer—imaginary or contrived though perhaps it must be—to Thomas Wolfe's sad cry that we can't go home again. Think of our American family pilgrimage, Thanksgiving, when we try to get "home for the holidays." Like other great rites of passage, pilgrimage has a tripartite, liminal structure in which we struggle toward and enter a sacred place, pass through strange and transforming experiences there (that nevertheless restore us to our true selves and our true community), and then are ushered back into our working lives and roles but revitalized now by an inner knowledge of the purpose of our work, and perhaps with some shreds of insight for how to change it for the better.

What is this "going home"? What elements make it up? We can get a very good idea of what human beings expect from the homecoming of pilgrimage, by looking at pilgrimage centers all over the world. I would divide what we find there into seven categories: 1) rest and recreation; 2) reclaiming the past; 3) community;

4) healing; 5) divination; 6) orientation; and (7) transcendence. These I will examine in the remainder of this chapter, as I compare them to the features we find on the Mall.

Rest and Recreation

A pilgrimage site will usually include a house of treasures—a repository of the major talismans of the tribe or a showplace for the arts of the community. Pilgrimage is an ancient form of tourism, and a good pilgrimage site should be a good tourist venue, too. There is something of the theme park, or even the freak show, about many pilgrimage centers. The shopping and restaurants are often good, featuring famous local specialties: in Santiago de Compostela, you can get little silver medallions of Saint James, and a sort of sweet lemon pie. Ancient Delphi had a whole mall of booths sponsored by different Greek cities, each booth acting as a showcase for local manufactures and market goods. When the Wife of Bath goes on her annual pilgrimage in Chaucer's *Canterbury Tales*, she is quite as much taking

the air and enjoying the food and looking for a new husband as she is purifying her soul. It is important at the outset not to be too puritanical about pilgrimage: if it doesn't have a lot of appeal to our lower selves, the higher spiritual goods it offers will have no somatic anchor and bodily associations to keep them in memory. "Home" is where we relax and have a good time.

In this respect, Washington does quite well; its magnificent museums, its good restaurants, its roaring trade in souvenirs, and its exhibits of sacred objects, such as the Constitution, the Gemini orbital module, the *Spirit of St. Louis*, and the First Folio editions of Shakespeare in the Folger Library are typical of the genre. Little more needs to be done here.

Reclaiming the Past

To go on a pilgrimage is to re-celebrate the founding of one's community. Often, and very importantly, it is an ancestral burial place. The burning ghats along the Ganges, where Hindus are cremated and returned to the sacred waters of Brahman;

or Mount Nebo, the burial place of Moses, in present-day Jordan; or the ancient tumuli of Neolithic Britain; or the pyramid burials of Egypt and Mayan Yucatán, attest to this profound function. Home is where our ancestors are buried.

The pilgrimage is not just to the tomb, however, but also to the womb. Delphi contained, and still does, an omphalos stone that symbolized the whole Greek world's umbilical connection to the mystery of origin. There is often something deeply female about the pilgrimage site—consider Medjugorje in the former Yugoslavia, Czestochowa in Poland, Guadalupe in Mexico, Lourdes in France, and Knock in Ireland, all dedicated to manifestations of the Virgin Mary; or consider Sarasvati in India and remember that the ancient oracles of Delphi and Cumae were priestesses. Home is the womb from which we came.

Together with the tomb and womb, the pilgrimage site is also a place of historical reenactment, especially of the heroic exploits of the community's past. And it is the place where the great martyrs are celebrated: Canterbury Cathedral, where Saint Thomas à Becket was murdered by King Henry's knights, is a good example.

Washington has a mixed score in regard to its past. It does certainly have important memorials to the dead; indeed, the main axis of the Mall itself points westward beyond the Lincoln Memorial to Arlington National Cemetery and the tombs of many heroes and leaders, including such figures as Oliver Wendell Holmes and John F. Kennedy. Likewise, the Jefferson Memorial anchors the south end of the minor axis, while the Ulysses S. Grant Memorial (fig. 33) acts as a frontispiece

to the Capitol itself. Among lesser-known monuments, there is also the very fine, if rather hidden, *tempietto,* to the east of the Reflecting Pool, honoring the dead of World War I (fig. 34). The Vietnam Veterans Memorial has been transformed by the people from a modernist abstraction in stone to a rich shrine to the dead. There is also plenty of reclaiming the past in Washington through historical reenactment, ranging from the fine murals in the Capitol to the Benjamin Franklin impersonators and the continuing pomp of public military ritual. And martyrs such as Lincoln are well celebrated in the city.

Tombs and monuments to the dead are plentiful here. But there is too little of the womb in Washington; not much that is female, embracing, mysterious, nurturing, transformative. We do not find on the Mall an equivalent of the many-breasted Diana of Ephesus or Rome's Cybele, mother of cities, or the mother wolf suckling the infant Romulus and Remus. There is no Marian rose window of Chartres, no virgin of Guadalupe, no Kuan-yin or Kannon or Lakshmi, not even a Lady Liberty. The Roman mint, the core of Rome's financial empire, was in the temple of Juno, and her priestesses controlled it; Juno's nickname was "Moneta," the counselor or adviser or admonisher, and from that name we get the words for money, mint, and monetary. In Washington, women are indeed commemorated but usually for their successes in what were previously considered masculine fields of achievement, such as politics, arts, and sciences. Neither men nor women are celebrated much in public art and ritual for their caring and nurturing and gently prosperous virtues.

Community

We go on a pilgrimage to renew our ties
with distant parts of our own community.
A pilgrimage needs to include some kind
of communal meal—a thanksgiving or
holy communion or sharing of the sacred
buffalo, a renewal of the family table. For
such a reason, *The Canterbury Tales* begins
and ends with a banquet. The founding

records of a society's laws are often preserved at the pilgrimage site—the Ark
of the Covenant, the Magna Carta, the
Qur'an. And a pilgrimage site also, paradoxically, often contains a place of asy-
lum, where the laws of society cannot
reach and punish—for society is not only
its laws but also its recognition of its own
people as being the purpose of its laws and
thus as possessing a sacredness that must
finally be placed above the law. Polynesian
temple platforms, for example, were both
the center of the legal system and also the
place where fugitives could shelter from
their enemies or debtors. Home is where
the table is spread for you and your kin,
where you find both justice and refuge
from justice.

In these respects, Washington does
fairly well. The National Archives, housing the Declaration of Independence and
the Constitution, bridges Constitution
Avenue and Pennsylvania Avenue, the legislative axis and the executive axis. The
founding of the nation is represented
not only in paper form but in the flesh
at the Supreme Court, which is located
at the head of the Mall composition. The
Supreme Court is a sort of sanctuary,
where a fugitive from the agents of justice
can be given a breathing space to plead his
case. But although the cuisine of Washington is quite tolerable, there is no sense of
the communal meal. The closest the place
gets to that is the mass picnicking on the
Mall on the Fourth of July; here, a brain
trust of liturgists, ritual anthropologists,
theater experts, and designers might find
ways to turn the popular forms into a transforming experience.

Healing

Very often, a pilgrimage site arose around a well of life-giving water, a sacred river, or a volcanic spring whose medicinal virtues were widely praised. In India and Japan, most pilgrimage sites include this feature; the source of the Seine, the Fontes Sequanae in France, is still littered with ancient votive figures, representing the diseased parts of the body that the water gods might heal. Saint John was baptized in the Jordan at Bethesda; the Buddha meditated beside his sacred spring. Our own fascination with the springs of Yellowstone National Park—and the local Indian groups' similar sense of sanctuary there—has much to do with our natural sense that our health can be renewed by those waters that flow out of the womb of the earth. We can be healed in soul as well as body; the sacred waters can purge us of sins and curses, and they symbolize and precipitate a psychological renewal. Often, a pilgrimage center is a place of miraculous healings by faith: the grotto at Lourdes is surrounded by discarded crutches and prostheses. Home is where one recovers from illness.

Here again, Washington has a mixed record. There is little if any sense of connection between the practical functions of the city's hospitals and the deeper spiritual sense of the nation's capital as a pilgrimage center. We may be healed of our wounds here but not of our sins—or at least, not in the same, mutually enhancing context. This is in some sense partly an architectural and city-planning issue; I offer it here as a puzzle to designers. But it is now well known that the so-called placebo effect is crucially important in heal-ing, and if the spiritual-physical connection might be made more convincingly, more patients might be induced to get well in the District of Columbia.

The waters of Washington have been used to fine effect as a decorative and reflective design element. The grotto spring in what is known as the Summer House, on the Capitol grounds, is not given the significance of, say, the grottos at Lourdes or Fatima. There are fine fountains, such as the Mellon Memorial Fountain near the National Gallery of Art and the Bartholdi Fountain at the foot of the Capitol near the U.S. Botanic Garden, and of course several reflecting pools and flowing water features, such as those at the Franklin Delano Roosevelt Memorial (fig. 35) and the Enid A. Haupt Garden behind the Smithsonian "Castle." But they do not have the quality of mysterious flow and healing purity that they might have; we feel that it would be a sort of desecration, or breach of decorum, to immerse ourselves in those waters or drink them.

This lack of public bathing places was not always the case. During the interwar decades and perhaps for some time thereafter, the Tidal Basin served as a huge municipal swimming pool in summer and a skating rink in winter. Other water features were used for unauthorized recreation. The Columbus Fountain fronting Union Station, for example, used to be a place where the poor kids living nearby could cool off.

The original inspiration of fountains needs, perhaps, to be recaptured—where are Washington's sacred caves, its hell mouths and healing springs? Our Water Gate is not sacred, and perhaps it should be.

THEY (WHO) SEEK TO ESTABLISH
SYSTEMS OF GOVERNMENT BASED ON
THE REGIMENTATION OF ALL HUMAN
BEINGS BY A HANDFUL OF INDIVIDUAL
RULERS... CALL THIS A NEW ORDER.
IT IS NOT NEW AND IT IS NOT ORDER.

FIG. 35
Franklin Delano Roosevelt
Memorial, by Lawrence Halprin,
dedicated 1997
Andrew McCartney

Divination

Less universal, but still a major feature of many pilgrimage centers, is the presence of an oracle, a voice of diagnosis, divination, and prophecy. Lakota Indians go to a holy place to "cry for a vision"; ancient Greeks traveled to Delphi and Romans to Cumae to get supernatural advice. Chinese pilgrims consulted the Shang oracle, interpreted from the cracks in burned bones inscribed with the pilgrim's question; Hebrews received oracles from a small, secret room in the Temple of Jerusalem. Individual and collective problems are faced, diagnosed, and given an often ambiguous response, but even the framing of such a question is itself psychologically useful. Home is where we get advice, wanted or unwanted; where we are told what is wrong with us and how to fix it.

Could Washington in some way serve such a function? Perhaps as a central clearinghouse for national statistics, military scenario gaming, market prognostication, demographic analysis, and the census, it does so on a collective level. The Park Service counts the numbers of persons involved in demonstrations on the Mall as an index of national sentiment. There is a certain ritual element in the lighting of the Capitol dome's lantern, visible from the Mall, on nights when the Congress is in session and matters are grave. On the individual level, there is little of a revelatory nature for the pilgrim; the National Institute of Mental Health probably does not qualify. What would a place of oracles look like in the context of a modern scientific society? There may be an oracular element in Supreme Court decisions, the president's State of the Union address, and Senate investigation committee reports, but these are political or forensic instruments of social structure, the powers of the strong, not messages from the antistructural underworld about its future—they do not represent the powers of the weak.

Orientation

Pilgrimage sites are important in another way: they are often the zero point of our geographical measuring systems, the *axis mundi*—the place where the central pole of the ceremonial tipi (or, in an older spelling, teepee) connects earth with heaven; the gateway to the underworld. All roads lead to Rome; all distances in the Roman empire were calculated from the city. The imperial city of Beijing was the center of the Chinese world and the criterion of its weights and measures; Greenwich Observatory in England is the marker of Greenwich Mean Time and the zero point of the global lines of longitude. Jerusalem was the center of the world in medieval Christian maps, Mecca in Muslim maps; the Jew prays toward Jerusalem, the Muslim toward Mecca. Chichén-Itzá was not only the center of a Mayan empire but the gateway to the underworld, where human sacrifices were flung into the great cenote to feed the world's fertility. Home is where we start, where the heart is, what any place is west or east of, above or below; what we measure things by.

Washington meets these criteria well. The zero mile marker of the nation is placed at the crossing of the two axes of the Mall, running north-south from the White House to the Jefferson Memorial and east-west from the Capitol to the Lincoln Memorial. The Washington Monument, a few dozen yards away from the crossing point, would have been built at that very spot if the ground had been firm enough there. Perhaps there is a good symbolism in the forced avoidance of this most central point, in harmony with the first president's refusal of the crown.

In practical terms, it is in Washington that the Bureau of Weights and Measures determines our basic units of measurement, the Federal Reserve Bank and the Bureau of Printing and Engraving our units of economic value. Perhaps our design challenge is not so much to enhance these pragmatic "orientation" features as to connect them symbolically and ritually with the other elements of the pilgrim city, affective and spiritual; again, a challenge for architects, curators, and masters of ceremonies.

Transcendence

Finally, a pilgrimage center is a place where we connect with the divine world. The center is often built around a sacrificial altar; ancient Jerusalem is, of course, the model here, monopolizing during the priestly period Israel's sacrificial duties on Mount Moriah, the site of Abraham's offered sacrifice of his son Isaac. But

FIG. 36
Interior of the Washington
Monument
Library of Congress, Prints and Pho-
tographs Division

almost all pilgrimage sites require sacrifice; if trade is the way humans in practice
communicate with each other (even con-
versation is a trading of words), sacrifice
is the way that humans communicate
with God—how we trade with him or her.
Teotihuacan, the greatest city of the pre-
Columbian Mesoamerican world, was
oriented around two gigantic altars, the
Pyramid of the Sun and the Pyramid of
the Moon, and a group of fifteen lesser
sacrificial pyramids. Beneath the Pyramid
of the Sun is a natural cave from which
Teotihuacanos perhaps believed their
ancestors first came.

A pilgrimage altar is not only a place of
sacrificial death; it is also a place of resurrection and rebirth. In the Cathedral of
Saint James in Santiago de Compostela,
pilgrims place their hands into a hole in
the statue of the saint then pass through
a narrow, claustrophobic passage behind
the altar. When I was there, I was reminded
of the earthen tunnel in the Central African Ndembu women's coming-out ceremony, through which the girl must crawl
almost naked in order to be born again as
a woman.

The pilgrimage site is the place where
we meet the messiah, the creator, the
prophet; it is where we are closest to our
God or gods. Our true home is where our
God is always to be found.

Yet Washington is the capital of an explicitly secular—or at least nonsectarian—
polity. It is not necessarily the spiritual
capital of a religious nation. The United
States may be a religious nation, but it does
not have a religious capital, nor should it.
Thus, despite such remnants of the founders' sturdy deism as the congressional
invocation and the presidential oath, an

explicit denominational cult would not
be appropriate. Washington has splendid
cathedrals, notably the noble Episcopa-
lian one on the hill (Washington National
Cathedral) and the very fine Byzantine-
style Catholic one in the city (Cathedral of
Saint Matthew the Apostle), not far from
the White House. But it also has a strong
collection of emblems signifying its secular national religion, of freedom and equal
justice. There is a sort of generalized mystical or transcendent experience possible
in Washington, perhaps similar to that
of Wordsworth on Westminster Bridge
(another *axis mundi*, of course):

> Earth has not anything to show more
>   fair;
> Dull would he be of soul who could
>   pass by
> A sight so touching in its majesty:
> This City now doth, like a garment, wear
> The beauty of the morning; silent, bare,
> Ships, towers, domes, theatres, and
>   temples lie
> Open unto the fields, and to the sky;
> All bright and glittering in the smokeless
>   air.
> Never did sun more beautifully steep
> In his first splendour valley, rock, or hill;
> Ne'er saw I, never felt, a calm so deep!
> The river glideth at his own sweet will:
> Dear God! the very houses seem asleep;
> And all that mighty heart is lying still!

The popular experience of entering the
interior of the Washington Monument
(fig. 36) and being taken to the top is perhaps a way of getting this mystical sense
of the whole. It should be noted once again
that several of the core Mall experiences
that do give a sense of wholeness—the

Vietnam Memorial offering, the carnival-style mass demonstration—were, basically, created by the people and not the designers; perhaps designers need to heed the folk wisdom of the pilgrims they serve.

Still, in the concept of Washington as a pilgrim center, what is the connection between such transcendence and the idea of sacrifice? America routinely permits the purely utilitarian killing of animals for food, as well as of humans in warfare and in the punishment of criminals. These, however, are not "sacrifices" in the understood sense of the term. The sacrifices of our warriors in battle are well celebrated. But beyond them, America has two main forms of sanctioned sacrifice as such: the killing for scientific purposes of experimental animals—explicitly referred to as "sacrifice" in the laboratory—and the practice of clinical abortion. In my opinion, both are true forms of sacrifice: one for the sake of scientific knowledge, and thus in pursuit of America's secular religion of nature; the other as a consequence of the legal definition of a human being, and thus in pursuit of America's secular religion of humanism. It is not my purpose here to question whether the secular religion of the nation is adequate by itself but simply to call a spade a spade: as the home of the Supreme Court, which is the final arbiter of the legality of human abortion, and the Congress, which ultimately sets the legal standards for the laboratory sacrifice of animals, Washington lives up to its ritual role as a pilgrimage altar. For the architect and designer, again, the noblest artistic and liturgical role would be to make explicit in all their rich complexity and ambivalence the meaning of these sacrifices and their connection with the other aspects of the pilgrim city as outlined here.

How did the rulers, architects, designers, and planners of the past and of other nations create successful pilgrimage cities? Obviously, by investing in grand and costly artifacts—buildings that stick up into the sky and inspire heroic thoughts and aspirations, noble sculpture, and great public pictures. The city of Washington has had plenty of advice in this regard, some good, some bad; it needs more. But it is in other respects that the nation's capital can perhaps learn from worldwide human tradition.

The following are some of the recurring elements of pilgrimage center design.

- Caves and grottos
- Flowing water
- Sacred groves
- Shrines of sacred objects and relics
- Architectural forms embodying female symbolism—arches, caves, enclosed spaces, secret passageways, places of dark and mystery and security
- Icons—that is, sacred pictures whose subjects are not safely separated from the picture's physical surface by means of devices such as perspective, but in which the physical surface actually participates in the holy magic of its subject
- Communal spaces in which status distinctions and other forms of power differentiation and social roles are nullified
- Distinct gated boundaries between sacred and mundane space, requiring purification or sacrifice before entry
- Concentric and chiastic structures, such as mazes, rendering in space the tripartite phases of the ritual process

FIG. 37
Vietnam Veterans Memorial,
dedicated 1982
*AP Images / Wide World Photo / Mark
Wilson*

- Places of fear, peril, experience,
transformation

It is for students of the design and architecture of Washington to decide which,
if any, of these features the city already
possesses adequately, which it needs, and
which it should avoid.

    Many of the necessary design elements
are already present: the Capitol grotto,
flowing and still waters, trees, shrines,
communal spaces, even a few concentric
structures, such as the beautiful but
mostly unvisited World War I *tempietto*.
The great art galleries, with their codes
of visitor behavior and their request for

financial support, act in a way as sacred
precincts requiring certain qualifications
for entry.

    There is, I believe, an appetite in the
American pilgrim for at least some of the
experiences such design elements can help
mediate. I think the Vietnam Memorial's
success derives partly from the simple but
affecting fact that people have to go below
ground level to see it (fig. 37). The Mall, as
Edith Turner argues in her essay, is obviously a marvelous, open-ended communal
space where status distinctions among
Americans are set aside and where new,
even disruptive, insights and emotions
can enrich the national experience. The

Mall has groves aplenty: are there ways to make them more numinous and sacred? Should parts of the city and its parks be left open to the future? Should other parts even be removed? Washington's great potential perhaps needs to be focused into moments where all the multitudinous significances it contains are connected and made explicit without reductiveness. Not ignoring its more explicit and heroic monuments, it needs to recognize the meaning of its mazes, grottos, and wombs, its passageways through into psychic metamorphosis, its oracles, its altars, its sacred precincts, its communal feasts, and its healing waters; when those elements are not sufficiently present, there is an artistic opportunity for creating them or bringing out their significance.

The idea of the pilgrimage city can, I believe, help guide planners and architects of the future. If these meditations are suggestive, if they stimulate the imaginations of such artists and professionals and open up some new perspectives, they have served their purpose. If they can help Washington become an even more beautiful city than it is already, they will have done more than that.

Culture of, by, and for the People

THE SMITHSONIAN FOLKLIFE FESTIVAL

Richard Kurin

❋ "FOREST LAWN ON THE POTOMAC"—that's how S. Dillon Ripley, the eighth secretary of the Smithsonian Institution, referred to the National Mall in the early 1960s.[1] The phrase blatantly, but cleverly, suggested the cemetery-like character of the capital's central space. A major thrust of Ripley's tenure was to rectify that by "livening up" the Mall and turning it into a "people's space." That he did through symbolic and practical actions, the most visible and enduring of which was establishing the Smithsonian Folklife Festival, held each year on the grounds of the Mall.

This essay examines the purposes and consequences of the festival, particularly with regard to issues of cultural representation. The insertion of the festival into the Mall itself, with the diverse peoples and traditions represented, reveals the role of culture in the capital and the place of those various cultures in the life of our nation. It also reveals some of the dynamic tensions between the Mall as a powerful symbolic space and an event designed to help realize an aspect of its symbolic purpose.

Background

Founded in 1967, the festival is an annual presentation of cultural traditions from across the United States and around the world. It takes place for two weeks overlapping the Fourth of July holiday and typically draws an audience of more than a million visitors. The festival, like other Smithsonian exhibitions, is based on research and is curated. It typically includes hundreds of musicians, artisans, storytellers, cooks, and others illustrating their traditions through concerts, demonstrations of craftsmanship and work skills, dance parties, cooking demonstrations, narrative sessions, and a variety of other formats. This "living exhibition" annually includes various context-setting features such as examples of vernacular architecture, crops and gardens, animals, and cultural icons; for example, a New Mexico–style adobe plaza, a Hawaiian taro patch, Tibetan yaks, and a tipi. The festival typically generates national, and sometimes worldwide, media attention. Though the festival is free to the public, it generates considerable revenue through the sale of food, crafts, books, and recordings—almost all of which goes back directly to the artists, musicians, authors, and concessionaires. The festival is produced by the Smithsonian's Center for Folklife and Cultural Heritage, which also produces Smithsonian Folkways Recordings and a variety of educational materials and activities, cares for a documentary archival collection, and works on cultural policy studies and issues. The cost of the event is supported through federal appropriations and Smithsonian trust funds, as well as by sponsors such as foundations, corporations, private donors, state and national governments, and grassroots community groups.

While the Smithsonian Folklife Festival is of relatively recent origin, organized festivity in the capital's core goes back to the early days of the Republic. The historian William Seale writes about Thomas Jefferson's administration in *The President's House:*

> The Fourth of July was a time to be outside. The President's Park—called the "common"—came alive at daybreak with the raising of tents and booths soon followed by crowds of people. A regular fair was held, selling food and drinks, as well as baskets, rugs, and other cottage products. There were horse races and tests of skill among the men. Cockfights and dogfights took place on the sidelines. In the bare "parade" kept clear in the middle, the Washington Militia and other military companies drilled between ten o'clock and noon. Music played as well, and guests were invited into the White House to greet the President and celebrate their independence.[2]

Public celebrations and performances, particularly musical ones, were held outdoors on the White House grounds during most of the nineteenth century. The Mall, in Jefferson's time and through much of the century, was not an attractive place for public gatherings—sodden as it was with drainage from Tiber Creek and issuing forth what people of the time referred to as "harmful" or "unhealthy vapors." This changed somewhat with the founding of the Smithsonian Institution and the development of parks and gardens on the Mall. The Mall as a place for leisure activities and exploration then began in earnest. Visitors could enjoy the winding garden paths, the so-called public museum of labeled trees and shrubs, the Smithsonian "Castle," the animals that made up the early National Zoo, and, by the 1880s, exhibits and collections in the newly built National Museum building (currently the Arts and Industries Building). During this period the bandstand near the south portico of the White House, which had long hosted many performances on the grounds of the Executive Mansion, was moved to the Mall. The move did not, however, produce a long-lasting program.

Though the remodeling of the Mall envisioned by the McMillan Commission was based on architectural ideas embodied in the 1893 World's Columbian Exposition in Chicago, it did not include the live performances and cultural programs that had animated that popular world's fair. Some 21 million visitors to Chicago had been entertained by the Ferris wheel, the dancing of Little Egypt, and "living ethnological villages"—designed by the father of American anthropology, Franz Boas, and Smithsonian scholars and curators.[3] None of these features or cognate programs were developed for the Mall in Washington. Indeed, no plan for outdoor cultural activity on the Mall took hold.

To be sure, people did gather on the Mall at times: the 1892 National Encampment of the Grand Army of the Republic, for example, or the 1932 "bonus army" mobilization, or the 1939 concert by Marian Anderson at the Lincoln Memorial.

These were protest events, organized and staged to bring attention to failings of government and gaps in democratic ideals. Indeed, the paradigmatic event for contemporary large-scale public gatherings on the Mall was the 1963 March on Washington, capped by the "I Have A Dream" speech of Dr. Martin Luther King Jr. That event included Marian Anderson singing "He's Got the Whole World in His Hands." It also featured several folk or protest performers of the time, Bob Dylan singing "Blowin' in the Wind" and Joan Baez. Fortuitously, it was the linking of the civil rights movement and the folk revival with the perceived need for museological innovation that led to the Smithsonian's festival.

Festival Origins and Development

Several museums in the early 1960s began to develop more active public programs: concerts, children's activities, skill demonstrations, living-history enactments that would supplement traditional exhibitions but also make them more engaging and more attractive to visitors. S. Dillon Ripley was a champion of this approach.

Ripley had come from the Peabody Museum at Yale and, as an ornithologist, fully understood the serious research purposes to be served by the museum. But, as Ripley wrote in *The Sacred Grove*, he also relished the educational role the museum could play. It could stimulate a sense of discovery. Visitors could be awed by artifacts and displays. The museum could be a lively place, engaging the senses and enlarging the mind. Unfortunately, the Smithsonian, Ripley wrote, "was someplace you visited after a heavy Sunday dinner."[4] It was anything but exciting when he took the helm in 1964.

As for the Mall, he saw it as dead space in the heart of the nation. Ripley, as a child, had been quite fond of the Tuileries Gardens, the great urban park in the middle of Paris, stretching from the Louvre to the Place de la Concorde. The park, with its paths, trees, and greenery in the midst of a great capital city, was full of life, with strollers, performers, food vendors, and children. Ripley saw the National Mall, in contrast, as bereft of people, civic life, and enjoyment.

Ripley turned his attention to the Mall, not only conceptually but also literally. The statue of the venerable first Smithsonian secretary, Joseph Henry, stood in front of the "Castle," facing toward the institution's first building and headquarters. Ripley turned it around, so it would face outward, toward the public and the broader society—thereby signaling a program of putting knowledge in public view for the enjoyment of all. Ripley supported the idea of a carousel on the Mall so that young people could enjoy the rides, the sounds, and the period workmanship of the wooden horses and carriages. As secretary, he initiated the establishment of the Smithsonian's Anacostia Neighborhood Museum, in the poorest of Washington's wards, so that its citizens could partake of the advantages museums had to offer.

Ripley's effort to liven up the Smithsonian had a profound democratic component. The institution had been founded for the "increase and diffusion of knowledge among mankind."[5] Ripley believed in this ideal of enlightenment and felt that museums could play a major role in bringing knowledge to the people. He sought various means by which to do so.

He hired James Morris in 1966 as director of museum services and shortly thereafter appointed him head of a new Division of Performing Arts. Morris came up with a broad program of performances that would enhance the range of experiences available to visitors. Morris developed barbershop-quartet concerts, theatrical performances, puppet shows, a "Rites of Spring" program, a "Summer in the Parks" program, and even for a brief time a nine-hundred-seat nylon-and-steel Theater-on-the-Mall. Plans were formulated for a Smithsonian sound and light show and other programs.

Morris, a trained operatic tenor, had organized the American Folk Festival in Asheville, North Carolina, in 1963. This was a staged performance of folk heritage involving Alan Lomax, Pete Seeger, and others. The early 1960s had seen the development of many folk festivals, including those at Swarthmore, the University of Chicago, and the famous Newport Folk Festival. Ripley loved the idea of a revitalized bandstand, outdoors on the National Mall. Recalling New England summer town-band concerts, he envisioned visitors listening to the music provided by the Smithsonian, spread out on the national town commons. Morris suggested that the Smithsonian organize something more ambitious, youthful, and, at the time, perhaps more popular—a folk festival.

Morris hired Ralph Rinzler (fig. 38), Newport's head of research and a musician in his own right, and Henry Glassie,

a folklorist and material culture expert from the University of Pennsylvania who had worked with Rinzler at Newport, to plan and organize the first festival, to be called the Festival of American Folklife. The festival would build on the Smithsonian's longstanding ethnographic research on American Indians at the Bureau of American Ethnology and Department of Anthropology and on the research of curators at the Museum of History and Technology (later to become the National Museum of American History). It would also expand on the precedent that the folklore scholar-advocates Scott Odell and Archie Green had established by staging performances on the museum terrace.

Rinzler became the first director of the festival. He had worked closely with Pete and Toshi Seeger at Newport. Bob Dylan was, with Rinzler, a pupil and fan of Woody Guthrie, learning tunes from him in New York City. Rinzler had experience in man-

aging artists—including Bill Monroe and Doc Watson—on the folk festival circuit. He was an experienced field documenter of musical traditions, inspired and mentored by Lomax, Charles Seeger, and Moses Asch.

Rinzler brought several lessons from Newport to the Mall. The Newport Folk Festival was produced in the midst of great mansions and the conspicuous display of wealth. With participants like the Student Nonviolent Coordinating Committee's Freedom Singers, Judy Collins, Joan Baez, and Dylan, the Newport festival offered a means for the young generation to make a protest statement to entrenched powers on behalf of the people.[6] Rinzler took this perspective to the Mall, albeit in tempered form. He also took to the Smithsonian the impact that appearances at Newport had made on the more traditional performers. He was moved by the appreciation that the outstanding Cajun musician Dewey Balfa felt when applauded by an audience of afflu-ent, urban, northern youth—a reaction much more positive than Balfa had been used to receiving back home. Energized, Balfa went on to revitalize Cajun music and culture, with Rinzler's support.[7]

The first Smithsonian festival was held in 1967 under several tents on a portion of the Mall and on the terrace of the Museum of History and Technology. Ripley's initial allocation was a few thousand dollars. The festival included eighty-four participants: Bessie Jones and the Georgia Sea Island-ers, Moving Star Hall singer Janie Hunter and coil basket maker Louise Jones of South Carolina, dulcimer maker Edd Presnell from North Carolina, Dejan's Olympia Brass Band from New Orleans, Navajo sand painter Harry Belone, Acoma Pueblo potter Marie Chino, the Yomo Toro Puerto Rican Band and the Irish Ceilidh Band from New York, cowboy singer Glenn Ohrlin, bluesman John Jackson, folk singer Libba Cotten, Russian *glinka* dancers from New Jersey, King Island Eskimo dancers from Alaska, and country blues singer Fred McDowell, among many others.[8] The festival attracted more than 430,000 visitors and the positive attention of Congress. Paul Richards wrote in the *Washington Post:* "The marble museums of the Smithsonian Institution are filled with beautiful handworn things made long ago by forgotten American crafts-men. Nostalgic reminders of our folk craft heritage, the museum exhibits are dis-cretely displayed, precisely labeled, and dead. But the folk tradition has not died. Yesterday it burst into life before the astonished eyes of hundreds of visitors on the Mall."[9]

Since then, more than twenty thousand culture-bearers from every region of the United States and some ninety other nations have participated in the festival for audiences numbering over 38 million people. The festival has mainly been held on the Mall between the Washington Monument and the Capitol. In the years 1973–76, it was held on the grounds of the Lincoln Memorial, around the reflecting pool and in Constitution Gardens, due to the construction of the Metro and the Smithsonian station. The festival has been held mainly in the summer, the last week of June and first week of July. In 1977–81, it was held in the autumn. Most years it has averaged ten days, but several times has been shorter.[10] The 1976 Bicentennial festival was exceptional and ran for three months and cost over $9 million. The 2006 festival cost $5 million.

Outdoor Festival versus Inside the Museum

The festival has always occupied an uncer-tain, ambiguous position vis-à-vis the Smithsonian's museums. When the festi-val was first announced in 1967, the *New York Times* headlined the story "Fresh Air for Nation's Attic," a reference to the Smithsonian's somewhat dusty museum image.[11] It was Ripley, though, who suc-cinctly characterized the relationship by describing the festival as a way to "take the instruments out of their cases and let them sing!"[12] This became the mantra for the festival. The relationship between the festival and Smithsonian museums was best captured by Undersecretary Dean

Anderson at the festival's opening ceremony in 1986. "Museum is a noun," he said; "the festival is a verb."[13]

There are, of course, many ways the festival is similar to the group of museums that surrounds it. Both are under the Smithsonian umbrella. Both are involved in similar professional and bureaucratic processes relating to budget, employment, procurement, sponsorship, ethical guidelines, operational procedures, and intellectual property rights. Both help legitimate or bring added value and attention to that which is exhibited—whether it be an artifact, work of art, or a cultural community and its living traditions.

The festival has engaged in a continuous dialogue with the museums from its founding. Rinzler and others early on faced the issue of whether the festival could be a serious format for the representation of culture. Some scholars in the museums were doubtful. First, historians and anthropologists questioned the scholarly status of folklore, which they perceived as being a less rigorous discipline than their own, less significant in the scope of human affairs, and of inferior academic standing. Second, the festival seemed like simple entertainment and, as such, of dubious educational value. Third, the festival had as its teachers and interlocutors people who were carriers of the traditions, not those who were expert in studying them. These folklife carriers, most lacking in formal higher education and specialized professional training, could not be counted on to give the public a high-quality, objective account of their culture. Fourth, many of them and the traditions they represented were of questionable authenticity. In contemporary times, some argued, the true form of these traditions had vanished. The danger was that the festival would present ersatz, revived, and barely surviving traditions—mere shadows of the real thing. Fifth, the festival was a throwback to the expositions of the late nineteenth and early twentieth centuries, in which people of non-Euro-American cultures were exhibited and displayed like ethnographic oddities. Was not the festival a contemporary form for the exhibition and display of living people—a somewhat unethical, neocolonialist, exploitative effort to create what might be called a human zoo for the voyeuristic pleasure of Washington's powerful? Finally, noting that the festival annually pitched its tents outdoors, some doubted how anything out on the Mall could possibly be considered a serious effort to convey knowledge.

These are all relevant arguments, and the festival has, either directly or indirectly, dealt with each of them over the years. From the beginning, Morris, Rinzler, and Glassie convened groups of distinguished scholars from a variety of disciplines to discuss the idea of the festival and develop its principles. The festival was always based on research, fieldwork, and documentation. Bernice Johnson Reagon saw the festival as a direct, unique way to present research results in a public format: "[The festival] is like walking through a major research project or term paper, and like a good book, one that you can't put down."[14] Over the years, thousands of reputable scholars, lay and academic, folklorists, ethnomusicologists, anthropologists, historians, and those in related cultural fields have conducted research for festival programs and helped present concerts, demonstrations, and other activities on the Mall. Festival programs are curated, just as museum exhibitions are, subject to layers of scholarly, technical, and institutional review. Researchers are instructed to follow specific guidelines in identifying and documenting cultural traditions and practitioners appropriate for the festival. The festival has developed a repertoire of practices for presenters—those academic and lay scholars who provide background on traditions, introduce performances and demonstrations, help translate when necessary, and lead discussions. Organizers conduct training for presenters and monitor their effectiveness. Beginning in its second year, the festival developed a program book, intended as a parallel, of sorts, to a museum's exhibition catalog.[15] Early on, the festival developed the practice of producing substantive, museum-quality signs with texts and photographs, along with photomurals designed for use outdoors, to inform visitors about the cultures presented. Such measures have sought to ensure the research-based quality of the festival.

Survey results year after year indicate that the public believes it learns from festival performances and presentations— more, in some ways, than from museum exhibitions or books or documentary films on cultural topics.[16] The festival's use of multisensory, participatory experiences has been increasingly adopted by museums as sound educational practice.

The festival has also been able to illustrate the dynamic nature of tradition, showing how it adapts to and changes with circumstances, and while the festival often presents the "best practices" of a tradition, it is not confined to some restrictively literal presentation of the past. Though perhaps initially focused on rural musical and handicraft traditions, the festival has fully and freely explored contemporary urban traditions as well, presenting, for example, talented craftspeople who may use electric tools, even if their ancestors did not. Within the Smithsonian, the festival has pioneered examinations of all sorts of cultural communities and types of traditions. It has been very strong in looking at American ethnic and minority cultures, Native Americans, and the work of a variety of occupational cultures—from coal miners, cowboys, taxicab drivers, farmers, and fishermen to trial lawyers, Broadway choreographers, urban architects, Wall Street traders, and even Smithsonian scientists.

Anthropology, social history, and other cultural-studies areas have caught up to the festival in the realization that tradition-bearers possess, and can convey, knowledge. In part, this realization emerges from developments in the social sciences and humanities that have questioned scholarly objectivity, raising the issue of interpretation in the presentation of ethnography and history, and examining the basis on which the authoritative voice is construed. Senator Mark Hatfield captured this sense when he said at the opening ceremony of the 1978 festival, "No curator can convey through a glass display case what the people themselves can say to us directly."[17] In this respect, the festival is multivocal, inviting many people— including culture-bearers, curators, presenters, volunteers, members of the visiting public, officials, and others—to speak. Rather than present a single, tightly scripted story, the festival is what has been called a "low-resolution medium" for conveying knowledge.[18] Many stories and ideas are offered, in whole and in part; some are straightforward; others teased out of experience. There is no "official" line or omniscient curator.

It goes without saying that festival participants do not feel they are part of some undignified, voyeuristic display. Indeed, they overwhelmingly indicate, through letters, surveys, and other feedback, that they feel they are well treated and well respected and they enjoy sharing their knowledge and talents with the public.[19] They approach what they do at the festival with all due seriousness, recognizing that it is their opportunity to have the stage and microphone to express what is important to them. This creates a sense of exuberance out on the Mall, a celebration of public communication. Margaret Mead, a strong supporter, noted, "The Festival is a people-to-people celebration in which all of us are participants—now as organizers, now as audience, as hosts and as guests, as friends and neighbors or as strangers finding that we can speak the same language of mutual enjoyment."[20]

When James Boon, an anthropologist and research fellow working in the National Museum of Natural History, visited the festival, he experienced a sharp contrast between it and the museum and was prompted to write an article entitled "Why Museums Make Me Sad."[21] The museum was quiet and sedate, a bit dark, old and rich. The festival was outside, open, loud, sensory, and youthful. In contrast to the museum, the festival offers

what one-time festival collaborator Victor W. Turner recognized as a "liminal" ritual space in which people could experience *communitas*, a sense of themselves as part of a larger whole (see the previous essay by his son Frederick Turner).[22] More than simply instructive, the festival was itself a rite of cultural democracy.

Cultural Democracy and Diversity

From its inception, the festival has pioneered the concern for diverse representation in cultural institutions and, certainly predating broad public consciousness of multiculturalism, has been a voice for the inclusion of a great range of peoples and perspectives in telling the cultural story of the United States and the larger world (fig. 39).

Ralph Rinzler developed his concept of cultural democracy from such teachers as Charles Seeger and Alan Lomax and through the folk music revival and the civil rights movement. Charles Seeger, the founder of ethnomusicology and a public documentarian, found in America's communities a diversity of cultural treasures embodying wisdom, artistry, history, and knowledge. Alan Lomax clearly saw the growing problem of "cultural gray-out"—the worldwide spread of a homogenized, commercial, mass culture at the expense of most local and regional cultures. Rinzler saw the problem of cultural disenfranchisement, as people lost touch with and power and control over their own cultural products. He found that in rural Appalachia and in Cajun Louisiana and in Texas, the spirited musical performances by old-

timers were underappreciated by their descendents but had achieved popularity among city youth in the Northeast. He saw the strength of cultural enfranchisement in the powerful role music played in the civil rights movement, where it mobilized people in community churches, on picket lines, and in the streets for a great, moral battle. The grassroots creation and continuity of culture in contemporary society was a building block of democracy. The democratic force of culture was raised to a new level on the National Mall with the March on Washington in 1963 and the Poor People's March in 1968.

The festival sought to honor musicians, artisans, and their cultural communities; enhance their cultural identity, standing, and practice; and convey knowledge to others, taking to heart Woody Guthrie's American populist sentiments in the song "This Land Is Your Land," which could easily be applied, quite literally, to the Mall. Guthrie presented the idea that everyone has an equal place as an American in this country and that no one owns the nation more than anyone else. Rinzler saw the Mall in the same way, as our foremost public space, where all people have the right to express themselves, to be included, and share with their fellow citizens.

In designing the festival, Rinzler did not want to recreate an older world of utilitarian crafts or purge music of electronic media or reconstitute the nation or world into villages. Rather, his project was to move the contemporary world toward more culturally democratic institutions. The project recognized that older aesthetic traditions, forms and systems of knowledge, values, and social relationships would not just inevitably and uniformly fade away. Instead, people could use them to design and build their own futures. The village might get bigger; the forms of communication more wide-ranging, the systems of exchange more complex, but skill, knowledge, and artistry based in human communities could still remain and prosper. If voices that could contribute to cultural democracy became silent, then everyone would lose.

The result has been a spotlighting of diverse forms of cultural expression on the Mall through the festival. Rinzler enlisted states to help support demonstrations of regional cultures on the Mall, Texas one year, Pennsylvania the next. The programs encouraged the local study of cultural traditions and aided the organization of arts and humanities programs in the National Endowments and the Library of Congress.[23] They promoted local crafts traditions, resulting in revivals of Southern potteries (fig. 40), for example, and catalyzed revaluations in local music and performance traditions.[24]

Scholars and community advocates lined up festival programs to illustrate "Old Ways in the New World," in which different ethnic communities in the United States would demonstrate their traditions alongside their cultural cousins from Europe and Asia. A group of activists developed an African Diaspora program to link peoples and traditions in Africa to those in the Caribbean, South America, and the United States. This program contributed, theoretically and practically, to the development of African American studies programs in colleges and universities, helped in the training of a generation of African American cultural scholars, and led to the development of a Black American program in the National Museum of American History.[25] Festival programs on Native Americans brought together Indian leaders and cultural advocates. Programs on occupational culture and work-lore stimulated research and training programs among labor unions and professional groups and helped develop a new area of scholarly study.[26]

The attention paid to these programs, in the community and in the media, heightens the participants' self-recognition and promotes the legitimacy of the culture itself. Said Edward Samarin, a 1995 festival participant:

> I grew up in a very Russian, very Molokan community in San Francisco. I never really thought of myself in any other way other than as a Russian Molokan. I guess we were very insular, and did not see our connections to anyone else. The [Folklife] Festival has now changed all this. Standing on the Mall, seeing the wealth of cultural heritage under those

FIG. 40
Kentucky potter Ernie Corneli-
son at the 1968 Folklife Festival
*Robert Yellin / Smithsonian
Institution*

Sometimes cultural assertion occurs in the glare of television cameras, as when the Dalai Lama (fig. 41) spoke on the Mall at the 2000 festival to a crowd of some forty thousand, expressing his hopes for the preservation of Tibetan culture, both within Tibet and in the diaspora. Carefully positioned with the Washington Monument at his back, it was the image of the Dalai Lama speaking to his audience and the United States that hit the front page of the *Washington Post* the next day and went out to the world. Many other cultural communities have also used the festival and their presence on the Mall creatively to advocate for their perceived rights, to redress grievances, or gain more mundane advantages, as in attracting tourists, selling their cultural products, or improving their public image.[28]

This model has been used by others. Festival staff have worked closely with the organizers of the Black Family Reunion, several presidential inaugural committees, the Atlanta Committee for the Olympic Games, the Smithsonian's own 150th anniversary committee, the American Battle Monuments Commission for the National World War II Memorial, and the National Museum of the American Indian for its opening in order to help organize and define presentations that allow for the cultural representation of various communities.[29]

The festival has also, on certain occasions, been in a position to unite different groups in a way that has enhanced our national life. In 1968, for example, the festival was the first large-scale public gathering after civic unrest in the wake of Dr. Martin Luther King Jr.'s assassination. A huge, diverse audience gathered on the

beautiful elms in the midst of Washington, I had the realization, and the feeling for the first time in my life that I too was an American. That I had a place here. And that my Russian Molokan heritage made me part of America, not separate from it.[27]

FIG. 41
The Dalai Lama at the Folklife
Festival, July 2, 2000
Smithsonian Institution

Mall for the final concert, hosted by Alan Lomax who declared: "This is the festival of the common man. This is the festival of the democratic art the American people have made out of their experience. In affairs like this we realize our strength. We realize how beautiful we are. Black is beautiful. Appalachia is beautiful and even old, tired, Washington sometimes is beautiful when the American people gather to sing and fall in love with each other again."[30]

In the early 1970s, with conflict raging between hardhats and hippies, Senator William Fulbright noted the festival's ability to bring people together. "The festival is the surest antidote for what ails America down deep. Too bad there isn't more of it," he declared.[31] In the 1980s, lamenting the vapid commercialization and standardization of our public life, a reporter for the *Richmond Times-Dispatch* suggested, "Just when it seems that the nation has been McNuggeted, Roseanned, and Classic Rocked into dull sameness, the Festival comes along to prove otherwise."[32] In the mid-1990s, commentator and *Washington Post* writer Henry Allen

wrote for *Life* magazine, "Going to the Festival is like attending a service at the First Church of the Great American idea."[33] In the summer of 2002, a *New York Times* editorial called the festival on the Mall, with its emphasis on the peoples of the Silk Road region, "the ideal place in Washington to find the meaning of America during the time of trial and terrorist threats."[34]

Juxtaposition as a Presentational Technique

The presentational techniques used at the festival are varied. Most—such as concerts, workshops, dance parties, discussion stages, hands-on demonstrations, artifact installations—are found in other types of events and exhibitions. The unique feature of the festival for presentational purposes, however, is the creative use of juxtaposition with the National Mall (fig. 42).

Festival installations and performances generally make sharp, disjunctive contrasts with the Mall. "To find Detroit, turn left at the Washington Monument," suggested *USA Today* in writing about the Michigan program in 1987.[35] A 1973 article in the *Washington Star* commented on the Kentucky program: "The statue in the Lincoln Memorial has seen a lot of things . . . but it's never seen a quarter-acre planting of Kentucky 14 Burley tobacco sprouting greenly within plug-spittin' distance until today."[36] A year later, the *Washington Post* reported, "Way down yonder in the temporary land of cotton, just east of the Lincoln Memorial, the Smithsonian planted a mini-cotton crop."[37] In 1984 the festival program on Alaska included an iceberg transported to the Mall. The mere presence of an iceberg there, slowly melting away day by day, occasioned streams of curious visitors and a daily *Washington Post* "iceberg watch." The festival creates its own make-believe world in the midst of monumental Washington. As Secretary of State Colin Powell prepared for his visit to the 2002 festival, his aides were told that "his limo should pull up at Samarkand, he'll later come out into Registan Square, walk through the China ceramics courtyard and the silk grove, cut across in front of the Bamiyan Buddha, and leave by the Istanbul Aya Sophia"—the itinerary for his twenty-minute walk on the Mall.[38]

Performances like Mardi Gras, Junkanoo, and Carnival processions, Maryland foxhunts, polo matches, an "Amateur Night at the Apollo" event organized with the landmark theater in Harlem, or a dinner on the grounds create disjunctions of space and time that show tradition in a special light. In 2001, for example, the Royal Bermuda Regiment played their bagpipes marching down the Mall in their bright British redcoats, the U.S. Capitol in the background. Perhaps not since the burning of Washington in 1812, if then, had anyone seen such a sight.

Sometimes the juxtapositions have other effects besides discord and close rather than enlarge symbolic distance. For example, at a 1989 festival program on American Indian cultural conservation, a presentation on the Hidatsa and Mandan Indians included several live buffalo on the Mall. (They were derived from the same stock as the buffalo on the Mall in the nineteenth century that formed the early menagerie for the National Zoo.)

One of the buffalo was pregnant and one night during the festival gave birth to a calf, as security guards, the U.S. Park Police, festival staff, and a zoo veterinarian looked on. Following the birth, several of the Indian participants wrote to Senator Daniel Inouye and then Smithsonian secretary Robert McCormick Adams. They noted the rarity of life actually being born on the Mall and the parallel between the birth of the buffalo and the symbolic birth that year of the new National Museum of the American Indian, the legislation for which had been recently passed and signed. The Indians suggested that the calf, when grown, reside in and alongside the new museum, providing a paradigm, of sorts, of the living museum. Having to nurture a living buffalo on the Mall would ensure that the fledgling museum, its governing bureaucracy, and the powers that be would have to respect life and create a new kind of museum.[39]

In another example, Rajeev Sethi, the designer of the 2002 festival on the Silk Road, sought to use the architecture of the Mall and festival constructions to close the distance between American culture and Asian civilizations. Festival partner Yo-Yo Ma had desired to create the experience of a journey. After walking the Mall with the architectural historian Elizabeth Moynihan, and being cognizant of the architectural interests of another participant, the Aga Khan, Sethi decided to manifest the Silk Road on the Mall in a direct, visual way. He recreated several dome structures for the festival, particularly representations of Istanbul's Hagia Sophia and Samarkand's Registan Square. He sited these structures on the Mall in a particular way so that the dome of the Hagia

Sophia was lined up with that atop the National Museum of Natural History and that the domes of Samarkand were lined up with the U.S. Capitol. For those visitors who noticed and made the connection, the arrangement of domes helped close geographical and historical distance and obviate cultural difference.

Challenges and Tensions on the Mall

Presenting culture on the National Mall poses special challenges and exposes various institutional and environmental tensions. The Mall is among the most heavily regulated spaces in the world. To do anything, you have to get the approval of the National Park Service, for they regulate and police the Mall. And they are not alone.

You can't fly over the Mall, at least not easily. To do so, you have to get permission from the Architect of the Capitol, the Pentagon, and the Secret Service—an arrangement attempted for the festival in 1997, to allow crop dusters from the Mississippi Delta to demonstrate their skills. If you want to release balloons or birds into the air, as was done for a Massachusetts saint's day parade in 1988, you have to alert air traffic control at National Airport and a variety of other agencies.

If you want to dig into the ground, as was done to set up an Oklahoma oil rig in the 1982 festival, you have to deal with the Metro. In 1986, festival staff built a giant rice paddy so that Japanese villagers could demonstrate their traditional planting dance. But to the amusement of the Japanese, the paddy could not be built into the

ground; it had to be built above the earth, on top of a huge sheet of plastic. Digging on the Mall unearths remarkable things including, one year, the remains of a railway car, likely discarded from the railroad terminal that was once located at the foot of the Capitol, and dumped into the old Washington City Canal.

If you build anything, at least for the festival, Smithsonian engineers and safety officers need to inspect it; and so do District of Columbia fire marshals and the Smithsonian's accessibility officers. Like the festival events themselves, this process, too, can lead to cross-cultural juxtapositions. The Romanian carpenters who built an exquisitely crafted, all wood, traditional Maramure church on the Mall in 1999 were confounded by safety and accessibility people, who insisted on creating another doorway to the church; festival staff had to take chainsaws to the hand-hewn timbers to brutally carve out the required safety door. Sometimes, there is concern that the enactments of traditional cultural practice will lead to real harm: in 1985, as the culmination of the "Mela: An Indian Fair," three forty-foot-high paper and bamboo statues of the demon king Ravana and his cohorts, full of fireworks, were burned on the Mall; some twenty fire trucks lined up to protect the neighboring area, lest fiery detritus drift in the air.

To sell anything, you have to deal with the district tax and business authorities. If you cook food and sell it, you have to deal with the Public Health Service and Guest Services, Inc., the National Park Service concessionaire. Regulations stipulate that food to be sold has to be traditional and ethnic. This, of course, leads to an annual

debate between Smithsonian curators and the National Park Service over the application of the concepts: is the pizza cooked by an Italian food concession at the festival "ethnic"? is a Nigerian concession's use of canned vegetables as raw material in stew "traditional"? and so on.

If the cooking or brewing is of alcohol, other agencies get in the act. In 1986, the festival wanted to show the folk chemistry involved in the "still"-made whisky of Tennessee; such activities may be illegal, and so a fine line had to be walked with the Bureau of Alcohol, Tobacco, and Firearms to assure that the participants, two very interesting characters covered at the time in a large front-page story in *USA Today*, would not be arrested as they demonstrated their art and science at the invitation of the national museum.[40] In the end, there was a compromise: the still was fabricated and alcohol was distilled, right on the Mall; the product, however, had to be disposed of and could not be shared with the public.

Selling alcohol is another matter. Wine sales have for some years been prohibited on the Mall, so try telling the French that the Smithsonian seeks to represent their culinary traditions—without wine. Beer is allowed but must be consumed in a fenced area immediately adjacent to the point of sale. Wisconsin football fanatics had a hard time understanding that rule, questioning why they couldn't have a beer while enjoying a Green Bay Packers tailgate party staged for the 1998 festival.

If you have animals out on the Mall, the U.S. Department of Agriculture gets involved. This holds for cows milked at a family farm program in the 1991 festival, pigs at an Iowa program in 1996, and sheep at a New Hampshire program in 1999. Having animals at the festival often entails specific building requirements. Programmatically, this may be something as grand as a racetrack down the middle of the Mall for an Oklahoma program demonstrating the horsemanship traditions of that state (fig. 43). Usually, it is simply a matter of providing adequate shade, water, and fencing, but sometimes the required services may be more specialized. Diana Parker, who succeeded Rinzler as festival director, tells the story of how in 1975 a calf got loose from its enclosure on the Mall. Efforts by staff to recapture the errant calf failed, as it took off for Constitution Avenue. One of the participating cowboys rode up on horseback to Parker and asked if she wanted him to retrieve the calf. "Yes," she replied, and off he rode, eventually roping the calf in the parking lot of the Kennedy Center and returning it to the Mall.[41]

Law enforcement is in the hands of the U.S. Park Police. If you need a street closed, they will take care of those running east-west. D.C. Metropolitan Police handle north-south streets. Of course, if a visiting international dignitary, such as the Dalai Lama, is participating, the Diplomatic Security Service gets involved; if it is the president or vice president, then it's the Secret Service. In 1999, the festival was told that then Vice President Al Gore and wife, Tipper, were to make a "quiet, private" visit, with one or two agents, but how do you manage that on the Mall, at the festival, among thousands of visitors, and when scores of reporters have been notified?

Anyone who is hurt or affected by the heat is given first aid by nurses hired by the festival; more serious treatment requires calling the D.C. ambulance service. Most of the time, injuries or afflic-tions are mundane. Sometimes, however, they are festival-made, as, for example, in 1989, when demonstrations of Haitian *voodun* ceremonies provoked random members of the audience into a state of trance; nurses and an ambulance had to be stationed next to the recreated *honfor*, or *voodun* compound, during times of performance so that affected visitors could be treated.

Maintenance on the Mall is done by the National Park Service, at least up to the surrounding streets, though there is an incredibly detailed map delineating where Smithsonian horticultural and maintenance services take over. The Mall's physical plant has its own challenges. Only a few individuals, long-serving employees of the National Park Service and the Smithsonian, know where water and sewage lines and other utilities are buried. The festival depends on water lines for various demonstrations and concessions. Some of these are decades old, and when they malfunction, they have to be replaced with specially made, one-of-a-kind, historical replicas.

All of these factors would make it complicated enough to produce a good-sized family reunion cookout, let alone an event as complicated as the festival. Rational regulations for running and maintaining an urban park do not necessarily make for rational ways of organizing a cultural program.

The biggest impact comes from regulations concerning the protection of the Mall's magnificent elm trees. The elms were planted in the 1930s, after the clear-cutting of all the trees, shrubs, and other vegetation that had previously populated the Mall more in the style of the Boston Common and New York's Central Park. Elms on the Mall, as in other places in Washington and the United States, have been subject to blights of disease; many have been lost, though new strains have been developed that are more disease resistant. In the 1980s, a study by the National Park Service suggested that soil compaction on the Mall was so great as to pose a danger to the elms. (Compacted soil stresses tree roots, making it harder for them to absorb water and nutrients.) The annual trudging on the ground by festival crowds was cited as a major cause of the compaction. A suggestion was made to ban all public events from the Mall—and surround the treed plots with a tasteful chain-link fence.

The Smithsonian and the National Park Service considered and debated the evidence and the recommendation. The festival commissioned a study carried out by the Agricultural Research Service and Clemson University scientists. That study, conducted in 1995 and repeated two years later, found that the Mall was indeed compacted but argued that that compaction could be managed and alleviated.[42] Significantly, it found that trees in areas of the Mall not used for the festival or any other high-impact activity were in the same state of health as those in high-use festival areas. As a preventive measure, the Smithsonian and the National Park Service agreed to adopt practices that would alleviate compaction near the elms. The festival would not locate high-volume activities near the trees; it would put big music stages and food services in the middle of the Mall, in non-treed areas; it would

not dig into the ground near the trees; it would not use the trees to hold or hang things; it would locate tents and structures outside the drip line of trees; it would not drive vehicles on the treed plot unless they had special tires; and so on.[43]

These measures had very real consequences for programming. Imagine a tradition, such as in parts of the Caribbean or Africa, where storytelling occurs under a tree. Now, the festival could not place a stage or small platform next to such a tree; it has to be out of the drip line. Imagine explaining this to a storyteller from the Virgin Islands or a *griot* from Senegal or Mali who, back home, sits under a village tree that has been alive for generations. Or the new measures, by forcing large-scale presentations of music, as well as food services, to the center of the Mall, necessitated covering those events with large tents; under Washington's brutal summer sun, it is on the average about ten to fifteen degrees hotter in the center of the Mall than it is under the shady trees. A tradition that might well be presented in the open air back home now has to be presented under a tent, lest hundreds of visitors, and performers, suffer heat stroke. Tents, for some people, are quite neutral; for others they have a negative cultural connotation, suggesting low-class, marginal, or stigmatized refugee status. Moving big events to the middle of the Mall also forced festival curators to disconnect food and music from other aspects of culture. Experienced curators know how to use spatial proximity to indicate social relations and make connections; for example, it might make perfect sense to present festive craft making—say of Mardi Gras—

next to festive music making, to show how the patterns of each are related. But, given the heat in the center of the Mall, even with tents, festival organizers are reluctant to let craftspeople sit there all day. Craftspeople, therefore, typically inhabit tents and other structures under the trees. The continuity of a tradition—the relationship between, say, food, music, and crafts—may be lost to the public because regulations for the Mall make it difficult or even impossible for them to be presented in proximity.

Other regulations also complicate the effort to make connections. Following a ruling in a court case involving the Hare Krishna organization, sales of crafts, recordings, and other items are no longer allowed on the Mall.[44] Only items deemed allowed by free speech—such as publications—can be sold. The Smithsonian cannot sell a recording of the "I Have a Dream" speech on the Mall, even though it is a speech, and a speech given on the Mall at that. It can sell the recording's liner notes—that is, the "publication"— but not the recording itself. Recorded speech is not considered "speech," but written speech is! As a result of this case, the festival usually sets up its shop on the Mall-side grounds of the National Museum of American History. Again, this isolates commerce from other aspects of culture. Trying to give visitors a sense of a bazaar or marketplace in a particular society, for example, is impeded when at the festival the sales occur on the grounds of the museum, the crafts are found under the trees, and performance traditions in the center of the Mall. The dispersal of traditions normally found together follows a logic not of the culture represented but rather of historical accident imposed on the Mall.

No Better Place to Celebrate

Every year, a luncheon is given on the opening day of the festival. Weather permitting, it is held on the rooftop terrace of the National Museum of American History. It is from this aerial vantage point that discussions about the general place of the Mall and the festival are typically triggered among Smithsonian staff, guests, and dignitaries. One international guest, noting the beauty and monumental scope of the Mall's greensward from the Capitol to the Washington Monument, shook his head and said: "People in my country don't understand. They think that when you are speaking of the National Mall it is some type of shopping mall." Observing the myriad of activities and people on the Mall, an American guest from the farm belt commented that the festival was like a "national county fair." A Chicagoan thought it looked more like a "national block party."

The festival makes an intriguing counterstatement about the Mall and its role in our civic life. The great greensward is not fenced off. There are no "keep off the grass" signs.[45] Amid the marble and granite, the great institutions of power that carry the weight of a nation's history, there are the people. People from all walks of life. People making bricks and molding pots. Cajuns and Navajo, Appalachians and Tajiks, making music; Hawaiians telling stories; Wall Street brokers teaching their sign language; Ndebele decorating a hut; Bolivians weaving; Iowans tending their corn. They share what they do with tourists from around the nation, kids from daycare, staffers from Congress, suburban families, diplomats, graduate students, and fellow musicians and artisans; all are engaged in a rite of cultural enjoyment.

I have often said to festival guests, "The National Mall of the United States is not Tiananmen Square nor Red Square." It is not an overbearing or intimidating space; it is, rather, a place where life and people are central. Though the National Park Service and its regulations do not make it easy to use the Mall for planned activities, it nonetheless welcomes, if reluctantly, not only the festival but a host of demonstrations and activities that represent the ideals, aspirations, and expressions of the American people. Annually more than two thousand groups request to use all or part of the Mall for events. The American people clearly recognize the importance and significance of the Mall, given its symbolic centrality, its proximity to institutions of power, and its perceived connection to memorialized history. If something happens on the Mall, it must be important, it must be meaningful, somehow, to our national life, or so numerous organizers believe.

The Smithsonian Folklife Festival explicitly builds on this belief. It is what I tell festival participants every year when they first come down to the Mall to see where they will set up their stuff and play their music. If people are on the Mall, then they must be important, and their message meaningful enough to merit national attention. The festival is deeply entwined with its location on the National Mall, inviting citizens of the nation and the world to gather and have their say. It is a vehicle for the assertion of cultural identity by people enjoying the liberty of free expression. A healthy democracy is a lively one, where the words of the people may be directly heard—sometimes loudly and dramatically, sometimes exquisitely and intriguingly, amid the heat, dust, sweat, and smells of throngs of people. The festival on the Mall does not disappoint in this regard, for, as Ralph Rinzler said, "There is no better place to celebrate the cultures of the American people, and those from around the world."[46]

PART 3

MONUMENTS
for the FUTURE

Monuments, Modernism, and the Mall
Nathan Glazer

❧ WHEN THE MCMILLAN Commission was doing its work, there was only one great monument on the Mall, the Washington Monument, and it had been completed and opened to the public only fifteen years earlier. Its vicissitudes—almost a century between an initial proposal for such a monument and its completion, forty years in the building, political conflict and controversy through much of that period, endless difficulties in securing the money, radical revision of the original plan—foreshadowed the story of almost all the great monuments that have subsequently been erected on the Mall or its precincts in fulfillment of the Senate Park Plan. But one moment in the history of these controversies marks a distinctive divide: it is the controversy over the Jefferson Memorial, which was to fulfill the proposals of the McMillan Commission for the completion of Washington's monumental center.

The commission had proposed balancing the Capitol with a monument to Abraham Lincoln at the other end of their plan's lengthened Mall. The Lincoln Memorial was built, in a classical style very much as they intended, in remarkably short order and was an enormous success. But on the cross axis defined by the White House to the north and the Washington Monument in its pivotal central location, they proposed another great monument to the south. They did not propose that it honor any specific figure, but there

FIG. 44
John Russell Pope's proposal for
the Jefferson Memorial (rendering, 1936)
*Papers of Howard Worth Smith, MSS
8731, Special Collections, University of
Virginia Library, Charlottesville*

was only one person in the epic of American democracy who deserved to stand
with Washington and Lincoln, and that
was clearly the author of the Declaration
of Independence, Thomas Jefferson. It
nevertheless took a Democratic president,
Franklin Delano Roosevelt, perhaps con-
templating the presence of two great
memorials on the Mall to Republican
presidents (there is the forgotten but enormous monument to Ulysses S. Grant at the
foot of the Capitol), and none to Demo-
crats, to restart the stalled process of a
monument to Jefferson in January 1934,
with a letter to the Commission of Fine
Arts proposing it consider such a monument. John Russell Pope, the classicist
American architect who was designing
the enormous National Gallery of Art for
the Mall, emerged as the architect for the
memorial. What could it be, one would
think in 1937, other than a classical monument, and preferably a domed structure

(fig. 44), something like the centerpiece of
Jefferson's great design for the University
of Virginia? But modernism in art and
architecture, somewhat belatedly it is
true, was rapidly gaining dominance
among American critics and artists and
architects. The National Gallery of Art
had surprisingly escaped severe criticism
while its design was being developed and
modified. But the storm broke over the
Jefferson Memorial.

Two streams have contributed to modernism in architecture, social criticism
and the aesthetic rejection of historicism;
not always in agreement, they joined in
the denunciation of Pope's design for the
Jefferson Memorial. "With the country
still in the midst of a serious depression,"
writes Pope's biographer, "the most vitu-
perative criticism came from a group composed largely of advocates for the housing
division of the Public Works Administration, including Catherine Bauer [later

Catherine Bauer Wurster], Carl Feiss, Talbot Hamlin, Joseph Hudnut, William Lescaze, and Lewis Mumford." Should such a monument be built, it was asked, "in light of the fact that two-thirds of the nation was inadequately clothed, housed, and fed." That is always a good argument against expensive building of monuments. But one suspects the rejection of all forms of historicism in architecture, which is the mark of modernism, played a greater role. "[A] torrent of letters opposing Pope's appointment as architect for the memorial was presented at a House hearing from a vast number of luminaries, including the director of the Museum of Modern Art, Alfred H. Barr, Jr." Frank Lloyd Wright, in a letter to President Roosevelt, attacked the design as an "arrogant insult to the memory of Thomas Jefferson." The faculty of the School of Architecture at Columbia University denounced it as "a lamentable misfit in time and place."[1]

It was "High Noon on the Mall," as Richard Guy Wilson describes the conflict between traditionalism and modernism, and the shoot-out came over the Jefferson Memorial.[2] The Commission of Fine Arts, created to carry out the McMillan Plan, was no longer fully dominated by traditionalists, not that any strong proponents of modernism were yet on it. Nevertheless, they were not enthusiastic. Gilmore Clarke, its chairman, hoped that the design "would bring out some of the new arts rather than transporting an ancient *parti* from Rome to this site in the form of the Pantheon." William Lamb, whose firm had designed the Empire State Building, said, "I myself do not believe that the reproduction of imperial Rome in the shape of the Pantheon would represent in

the slightest degree that simplicity, honesty of character that he [Jefferson] stood for." And another member of the commission complained: "I feel it is rather a dreary thing as it stands. . . . I regret that this has not been exposed to the full possibility of American design today."[3] As we know, the project went ahead, and the classical monument, dome and columns and statue, went up.

But then, one may ask sixty years later, and in the light of what has transpired with monuments and modernism since, if it had been a design expressing contemporary modernism, what would it have been like, and would we have preferred it to what was then built? One may doubt it. There is the rub: modernism and monuments do not marry well.

The Death of the Monument

While the Jefferson Memorial debate was going on, Lewis Mumford's *The Culture of Cities* was published, and there he put the matter quite starkly: "If it is a monument it is not modern, and if it is modern, it cannot be a monument." Mumford was certainly the most important American critic of urban form and design during the middle of the twentieth century, between the 1930s and the 1960s. Before him, the most prominent figures in urbanism were the promoters of the city beautiful movement: Daniel Burnham; the firm of McKim, Mead & White; Frederick Law Olmsted, senior and junior; and the other figures who created the World's Columbian Exposition in Chicago in 1893 and who in time composed the McMillan Commission. After him was Jane Jacobs and advocates for the various forms of postmodernism. For the proponents of the city beautiful, the ideal city seemed to be nothing but monuments. For Jane Jacobs, committed to the lively and mixed-use city neighborhood, the monument just didn't exist. Mumford excoriated the advocates of the city beautiful but was disdainful of Jane Jacobs's prescriptions.

But what was the problem for Mumford? Why was there this fundamental contradiction between modernism and monuments?

Mumford writes, in a section of *The Culture of Cities* titled "The Death of the Monument," that monuments celebrate power and death while modernism celebrates democracy and life: "One of the most important attributes of a vital urban civilization is one that has rarely been achieved in past civilizations: the capacity for renewal. Against the fixed shell and the static monument, the new architecture"—he is talking about modernism—"places its faith in the powers of social adaptation and reproduction. The sign of the older order of architecture, in almost every culture, was the House of the Dead; in modern culture, it is the dwelling house, or House of the Living."

Architecture in the past was defined by its monuments to the dead: "The primitive burial mounds, the big stones of the Salisbury Plains or Brittany, the Pyramids and Sphinxes of Egypt, the grandiose gestures of a Sargon or Ozymandias, of a Louis XIV or a Peter the Great; these represent that respect for death which is essentially a fear of life."

He decries the cult of death, "thanks to [which], permanence comes in the structures of the city." Let me emphasize that word, *permanence*. But today,

instead of being oriented toward death and fixity, we are oriented to the cycle of life, with its never-ending process of birth and growth and renewal and death. . . . [T]he idea of fixity has been slow to resist change. . . . The truth is, however, that the notion of material survival by means of the monument no longer represents the impulses of our civilization, and in fact it defies our closest convictions. These Valhallas and Lincoln Memorials, these Victor Emmanuel Monuments and Vimy Ridge Memorials, these "Eternal Lights" that go out when the electric power station breaks down or the bulb blows out—how many buildings of the last century, that pretend to be august and monumental, have a touch of the modern spirit in them? They are all the hollow echoes of an expiring breath, which either curb and confine the works of the living, like the New York Public Library, or are completely irrelevant to our beliefs and demands.

Then comes that comment I have already quoted; "If it is a monument it is not modern, and if it is modern, it is not a monument."

Now, his reference to a number of monuments that would have been known, or might have been known, to his readers points up some problems with Mumford's dictum. Some of these monuments seem to us clearly worthier and more successful than others. The Victor Emmanuel monument (fig. 45) in Rome is a huge "wedding cake" of classical, Baroque, and Rococo elements that no one has a good word for today. But the Lincoln Memorial? Vimy Ridge, one of the sober monuments to the dead of World War I? The New York Public Library? All these monuments of

FIG. 45
Victor Emmanuel monument,
Rome, built 1885–1911
Richard Glover / Corbis

presumed permanence, drawn from the architectural library of the past, were equally anathema to him. These days we would, and do, make distinctions among them. I see a considerable difference between the Lincoln Memorial and the Victor Emmanuel monument and not only a difference in the quality of the two men who were being memorialized. And today, I think, many would be taken aback by such a dismissive reference to the New York Public Library, a building that does so much for New York, as a major element in its urban fabric, and not only because it is a great public library.

So, then, were there to be no monuments in Mumford's ideal city? Well, not quite:

This is not to say that a hospital or power station or an air beacon [today we would call it a control tower] may not be treated as a monument to a person or an event; nor is it to deny that a contemporary structure might not easily last 200 years or even two thousand: that is not the point. What will make the hospital or the air beacon a good memorial is the fact that it has been well designed for the succor of those who are ill, or for the guidance of the piloting airplanes. . . . The death of the monument . . . has implications that go far beyond the conception of individual tombs, memorials, or public buildings; it affects . . . the very texture of urban life. Why, for example, should each generation go on living in the quarters that were built by its ancestors? These quarters . . . were planned for other uses, other habits, other modes of living.[4]

Enough for Mumford. But he was pointing to aspects of modernism—in architecture, urbanism, and design—that are still with us and continue to create enormous problems for monuments and memorials being planned and built today. I would point to four aspects of modernism that contradict by their nature the idea of the monument: functionalism, lightness, impermanence, and the penchant for new materials. All of these play a part in Mumford's—and modernism's—rejection of the monument.

What, after all, is the function of the monument? And without a clear function, a program, what does the modern architect do? The form of the monument is not dictated by any mundane uses. It is true that people have to be gotten to it and through it and out of it, and comfort stations must be provided, and regarding these needs there are certainly functional requirements. But despite Mumford, a monument is not a hospital or a school or a dwelling; it is meant to celebrate, to recall, or to honor. How does that connect with modernism's commitment to the functional, to the meeting of a need, without doing anything more or anything less? And so in modernism we have the undecorated window without a frame that looks as if it had been punched out of a wall, the modest and almost invisible entry, the flat roof, the undecorated cornice.

Then there is the leaning toward the light and impermanent, as against the heavy and the solid. One of the most talked-about buildings of the last few years was the "blur" building of Elizabeth Diller and Ricardo Scofidio—the building itself, whatever there was of it, disappeared in a permanent mist. The perfect embodiment of the modernist spirit! A leading proposal for a memorial to the World Trade Center victims was for a time two columns of light recalling the buildings, realized as the "Tribute in Light" on view for one month in 2002 and on anniversary dates since then. One of the idols and prophets of modernism, Buckminster Fuller, emphasized that progress lay in reducing the weight of objects. His most successful invention was a light but strong dome of metal rods that could be taken apart and moved, and when in use could be covered in fabric. Other contemporary expressions of the modern are buildings whose surfaces are ever-changing patterns of color or graphics, projected images. Buildings that can be dismantled or look as if they can be (remember the Millennium Dome) are among those favored by advanced architectural theorists. As well as buildings that look as if they can shoot off into space, though as yet the mobile aerodynamic building is more theory than reality. All this favors new materials—fabric, plastics, illusions created by the manipulation of light.

But there is another and deeper problem with modernism when it comes to monuments, a problem aside from its formal and aesthetic characteristics. Modernism begins with an emphasis on the functional; it denies that it is part of the history of style, that it *is* a style or a family of styles. No, modernism asserts, its penchant for the functional, the impermanent, the changing, the new simply reflects the reality of our culture and civilization, the steady and always shifting impacts of new technology and new needs. It reflects too a new social aim: we are no longer dominated by priests and princes; we abhor war and hope for eternal peace. Our societies aim toward a stable democracy and a widespread equality, and architecture should serve those new objectives. So modern architecture's most prominent early achievements are in mass housing for the working classes and the poor and well-designed factories. Its objectives were better dwellings, schools, and factories, not grander palaces and tombs. How, then, can the desire for celebration and memorialization be satisfied by such a movement?

Despite its claim that it was the end of the history of architecture, modernism was also a style, time-bound, a rebellion against earlier styles, and part of the history of art and design rather than the end of art and design. As such, it is also part of what art and design have become in the past hundred years or so—that is, the celebration of the individual artist as a rebel against the past, against whatever is, and for the creation of something new and startling and outrageous. The monument must draw not only on the architect but also on the artist, and the artist has become someone whose very being is antithetical to the notion of the monument in its aspect as a memorial that represents and reflects and is suited to a community. The artist has become a rebel against community. The architect much less so, except that in his aspect as artist he also apes the posture of rejection of the given and the celebration of the new and rebellious.

This problem was sharply pointed up

when the leaders of modernism in Europe first pondered the problem of monuments in World War II. As the war progressed, they realized that monuments would certainly be built after the war. If modernism rejected the monument, would not its role in the rebuilding of cities, in the expression of the desires of the public, be sharply reduced? And so a debate began on how modernism could come to terms with monuments. A leading figure in guiding that debate was the distinguished architectural historian Sigfried Giedion, who was the most authoritative historian of modernism in his books *Space, Time, and Architecture* (1941) and *Mechanization Takes Command* (1948). He was also secretary general of the Congrès Internationaux d'Architecture Moderne (CIAM), the major international organization of modern architects. In 1943, during the war, Giedion, the architect Josep Lluis Sert— who was in time to become chairman of architecture and dean at the Harvard Graduate School of Design—and the French modernist painter Fernand Léger wrote "Nine Points on Monumentality." They took a more positive view toward monuments than Mumford had a few years before. They wrote: "Monuments are human landmarks which men have created as symbols for their ideals, for their aims, and for their actions. They are intended to outlive the period which originated them, and constitute a heritage for future generations. As such, they form a link between the past and the future. . . . Monuments are the expression of man's highest needs."

So they agreed monuments are needed. But the monuments of the recent past, they argue, "have become empty shells."

Can modernism help? They acknowledge it has not yet been much help when it comes to monuments. But they explain: "Modern architecture, like modern painting and sculpture, had to start the hard way. It began by tackling the simple problems, the more utilitarian buildings like low-rent housing, schools, office buildings, hospitals, and similar structures." But as modern architecture takes up the task of city rebuilding, it has to grow up to the task of designing and incorporating monuments, and it can. They recognize this is no easy task. They call for the collaboration of planners, architects, painters, and sculptors. They call for using modern materials and new techniques: "light metal structures, laminated wooden arches, panels of different textures, colors and sizes, light elements like ceilings that can be suspended from big trusses covering practically unlimited spans. Mobile elements can constantly vary the aspects of the buildings. These mobile elements, changing positions and casting different shadows when acted upon by wind or machinery, can be the source of new architectural effects. During night hours, color and forms can be projected on vast surfaces. . . . Monumental architecture will be something more than functional."[5]

But is there not a contradiction between the earlier part of their manifesto—the notion that monuments "are intended to outlive the period which created them, and constitute a heritage for future generations. . . . They have to satisfy the eternal demand of the people for translation of their collective force into symbols"—and the means they favor when they describe what the modern monument will be?

And there is another contradiction: they wish to employ modern artists and sculptors. These are ready to come out of the gallery and the museum and into the public sphere. Giedion refers to Constantin Brancusi, Hans Arp, Naum Gabo, Alberto Giacometti, Pablo Picasso.

But the modern artist does not easily lend himself to satisfying "the eternal demand of the people for the translation of their collective force into symbols." Artists have created their own unique symbols, symbols that identify *them*, that become their trademark. When we see a Brancusi, an Arp, a Giacometti, a Picasso as part of a monument, what will we think?

We will think, "There is a Brancusi," and so forth. Will we think of the collective effort they have been commissioned to celebrate, the tragedy they have been asked to commemorate, the hero to whom a monument for the ages is being raised? Not very likely.

The dilemma of modernism in dealing with the monument is that while it begins—at least in architecture—with the idea that it will accommodate the needs and uses of ordinary men and women, economically and directly, it has undergone an evolution and development in which the architect and artist become creators of the new and astonishing. They do not find it easy to celebrate the common ideals and emotions of a community. It is more likely that they will celebrate themselves or their own ideas and emotions.

A few examples of this dilemma: three leading modern artists were commissioned to produce works of art for the Holocaust Memorial Museum in Washington, works of art presumably in some way related to its theme. They were Richard Serra (fig. 46), Sol LeWitt, and Ellsworth Kelly. As one might expect, the three works are a Serra, a LeWitt, and a Kelly, easily identifiable as such. What they have to do with the Holocaust is not easy to divine.

There is in Warsaw a monument to the 1943 Jewish uprising in the ghetto. It is by a Polish Jewish sculptor, Nathan Rapoport, who spent the war years in the Soviet Union. It is a great block of a monument, with figures of the ghetto's heroes and victims along the side. James E. Young, the author of a fine book on Holocaust memorials, reports Rapoport saying in defense of his monument: "Could I have made a

FIG. 47
The World War II Memorial
opens to visitors, April 29, 2004
Gary Hershorn / Corbis

rock with [a] hole in it and said, 'Voilà! The heroism of the Jews'?"[6] He is clearly referring to his famous contemporary, Henry Moore, who unquestionably would have done something very much like that.

The issue is, or one issue is, that we have a storehouse of forms and emblems from the historic past, and they evoke something: obelisks, pyramids, columns, wreaths, steeples . . . Sometimes they have become kitsch, and we just don't want to use the form any more. This is the case, undoubtedly, with the man on horseback. It isn't just that that is not the way people go into war or review troops any more; the symbol simply just doesn't jibe with contemporary life. Or the various nymphs or sylphs on many monuments representing the Continents, the Winds, the Directions, the Virtues, the Vices, or what have you. They once meant something to us— they don't anymore. We can no longer read the language of classicism. Sometimes, we're not sure whether the symbols still work or not. That is the problem with the World War II Memorial (fig. 47)—a huge oval of columns, with something like wreaths on top, and with two triumphal arches at the short ends. It does seem like a throwback. But what could a truly modern World War II memorial be?

Making Modern Memorials

There are many traditional forms and emblems that are not yet, I would think, exhausted and do serve to communicate something to people. In any case, the new forms of modern art and modernism either have their own kitschy meaning, like flat roofs or metal beams agonizing with each other, or mean nothing at all. Perhaps the sophisticates can distinguish one construction of beams from another, one set of whorled metal sheets from another, so that one might mean triumph and another defeat, but most of us can't and are left to say, "Huh?"

I find an exquisite summary of the dilemma of modernism and memorials in a 1992 book by Harriet Senie, *Contemporary Public Sculpture: Tradition, Transformation, and Controversy*. In the two first sentences, she writes: "The problems endemic to public art in a democracy begin with its definition. How can something be public (democratic) and art (elitist)?"[7] The implicit and taken-for-granted assumption is that art must be elitist and therefore will be incomprehensible to a democratic public. What a strange, what a modern, assumption! Would Michelangelo or Bernini or Lutyens have ever had such a thought? They would not have contemplated such a thought not because their publics were better educated than we are today (they might have been) but because they took it for granted that they were distinguished from their fellows by their skill and genius, not by their assumptions and values and ideals.

One way the contemporary artist overcomes the problem is by turning his or her art into a joke. So on the dust jacket of the book *Contemporary Public Sculpture*, one will see an enormous clothespin erected in front of the huge Philadelphia City Hall, which was built in Second Empire style. The sculpture is by Claes Oldenburg (fig. 48), who has proposed many such modern monuments and built a few. Alexander

FIG. 48
Claes Oldenburg, *Clothespin* (2002), Philadelphia
AP Images / Wide World Photos

Calder's mobiles and stabiles are gentler jokes. One can see one on the west side of the National Museum of American History (fig. 49), a homage to Gwendolyn Cafritz, a benefactor of Washington art. This will work to some extent; it will not work, however, for a serious monument or memorial to note events or people that we do not consider matters for amusement.

And yet, memorials must be built—people demand them—by modern architects and artists, and sometimes the dilemma is resolved and transcended, and we have a monument that is, despite Mumford, both modern and a monument. This is preeminently the case with the Vietnam Veterans Memorial in Washington.

But the road to the successful modern monument was not an easy one. The story of the Franklin Delano Roosevelt memorial, the first presidential memorial to be built since the Jefferson, shows how difficult it was to find a modern design that might gain approval, even from modernist architects and artists. Roosevelt himself, while he still lived, had called Felix Frankfurter to his office, and said, this is all I want after I am gone—something this big (indicating his desk), and with the simple inscription "Franklin Delano Roosevelt" and his dates. This went up in short order, and this sober and modest monument may be seen in front of the Archives building on Pennsylvania Avenue. Clearly this was not enough, in the eyes of his countrymen, for the man who had been elected president four times and who had led the nation through Depression and war. In 1955 Congress established a Franklin Delano Roosevelt Memorial Commission, and an act of Congress in 1959 authorized

a competition. The monument was to be located on the Tidal Basin, north of the Jefferson Memorial. There were six hundred participants, and a winning design was selected in December 1960. It consisted of eight huge concrete stelae, up to 167 feet in height, with suitable inscriptions. The Commission of Fine Arts did not approve. As one member said, "But what does it mean?" That is a generic problem for the modern monument.

After revisions, the proposal won the approval of the CFA in 1964—but the Roosevelt family did not approve of the monument, and it did not go ahead. The FDR Memorial Commission now went to one of the major figures of modernist architecture, Marcel Breuer, and asked him for a design. Breuer's Whitney Museum had just opened in New York City, and he seemed ideal as the designer of a modern monument. "While the artists, architects, and critics who made up the Commission of Fine Arts," we are told by Isabelle Hyman, who has researched this story, "were committed through their work or their writings to abstract art as it had been formulated in America through the 1940's and 1950's, and while the government officially supported Modernism through the designs approved for many of its institutions . . . a memorial structure was a different matter altogether." Breuer came up with seven giant triangles of stone, in a pinwheel arrangement, their extended narrow angles pointing to a 32–foot cube of dark granite on whose face was inscribed a high-tech version of a portrait of FDR. His words would be heard over the site through loudspeakers. The designers were responsive to, among other things, the significance of the radio for

Roosevelt: his fireside chats were a unique manifestation of his leadership.

Nevertheless, the CFA—which then included William Walton as chairman, the critic Aline Saarinen, Gordon Bunshaft, John Carl Warnecke, Burnham Kelly, Theodore Roszak, and Hideo Sasaki, a group very far from the Beaux-Arts and city-beautiful architects and artists who made up the CFA at its founding—did not approve. By now there were various versions of modernism in tension with each other. For Theodore Roszak, "This might have been all right for the Cabinet of Dr. Caligari but I don't think it has much to do with today." Two years later, in 1969, at the urging of the FDR Memorial Commission, the CFA reconsidered the design, and again said no. Finally in 1990, a design by the landscape architect Lawrence Halprin won the approval of the CFA, and construction began in 1994, forty years after the process was begun, on the monument that we see today.[8] As it was being built, the conflicts shifted from the issues of what kind of design, to what kind of content. The world had changed; various veto groups now wielded substantial power. The advocates of the disabled insisted that Roosevelt must be seen on the wheelchair that he had not allowed to be photographed and whose necessary use was never noted while he lived, and they succeeded in having an addition made to the completed monument, a group of outdoor rooms representing Roosevelt's four terms. A forecourt now shows Roosevelt on a wheelchair.

But then, as against all these variously troubled monuments, there is the enormously successful and modernist Vietnam Veterans Memorial. The design, which emerged from a competition, was denounced by many supporters of the plan for a memorial for its black stone shaping a descent into the earth, for its avoidance of any suggestion of representation, for its entirely abstract design, for the absence of any recognizable symbol that might represent war, or loss, or tragedy. Yet despite the conflict that raged about it, it was built as proposed in the competition for the memorial and has become the most moving monument on the Mall, matching, in its impact on its many visitors, the Lincoln Memorial. Not the least astonishing thing about it is that it was designed by a twenty-one-year-old who had designed nothing that had been built before. It is worth studying: why does this modern monument succeed when so many others fail? And many have studied and pondered the amazing story of its success.

I think there are three reasons why the Vietnam Veterans Memorial is able to transcend Mumford's dictum. One is that it is not a work by a "trademark" modern artist. The artist's personality and style do not get in the way. Maya Lin (fig. 50) was too young and unknown to have a trademarked and recognizable style. (Nor, of course, does every contemporary artist develop a trademark style.) So we don't think of the artist when we visit it, even though many of the visitors must be aware of the remarkable story of its design.

A second is that it was a stroke of near genius to place the names of the dead on the monument by *date*, in the order in which they died. This meant we did not have the problem of columns of Smiths and Joneses and Gonzalezes, which would have depreciated the individual character of each sacrifice and each death. It meant

further that those looking for a name would have to consult an alphabetical directory to find out where the name they looked for on the monument was located, and then go searching along that long wall, descending deeper into the earth and ascending out of it. It offered what few monuments do, a degree of legitimate interaction (not the kind of interaction through a television or video that keeps breaking down, which is today all too common in exhibits and artworks)—one has to look up the name in a directory and search for it along a wall; and then there is an additional form of interaction that may not have been in the mind of the designer: the tracing out of the letters with a finger, or the making of a paper tracing of the name. I note in a picture I have seen of the Kobe earthquake memorial that the names of the victims are also listed, and people are looking for them.

And a third reason I would warrant for its success: its silence. Is there any other monument that refuses to say anything at all? There is not a single word aside from the names. Of course it suits the minimalism of some modern art, which eschews inscriptions. But in this case, the reticence of modern art also suits the subject it is dealing with. It fits our ambivalence over the war—there is nothing to be said, and nothing is said. Neither that it was a victory or a defeat, nor that it was worth fighting and dying for or not, nor that it was heroic or its opposite. (I don't think this reticence was compromised by the addition of the figures of three weary soldiers to the monument site. The addition of more figures is definitely a problem.)

But of course one cannot escape the skill or genius of the design itself. Minimal, as most modern art is, without reference to anything else, it draws one into the declivity it creates, and evokes a mixed emotion suitable to the event it memorializes. All art, whether historicist, or classicist, or contemporary, has to depend on the skill or genius of the creator. It is only much, much harder when all historical reference, when the storehouse of symbols and memories, is abandoned, and everything has to be created anew. That is the problem that modernism faces when it deals with monuments and memorials.

A good deal has changed since the shoot-out on the Mall in 1937 and 1938. Modernism in architecture has lost some of its self-confidence. With a track record now of nearly a century, it can point to its masterpieces, but these are overwhelmed by a sea of dullness and idiosyncrasy. It turned out it was not so easy to speak to the spirit of man, to celebrate the great, to mourn catastrophe and disaster, without some help from the past. Even John Russell Pope is no longer universally execrated. Joseph Hudnut wrote in 1941 of Pope's National Gallery of Art: "[S]urely the time cannot be far distant when we shall understand how inadequate is the death-mask of an ancient culture to express the heroic soul of America."[9] It was denounced as a "pink marble whorehouse" and a "costly mummy." Today, when we see what some followers of modernism have produced in the way of museums on the Mall— the Hirshhorn and the Air and Space Museum—we are somewhat more tolerant. Indeed, when I. M. Pei was designing the East Building addition to the National Gallery of Art, we are told by J. Carter Brown, he "insisted that the Pope building

not be touched. He loved the building, its great interior spaces, and its detailing."[10]

We even find the Jefferson Memorial today dignified and suitable to its purposes, and we may think even better of it when we ask ourselves, what might a contemporary design of the later 1930s have been like, and would it have aged and survived as well?

The shoot-out continues, and we have additional major monuments to contemplate in this ongoing clash between traditionalism, of some sort, and modernism, of some sort, in the Franklin D. Roosevelt Memorial, the Korean War Memorial, and the World War II Memorial, and in time we will undoubtedly have to consider someday a memorial to Presidents John and John Quincy Adams and to Abigail Adams. It is questionable whether there will be any room on the Mall for it.

We have veered furthest back to traditionalism with the World War II Memorial, which raises many questions aside from its traditionalism, in particular, its disruption of a vista that, to the members of the McMillan Commission, would have been already complete.

But then, what might a "contemporary" World War II memorial have been like? Although alternatives to the winning design by Friedrich St. Florian have not been given much publicity, there seems to have been no great modernist design submitted in the competition for the memorial.[11] Wondering what that modernist possibility might have been, I think of the largest contemporary monument that has been erected recently; it is to be found in Berlin, and it is the monument to the murdered Jews of Europe (fig. 51). It consists of a field of thousands of catafalques—they are also called columns, and stelae, but it is the catafalque they most closely resemble. These rectangular, columnar forms are closely spaced together, with just enough room separating them—three feet—for two people perhaps to squeeze past each other. The columns are of variable height, and look from above as if a giant scythe had swept over them, reducing them in some sections of the field to a foot or two in height, while others are ten feet tall. It was designed by the architect Peter Eisenman and the sculptor Richard Serra. Serra dropped out when the German sponsors asked for a reduction in the number of catafalques, and for trees along the side to soften the unforgiving field of concrete. He would not accept any modification in the design. Eisenman was more flexible, as architects are bound to be.

Does it work? One wonders whether and why people are drawn into the labyrinth of paths it forms, and what they will do when they get there. In contrast, at the Vietnam Veterans Memorial, there is a reason to go down into the declivity, and there is something to do when one gets there—make a tracing, leave a memento. The Holocaust memorial is, like almost all modern monuments, mute. But the muteness of the successful Vietnam Veterans Memorial is not absolute—there are the names. There was no way of solving the problem of introducing names in the Berlin memorial—there were too many, an alphabetical order would have been ridiculous, there was no way of knowing when they died. I think the Holocaust memorial does not succeed in the enormously difficult task of making a monument that is modern. But I also have my doubts whether the forms drawn upon for the

World War II Memorial, a very different kind of memorial, still have the power to move.

The strongest argument in favor of monuments hewing to established traditions remains our fear as to what the alternative would be like. Modernism has become individualistic, eccentric, "self-referential," as the fashionable term today puts it. It is the expression of the "me," when what we want in our memorials is the expression of the "us." That is what makes us more friendly to the Jefferson Memorial today.

FIG. 52
Construction fences on the Mall,
2004
Judy Feldman

Turning Point

THE PROBLEMATICS OF BUILDING ON THE MALL TODAY

Judy Scott Feldman

❋ WALKING ON THE MALL in early 2004, I wondered if the McMillan Plan's vision that gave the nation this great symbolic landscape had lost its power, in Daniel Burnham's words, "to stir men's blood." The Mall appeared to be undergoing a seismic change (fig. 52; see also fig. 66). Behind tall plywood construction fences surrounding the Washington Monument, the grounds were being regraded to accommodate new security barrier walls and curvilinear walkways at the heart of the Mall's symbolic cross axis. The World War II Memorial's pylons and triumphal arches were rising at the site of the Lincoln Memorial's Rainbow Pool, a completed element of the McMillan Plan. Concrete barriers, surveillance cameras, and police cars surrounded monuments and museums. Pedestrians maneuvered the maze on crumbling walkways and sparse grass rutted with tire tracks.[1]

Three years later, the transformation continues, with no end in sight. Near the Lincoln Memorial, new security barriers and food and gift concessions soon will be joined by an underground Vietnam Veterans Memorial Visitor Center. The open space next to the National Museum of American History, at the foot of the Washington Monument, has been selected for the new National Museum of African American History and Culture. Large tents, construction equipment, and trucks regularly transform the open space between the Capitol and the monument into a fairground, destroying the grass and marring the vista.

Fifteen years ago, at the two hundredth anniversary of the Mall's conception, changes to its design were viewed benevolently, even approvingly, as evolutions of the L'Enfant and McMillan plans and of the Mall's place in American civic life.[2] Today, however, they signal a change in values and concept. The Mall is increasingly divided in two, physically and symbolically. Near the Capitol and the museums, it retains its open greensward and axial vistas. Yet west of the Washington Monument, the new World War II Memorial bisects the open landscape and occludes the connection between the monuments to Presidents Washington and Lincoln. At the same time, the area around the Lincoln Memorial is becoming a "memorial park," where multiacre war memorials with themes of military valor and sacrifice—dedicated to the veterans of the Vietnam War and the Korean War, and now to World War II—transpose the iconography of Arlington National Cemetery into the civic landscape, creating, in effect, an Arlington East. Public access is increasingly curtailed by walls and barriers, by chain fences that mark off consecrated zones around veterans' memorials, and by the gradual implementation of policies that will restrict the nature and scope of public events.

The Mall is not just a park; it is a democratic idea. What happens to it, and on it, is a physical expression of the nation's historical memory, its cultural values, hopes, and sense of the future. L'Enfant's plan expressed the optimism of the new nation in 1791. One hundred years later,

the McMillan Plan embodied a renewed sense of national identity—of unity restored under Lincoln and confidence in the growing power of democratic government—in the people's park. Throughout the twentieth century the public animated that open space, transforming it into a civic stage for celebrations, First Amendment activities, and recreation. But today the historic L'Enfant and McMillan visions are slowly being altered and lost; the public open space is increasingly buried beneath concrete and stone. The Mall seems guided less by a vision than by a capitulation to political expediency, changing fashion, and, now, the requirements of antiterrorism.

The World War II Memorial marked a turning point. Editorial writers and critics from across the political spectrum decried its location on the Capitol–Lincoln Memorial axis as a "monumental mistake," an "ambush" and "mauling" of the Mall. Other problems followed. Congress and local media reacted in outrage, with charges of "marketing the Mall," to the "NFL Kickoff Festival, Live from the National Mall, Presented by Pepsi Vanilla," in September 2003 when many parts of the Mall were closed off behind fences adorned with commercial advertisement. That same year, the proposed Vietnam Veterans Memorial Visitor Center on the Mall inspired the art critic Christopher Knight to compare the desecration of the Mall's historical open space to the looting of cultural treasures at Baghdad's National Museum of Iraq. "If the nation's politicians won't protect it, the public must," he asserted. In fact, a citizens movement had already begun to take up the challenge.[3]

How did we come to this point? In this essay, I examine the competing forces for preservation and change on the Mall, and how they play out in real life. What is the process for change? Who are the decision makers? What roles do Congress, government review agencies, and the public play? Which parts of the process work, and which do not? If the historical concepts for the Mall are no longer capable of meeting modern social, cultural, and political needs, what are the alternatives? What can be done to fix or improve the way the Mall is cared for as it grows and changes?

I use three recent controversial projects as case studies: the Security Improvement Plan for the Washington Monument; the Visitor Center for the Vietnam Veterans Memorial; and the World War II Memorial. From Congressional authorization to site selection and design review, these examples illustrate in varying ways the day-to-day reality of decision making. (The Capitol visitor center, now under construction, another expensive and controversial project meriting discussion, is administered solely by the Architect of the Capitol and so falls outside the jurisdiction of the other government review agencies.) Each project in its own way represents a disregard of, or an intentional departure from, the L'Enfant and McMillan plans. In each case, public controversy regarding site and design decisions reveals a struggle among competing ideas about what the Mall is for. The nature of the debate goes to the heart of the Mall's perceived role as a place of history and memory and as a public space dedicated to the American people.

The Washington Monument Security Improvement Plan

This project puts security front and center on the Mall. It introduces a new curvilinear design scheme at the heart of the cross axis. It epitomizes what can happen when careful planning, oversight, and historic preservation are sacrificed in the name of a security "emergency."

The National Park Service (NPS) had installed temporary concrete "Jersey" barriers around the base of the monument in 1998, after the bombings of U.S. embassies in Africa, and in early 2001 added an interim visitor-screening structure at its eastern entrance. Immediately following September 11, 2001, the NPS used emergency congressional funding and put forward a permanent security plan with two major components: stone retaining walls to stop potentially bomb-laden vehicles and a new underground visitor-screening facility and tunnel entrance.

The plan called for thirty-inch-high barrier retaining walls, or ha-has, located approximately four hundred feet out from the monument's base. The walls, lining new curvilinear sidewalks, formed interlocking oval shapes with four openings to permit pedestrian access to the monument. Visitors who wish to ascend the monument would no longer be permitted to enter through the door but would be directed to a visitor screening facility at the historic stone lodge at Fifteenth Street, four hundred feet east of the monument. After entering the lodge and proceeding into a new glass addition for security screening, they would descend into an underground visitor center and from there walk through a long tunnel to reach the monument's elevator. They would exit the monument through the existing door.

The Security Improvement Plan was an amalgam of disparate parts from earlier, unfunded National Park Service plans, including a 1973 proposal for an underground visitor center and tunnel into the monument; 1982 landscape improvements; a 1986 above-ground visitor center that had been rejected by the federal review agencies; and a 1993 concept that added handicapped-accessible walkways and funded restoration of the monument lodge to make it the entrance for a new underground visitor facility.[4] In a design competition hastily put together following September 11, the Park Service sought a concept that transformed the visitor center idea into a screening facility and the walkways into integral components of a security retaining-wall system, thus justifying the elements as part of a unified emergency program.

The hasty reworking and consolidation of the earlier plans produced a predictable muddle. Critics, including the chairmen of the Commission of Fine Arts (CFA) and National Capital Planning Commission (NCPC), questioned many of its elements: the concept of a tunnel as a desirable security solution; the symbolism of forcing visitors into an underground approach to the great obelisk; the new glass addition to the lodge, which would more than double the size of that structure directly on the Capitol axis; the potential destabilizing of the monument itself during construction; and the location of walls on the monument's grassy mound where they would interfere with pedestrian access and traditional large public gatherings.[5]

The National Park Service began a series of redesigns of the lodge addition but rejected most of the other criticisms. Ultimately, the agency circumvented part of the federal review process so that it could proceed with construction of the walls. After the Commission of Fine Arts questioned the tunnel concept and the glass screening facility and raised concerns about the location of the walls, the NPS determined that it would proceed without the CFA's final approval. It secured approval from the NCPC for one piece of the project, the landscape elements, and went ahead with construction—regrading the mound, adding trees, and building the new sidewalks and retaining walls.[6] The walls were completed in 2005. The lodge addition and underground elements, however, were abandoned in 2003 after Congress withdrew funding amid unanswered questions of cost. As a result of piecemeal development and approval, the total security plan was never completed and instead the temporary screening facility—a major reason the NPS cited for moving ahead with the plan in the first place—was returned to the monument entrance. Word is that the lodge is simply being restored to serve as a ticket office and visitor center for the monument.

If security had been the only concern, less intrusive alternatives were available. Local citizens and preservation groups who participated in the public consultation process proposed locating the security barriers at street or sidewalk level, as is done at other federal buildings, instead of on the open landscape. Another idea was to conduct visitor screening inside the entrance, where, according to engineers, the fifteen-foot-thick solid masonry walls afforded substantial protection against any handheld explosive device. The Park Service, however, refused to consider security measures that did not incorporate the underground visitor center and walkway components of the 1993 concept, and the NCPC deferred to the NPS decision.

While the most obtrusive elements of the plan were not built, and the security walls have been cited by the NCPC and American Society of Landscape Architects as a model of sensitive security design, nonetheless the walls and accompanying curvilinear walkways have significantly altered both the look and the visitor experience of the Washington Monument grounds, as well as its relationship to the larger Mall. The monument's gentle slope has been subtly but noticeably reshaped above the dark line of the low stone walls. The new curvilinear walls and walkways, replacing walks that led more directly to the monument's base, guide pedestrians in an arc around its base and off the main vista (when I lead tours to and from the monument, I maneuver my group off the curving paths and onto the open grass so that we can keep the Capitol and Lincoln Memorial in view). The public safety effect of these walls on what has traditionally been a meeting ground for large public events and marches has not yet been evaluated.

In the end, the landscape design represents a challenge to the L'Enfant and McMillan plans by introducing a curvilinear design scheme at the heart of the Mall's cross axis. The McMillan Plan's formal terraced concept for the grounds—although never built, due to congressional concern that the required excavations could destabilize the monument—reinforced L'Enfant's concept of the monument at the nexus of the Mall's cross axis. It envisioned a round pool at the monument's originally intended location, aligned with the Capitol and the White House. Today, that site is marked by the Jefferson Pier, the granite marker about four hundred feet northwest of the monument. The new walkways and walls, however, obscure the axial spine of the L'Enfant and McMillan plans. The status of the Jefferson Pier is permanently altered and minimized (tourists who used to visit it, wondering what it was, no longer do so) by its being set inside the curving walls, in a gulley where it collects water and mud. The new design introduces, instead, a new variation on nineteenth-century Downing-esque garden design. Indeed, in a presentation before the NCPC in 2003, the designer, landscape architect Laurie Olin, likened this concept favorably to Andrew Jackson Downing's naturalistic design scheme for the Mall. (Paradoxically, in 1981 a National Park Service report criticized the Downing plan as having "obliterated" the L'Enfant concept.)[7]

If any place on the National Mall calls for the most intelligent, careful, and historically sensitive design solution, it is the Washington Monument grounds. Instead, the redesigned landscape at the heart of the Mall's cross axis is a testament to the allure of security funding, political expediency on the part of the National Park Service, and the weakness of preservation laws and the review agencies to enforce those laws, especially in the face of a so-called security emergency. Even the judge addressing a lawsuit brought against the project declined to step into a situation the Park Service called an "emergency." The L'Enfant and McMillan plans simply could not compete.

The Vietnam Veterans Memorial Visitor Center

The purpose of this visitor center is "to better inform and educate the public about the Vietnam Veterans Memorial and the Vietnam War." Proposed by the Vietnam Veterans Memorial Fund in 2000, authorized by Congress in November 2003, and approved for a site on the National Mall north of the Lincoln Memorial in 2006 (fig. 53), the controversial project exemplifies the weakness, in the face of powerful political interests, of current laws intended to protect the Mall's historical design, symbolism, and public open space. It has been sharply criticized, including by some veterans as unnecessary and a distraction, given that the Vietnam Veterans Memorial is the most popular memorial on the Mall; as an intrusion on the Lincoln Memorial grounds; as insulting to veterans because of its underground, bunker-like design; and as setting a bad precedent that could encourage additional visitor centers at the nearby Korean Veterans Memorial and the World War II Memorial.[8]

The visitor center will be the latest of several additions to Maya Lin's original design, dedicated in 1982, that include the flagpole and *Three Soldiers* statue group (1984); the Vietnam Women's Memorial (1993); and a plaque dedicated to those who died later as a result of inju-

ries suffered during the war (2004). The original legislation proposed a temporary, relatively small (twelve hundred square feet) "education center" that would be reevaluated (and possibly removed or moved) after ten years. By the time the bill, sponsored by influential Vietnam veterans in Congress, was enacted in 2003 as Public Law 108-126, the project had grown in scope and scale: it was now to be a permanent facility; it was to be constructed underground; after being built with private Vietnam Veterans Memorial Fund money, it would be transferred to the jurisdiction of the National Park Service; and it was now called a "visitor" center, which implies additional purposes beyond the original purely educational function. And it continues to grow. While the legislation states that its size was to be "limited to the minimum necessary" so as not to encroach on the memorial itself and the open space, the May 2006 Environmental Assessment states that "the building program is estimated to require approximately 25,000 square feet of exhibit and exhibit support space, maintenance and mechanical space, public entry and visitor services spaces, educational programming space, and administrative space."[9]

Choosing a location for the visitor center was at the heart of the controversy that went all the way to the halls of Congress. The Senate Energy Committee wanted a moratorium on any new memorials or visitor centers on the Mall; the House Resources Committee was supporting legislation to put the visitor center "on or near" the Mall. The compromise law (PL 108-126) imposed a moratorium on future memorials and visitor centers and,

Constitution Avenue

SITE A

Henry Bacon Drive

Vietnam Veterans
Memorial

Lincoln Memorial

Reflecting Pool

FIG. 53
Environmental assessment map
showing site A, selected for the
Vietnam Veterans Memorial
Visitor Center
*National Capital Planning
Commission*

in the very same measure, exempted the Vietnam visitor center from the moratorium. The controversy heated up again in 2006 when the Vietnam Veterans Fund, having chosen its preferred site on the Mall near the Lincoln Memorial, encountered opposition from government review agencies and the public. The House of Representatives reacted by passing legislation that mandated the Mall site. The NCPC and Commission of Fine Arts, stripped of their review authority in the House and facing similar legislation in the Senate, retreated

and voted approval. The review agencies, the public process, and historic preservation laws were no match for the Vietnam Veterans Fund and its friends in Congress.

Ironically, even while the visitor center generated controversy, little attention was given to the National Park Service's own plan to build two new food and gift concession structures near the Lincoln Memorial, one of them on the same plot of land as the visitor center. While the center is required to be built underground, the large new Park Service concession—for which the NPS never sought congressional authorization and thus avoided similar scrutiny—stands prominently across the street from the Vietnam Veterans Memorial.

The World War II Memorial

The World War II Memorial (figs. 54 and 55) represents the most significant change in recent years to the Mall's historical concept. The controversy over the location and design of this memorial pitted powerful veterans groups against any and all opponents, government agencies against one another, and Congress against citizens who brought a lawsuit against the memorial approvals. More than any recent event, it finally persuaded Congress in 2003 to declare the Mall a "substantially completed work of civic art" and impose a moratorium on any new memorials or visitor centers.

The 7.4-acre site is directly on the east-west Capitol-to-Lincoln-Memorial axis, between the Washington Monument and Lincoln Memorial. The design as finally approved in late 2000 required the destruction of the Rainbow Pool—a completed element of the McMillan Plan and an integral component of the landscape designed for the Lincoln Memorial by Frederick Law Olmsted Jr. The memorial plaza, lowered seven feet below grade, contains a smaller pool at its center, fifty-six granite pylons, and two triumphal arches set into the tree line to the north and south. Critics charged that the memorial would compete with the Mall's transcendent design, symbolism, continuous public open space, and axial vistas; that it would interject incongruously a twentieth-century world war into the midst of the monuments to American government; that because it is fully enclosed it would restrict free pedestrian access through an area historically associated with large public demonstrations and marches, including civil rights and anti–Vietnam War demonstrations.[10]

As the memorial moved toward almost certain final approval in 2000, despite growing media and public opposition, one government agency stepped into the fray and issued a formal finding that should have brought a much-needed reevaluation. The Advisory Council on Historic Preservation, a federal office created in the 1960s to advise the White House on matters of historic preservation, held a public hearing and, on September 5, 2000, issued a formal finding that called for rejection of the design. In a letter to Interior Secretary Bruce Babbitt (whose jurisdiction included the National Park Service and whose authority included approving memorial sites and designs and signing construction permits), the council summed up the objections to the memorial:

[T]he Memorial's overall scale and complexity create a tension with the transcendent symbolic significance and fundamental simplicity of the National Mall. In particular, the visual screen of 56 ornamented pillars, while enclosing the plaza, violate the open feeling of the Mall and intrude upon the uncluttered historic vistas. . . . In the Council's view, it is of utmost importance that the National World War II Memorial complement and not compete with the Mall's transcendent historic and cultural values and that the Mall remain

FIG. 54
The World War II Memorial,
May 26, 2004
*Associated Press, American Battle
Monuments Commission*

genuinely the common ground that it has been historically. . . . We urge reconsideration of the current Memorial design to preserve the distinctive character of this national treasure.[11]

But this ruling was apparently too little, too late, for a memorial that, according to its politically powerful supporters, needed to be completed while the remaining World War II veterans were still alive. Secretary Babbitt rejected the findings.

FIG. 55
The World War II Memorial
Judy Feldman

The NCPC and CFA gave the memorial final approval. A lawsuit brought by local preservation groups, based on the Advisory Council's finding, was nullified after Congress, impatient with any delay, exempted the project from all laws governing site and design approvals. The memorial was dedicated on Memorial Day 2004.

The memorial had been troubled from the start. Legislation authorizing a World War II memorial, first proposed in 1987 by Rep. Marcy Kaptur of Ohio, was signed into law (Public Law 103-32) by President Clinton in 1993. Two years later, choosing from among seven potential sites identi-

fied by the Park Service and analyzed in a World War II Memorial site selection study, the memorial sponsor, the American Battle Monuments Commission (ABMC), unanimously picked a four-acre site at the east end of Constitution Gardens (just north of the current site), overlooking the lake. The National Capital Planning Commission approved that location, but the influential chairman of the Commission of Fine Arts, J. Carter Brown, rejected it, stating that it was not prominent enough to memorialize an event of the magnitude of World War II. With a scheduled dedication of a site by President Clinton on Veterans Day 1995 fast approaching, in September the ABMC and other government agencies met in private to resolve their differences. They selected the Rainbow Pool, a site not previously considered and never subjected to public review. The CFA then approved the site, and the NCPC, after rescinding its earlier vote, approved the new location in October 1995, barely a month before the site's dedication on Veterans Day. The public process had been circumvented but the consequences of a lack of proper scrutiny were not apparent until 1997, when the announcement of the competition-winning design by the architect Friedrich St. Florian was greeted by congressional, public, and media outcry.[12]

The problems with the site became clear. That original design—consisting of a plaza, lowered fifteen feet below grade and enclosed at the north and south by fifty-foot-high earthen berms housing museum space and rows of forty-foot-high columns—would have required the removal of dozens of elms and the obstruction of vistas through and around the Rainbow Pool and Reflecting Pool. In the face of strong opposition that included members of Congress on both sides of the aisle, the CFA and the NCPC rejected the design as too large and overbearing for the Mall site. This was the opportunity for the memorial sponsor and review agencies to reconsider the site, a decision that ultimately would have freed the design from constraints forced on it by the location between the Washington Monument and Lincoln Memorial. The review agencies refused, however, to reconsider the memorial's location, and over the next two years the ABMC struggled with a succession of designs and redesigns.

The design first was scaled back and then enlarged, ultimately drawing government review agencies into a confrontation over the memorial's adverse impact on the sensitive historical site. In 1998, St. Florian returned to the review commissions with a new, smaller concept, which avoided controversy, won preliminary approval, and then eventually evolved into the final design. The 1998 concept envisioned a plaza, lowered seven feet below grade and surrounded by a "transparent" metal fence, with two triumphal arches located to the north and south, inside the curve of the historical elms framing the pool. In 1999, the metallic fence was replaced by new vertical elements, the fifty-six seventeen-foot-high pylons inscribed with the names of the states and American territories during the war. The memorial focal point, at the western end of the plaza, featured a stone "cenotaph," resembling a sarcophagus, and an eternal flame. By 2000, and in response to criticism, the cenotaph and flame were abandoned, to be replaced by a wall of four thousand golden stars, each intended to represent one hundred military dead.

Throughout design development, St. Florian responded to criticism of the memorial's lack of cohesive idea or iconography by promising a yet-to-be-defined "central sculptural element," which was to be located in or over the reconstructed Rainbow Pool. In the end, that element was abandoned. By the time the Advisory Council on Historic Preservation in 2000 issued its finding against the massive, enclosed plaza design, the memorial had not only grown vertically with pillars and triumphal arches. It also included, north of the plaza, a small, walled "contemplative area" and, south of it, a new road for bus drop-off and handicapped parking, restrooms (oddly, housed in an imposing granite structure that looks as though it is part of the memorial itself), and a visitor kiosk.

The lawsuit brought by preservation groups against the memorial was based on the Advisory Council's finding, preservation law, and the Commemorative Works Act (discussed below). In preparing its own defense, the NCPC discovered that it had to retake its final votes. With a new, independent-minded chairman actively seeking changes in the design, a reevaluation seemed possible. That was when Congress stepped in and, by unanimous consent, exempted the project from all laws. Public Law 107-11 was in effect a tacit acknowledgment that the World War II Memorial violated existing statutes intended to protect the Mall's historic plans and public open space.

That decision, the most egregious among the three case studies, marked a turning point in the Mall's history. Existing laws and public review processes intended to protect the Mall's historical and cultural integrity were ignored, circumvented, or overturned. Historic preservation and forces for change were at war, and preservation lost. So, what can be done to restore the Mall's capacity to respond to change? To compel Congress, memorial sponsors, and government agencies to follow the laws and processes that protect the integrity of the Mall and put its well-being above special interests? To find answers, we need to understand the strengths and shortcomings of current laws, management, and policies and to identify remedies and new approaches.

The Failure of the Commemorative Works Act and Other Preservation Measures

Congress and the federal agencies have attempted over the past twenty years to protect the Mall's historical integrity with laws, plans, and policies. But clearly, these measures are not working and, furthermore, are not enforceable.

Congress passed the Commemorative Works Act (Public Law 99-652) in 1986 precisely to control future memorial growth; it amended and strengthened the act in 2003 by declaring the Mall a "substantially completed work of civic art" and imposing a moratorium (the Commemorative Works Clarification and Revision Act of 2003, Public Law 108-126) (fig. 56). Congress was reacting in the 1980s to the "monumental chaos" over the Vietnam Veterans Memorial and to the lack of guidelines and public process for the subject matter, location, and design of memorials.[13] The act's purpose is to protect the L'Enfant and McMillan plans and public open space in the nation's capital, especially on the Mall, and to bring order to the memorial building process. It requires congressional authorization of any new memorial in the nation's capital and, to afford extra protection, mandates that only memorials of "preeminent historical and lasting significance to the Nation" are to be permitted on the Mall. It stipulates a twenty-five-year waiting period after the death of an individual to be commemorated before a memorial can be authorized and puts limits on military memorials. Memorial sponsors are required to consult with the National Capital Memorial Commission on site selection and to submit site and design review to the Commission of Fine Arts, the National Capital Planning Commission, and the National Park Service.

The act has sometimes succeeded in encouraging memorial sponsors to seek sites off the Mall. Examples include the Women in Military Service to America Memorial at Arlington Cemetery, the African American Civil War Memorial, the Disabled Veterans Memorial, and the Victims of Communism Memorial. The National Capital Planning Commission's 1997 Legacy Plan and 2001 Memorials and Museums Master Plan provide a planning framework to help guide sponsors to one hundred off-Mall sites (see the essay by Patricia Gallagher). But just as often, groups hold out for a Mall site and, as recent history shows, succeed.

The weakness of the Commemorative Works Act in controlling development is evident in the prodigious growth in the number and size of memorials since 1986. After the Vietnam Veterans Memorial, Congress authorized the Korean Veterans Memorial, also near the Lincoln Memorial. The Vietnam complex grew, with the addition of the *Three Soldiers* statue group and the Vietnam Women's Memorial, to occupy a large triangular area of Constitution Gardens; the visitor center will extend the memorial's reach onto yet another parcel. The trend toward more and ever larger memorials intensified with the 7.4-acre FDR Memorial at the Tidal

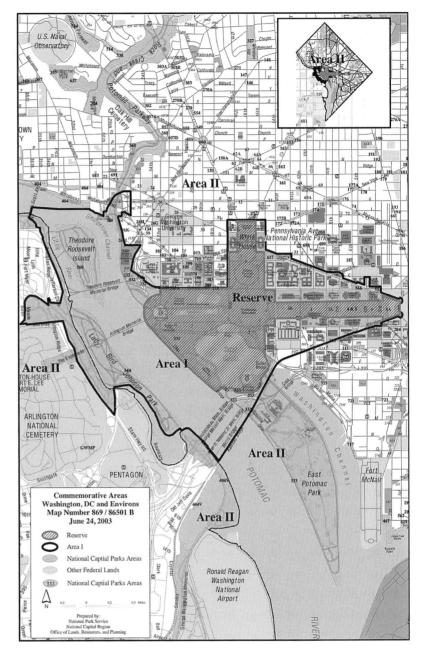

FIG. 56
Reserve map showing commemorative areas, Washington and environs, as of June 24, 2003

Basin (fig. 57), the 4-acre Martin Luther King Jr. Memorial planned nearby, and the 7.4-acre World War II Memorial.

The effectiveness of the Commemorative Works Act ultimately depends on Congress, the federal agencies, and memo-

rial sponsors properly and consistently applying and enforcing it. But Congress has demonstrated its own ambivalence about applying the act. It exempted the World War II Memorial from it in 2000, imposed a moratorium but exempted the Vietnam visitor center from it in 2003, and authorized the Smithsonian to choose a site on the Mall, next to the National Museum of American History, for the future National Museum of African American History and Culture. Congress seems incapable of turning away memorial and museum sponsors who want a place "on the Mall." Thus, from a purely practical perspective, the moratorium is not a realistic preservation solution.

So, if the act's restrictions and the moratorium cannot control growth, what can? How can the Mall accommodate two seemingly conflicting needs: preservation, on the one hand, and on the other, additional space for new memorials and museums? A logical solution is to let the Mall grow, as it did a century ago when the McMillan Commission extended the extant Mall onto landfill to create a place for the Lincoln Memorial and vast new public parkland. The Mall can now expand onto contiguous land in East Potomac Park, L'Enfant Promenade, and South Capitol Street, areas already identified by NCPC as preferred locations for future museums and memorials. Expansion would relieve pressure on the existing Mall and allow American history to continue to unfold on the Mall. Of course, an updated master plan would be needed to ensure that the iconic quality of the National Mall is protected and extended into the new areas.

The act also needs to be amended to eliminate a built-in conflict of interest that has worked against Mall preservation. The conflict is in the almost absolute control Congress has assigned to the National Park Service. It works at two levels. As described in "24 Steps to Erecting a Memorial in Washington, D.C.," a document the Park Service distributes to potential memorial sponsors, the Commemorative Works Act gives the Interior Department (and the National Park Service under its control) a crucial role as advocate, judge, and jury for new memorial projects. The Park Service co-sponsors new memorial projects (for example, the environmental assessment for the Vietnam visitor center opens: "The National Park Service, on behalf of the Vietnam Veterans Memorial Fund, proposes to secure a site . . ."); determines, in its role as chair of the National Capital Memorials Commission (NCMC), if the memorial warrants a place on or near the Mall; and selects the preferred site. Then, the National Park Service presents the site and design to the review agencies, votes on those decisions as commissioner on the NCPC, and ultimately authorizes (through the Interior Department) the construction permit. When asked to recuse himself from voting on memorial projects at NCPC, the Park Service representative has refused, pointing out that Congress intended it that way.

The Park Service not only dominates decision making for privately sponsored projects. It also makes key decisions on the applicability of the Commemorative Works Act to its own projects, as was the case with the Washington Monument security plan. In his role as chair of the NCMC, the Park Service official privately

Dedication of the Women in Military Service for America Memorial at Arlington
National Cemetery, October 1997
AP Images / Ken Cedeno

determined that the act—with its important requirement for congressional authorization of a project—did not apply to his agency's Washington Monument project, which included both above-ground and below-ground security and visitor-screening components, or to its concession buildings at the Lincoln Memorial but that it did apply to the Vietnam Veteran Funds' underground Vietnam visitor center.

At another level, the act puts the National Park Service at odds with its core mission. The mission of the agency, as described in the Organic Act that created it in 1916, is "to conserve the scenery and the natural and historic objects . . . and to provide for the enjoyment of the same in such manner and by such means as will leave them unimpaired for the enjoyment of future generations." Yet, as co-sponsor of new memorials, park officials are required to advocate for and approve changes that challenge their preservation role. When Congress gets into the act, as it did by mandating a site on the Mall for the World War II Memorial and the Vietnam visitor center, the agency is put in an untenable position. The way to solve this dilemma is to remove the memorial building process from National Park Service control.

Money also can undermine Mall preservation, and this, too, can be remedied by amending the act to require more public funding and oversight. Most memorials today are privately funded. The act requires memorial sponsors to provide 10 percent of the total construction cost to the National Park Service for future maintenance. The lack of public funding lessens the pressure for strong congressional oversight. Alternatively, well-funded memorials can be seen by the Park Service as a way to carry out costly but unfunded maintenance and restoration projects. Two memorials that serve double duty this way—one for better, the other for worse— are the Women in Military Service for America memorial (fig. 58), which restored the Hemicycle at the ceremonial entrance to Arlington National Cemetery and uses its interior space for a museum; and the World War II Memorial, which required the destruction and reconstruction of the Rainbow Pool in the new setting of the Memorial's granite walls, pillars, and triumphal arches. By requiring substantial public investment in all new memorials, Congress would increase public accountability at all levels, from authorization to site selection and final design approval.

Missing: Agreement on the Mall's Definition and Purpose

Ask visitors to Washington, "What is the National Mall?" and you are likely to hear a general consensus that it includes the Capitol, the Washington Monument, and the Lincoln Memorial. Ask the same question of the government agencies that administer the Mall, however, and there is no easy agreement. As astonishing as it may seem, there is no official map, definition, and agreed-upon purpose for the National Mall. Conflicting definitions are both a symptom and a cause of the Mall's problems, especially its increasing divergence from the McMillan Plan concept.

A 2003 Congressional Research Services report that attempted to identify the statutory definition of the Mall concluded that there is no single official definition, although the McMillan Plan comes closest to one.[14] Congress described the Mall, in the Commemorative Works Clarification and Revision Act of 2003, as "the great cross-axis, which generally extends from the United States Capitol to the Lincoln Memorial, and from the White House to the Jefferson Memorial." This is consistent with the McMillan Plan in general, although it leaves open the question of geographical boundaries: does the Mall include the FDR Memorial and Constitution Gardens; the entire kite-shaped area including Pennsylvania and Maryland Avenues? Congress does not say. The National Park Service defines the Mall in several ways, some consistent with Congress, others not. For example, it is not unusual to hear representatives of the Park Service state that the Washington Monument is not on the Mall and that the Lincoln Memorial is not on the Mall but, instead, in West Potomac Park.[15] Why the conflicting definitions?

The National Park Service's last master plan, developed in the 1960s and 1970s with the architectural firm Skidmore, Owings & Merrill, incorporated the cross axis from the Capitol to the Lincoln Memorial and the White House to the Jefferson Memorial. At an April 2005 Senate oversight hearing, a park official testified that the National Mall includes the cross axis, as defined by Congress. But in day-to-day operations, the agency uses a different set of definitions. These are based on the Park Service's 1960s-era division of the Mall into manageable separate units for administrative and maintenance purposes; the units are shown in the official map of the "Park System of the Nation's

Capital and Environs" (also known as "Map A"). "The Mall" proper is identified as the area between First and Fourteenth Streets; the Washington Monument grounds lie between Fourteenth and Seventeenth Streets; the White House and Ellipse are between Fifteenth and Seventeenth Streets, north of Constitution Avenue; and West Potomac Park encompasses the Lincoln Memorial and the expanse of parkland along the Potomac River. These definitions put into context recent statements by park officials and in official documents that appear to reject the holistic McMillan Plan concept of the Mall for a narrower interpretation based solely on areas under Park Service jurisdiction: "While the term 'The Mall' is sometimes used informally to describe the axial landscape between the Lincoln Memorial and the Capitol, the Mall is officially defined by the National Capital Planning Commission [sic] as the land bounded by Constitution Avenue on the north, Independence Avenue on the south, the Capitol on the east, and 14th Street, N.W. on the west. The Washington Monument grounds lie immediately west of the Mall, between Constitution and Independence avenues, and from 17th Street, N.W., to 14th Street, N.W."[16]

A perusal of National Park Service documents, its official website, and pronouncements during public hearings uncover multiple, sometimes conflicting, definitions of the Mall. The National Register of Historic Places locates the Washington Monument on "The Mall, between 14th and 17th Sts., N.W." Documents and support materials, including a glossary, released in November 2006 at the announcement of the agency's National Mall Plan

(an update of the 1960s-era management plan), by contrast, limit the definition of the Mall to the greensward—"the area west of the United States Capitol between Madison and Jefferson Drives from 1st to 14th streets NW/SW"—not including the Capitol, the Smithsonian, or the Washington Monument. The "National Mall" is different from the "Mall." It is "the area comprised of the Mall, the Washington Monument, and West Potomac Park" (but not the Capitol or White House).[17]

What does this matter? At the very least, the National Park Service's (inconsistent) way of defining the Mall as a collection of memorial parks breeds confusion among government agencies, Congress, the media, and the public about what and where the Mall is. Because the National Park Service is a primary steward of the Mall, Congress depends on, and defers to, its judgment. In 2005, the Park Service codified this segmented concept of the Mall by renaming its "National Capital Central" administrative district "National Mall and Memorial Parks." The NPS definitions also raise questions of jurisdiction. By defining the Mall only in terms of its own jurisdiction, the Park Service can and does claim that it has exclusive administrative and planning authority for the Mall, when in actuality the agency's administrative authority does not extend to the Capitol, Smithsonian, National Gallery of Art, and other areas.

More serious, the National Park Service justifies a piecemeal approach to planning for the Mall, as happened with the Washington Monument security project and the World War II Memorial. For the former, park officials ignored or rejected concerns that the curvilinear walls, proposed addition to the lodge, and diminished status of the Jefferson Pier violated the sanctity of the monument as the nexus of the Mall's great cross axis. By disassociating the Washington Monument from historical concept of a continuous open space—especially by separating it from "the Mall" across Fourteenth Street—the National Park Service apparently felt free to design the monument grounds as a discrete element, separate from the larger whole. Park officials openly pronounced that "the Monument is not on the Mall." With regard to the World War II Memorial, Park Service officials described the site as being part of West Potomac Park, assiduously avoiding any discussion of potential adverse effects to the Mall as a whole and the McMillan Plan. The NCPC and Commission of Fine Arts deferred to the NPS's approach.

If the Mall is not to be further degraded into a series of separately designed miniparks, Congress and the Mall-managing agencies need to agree on a unified, coherent definition. That definition should be based in the historical L'Enfant and McMillan plans, not administrative jurisdictions, and its integrity should be upheld by the planning and review agencies. Since the geographic boundaries have never been clear, in part because the McMillan Plan's kite-shaped area includes the Federal Triangle and other areas not traditionally associated with the Mall, this will afford an opportunity to reexamine the McMillan Commission's ideas and to what extent today's Mall conforms to it. It is also an opportunity to examine areas for future Mall expansion.

Just as critical is the need to define the Mall's purpose. The Mall's physical definition is inextricably tied to its evolving function. In recent decades, with the addition of war memorials, security, new museums, and large public events, the Mall has taken on new qualities and public uses. In particular, the public has given the Mall new meaning as the people's place and civic stage. Yet the government has not recognized that evolving function as the basis for planning the open space.

Instead, the National Park Service has developed its own vision—the Mall as theme park. Park officials have spoken about "overuse" and the agency's long-term goals to move larger public rallies to RFK Memorial Stadium or Pennsylvania Avenue, consign cars and buses to satellite parking lots, and put tourists on shuttle buses: "Just like at Disneyland. . . . Nobody drives through Disneyland, [because] they're not allowed. And we've got the better theme park."[18] Several recent changes look like part of a larger plan to restrict public use of the open space: closing parking lots at the Washington Monument and Jefferson Memorial; restricting public activities permitted around the war memorials' "sacred" precincts; providing only one twenty-dollar-per-person Mall-wide transport system; locating new food and gift concessions at Tourmobile stops instead of along pedestrian walkways; and neglecting public amenities, including good food, restrooms, and convenient parking, to the point that the Mall has become a hostile pedestrian environment. The Park Service is notoriously underfunded by Congress, but its theme park response to burgeoning use is shortsighted and threatens to undermine the Mall's active democratic purpose.

The confusion over the Mall's definition and purpose is perhaps not surprising following a century of dramatic change and growth. Since the McMillan Plan was essentially achieved in the 1970s, new memorials and museums, as well as growing public use, have altered the Mall in ways never envisioned a century ago. Congress has apportioned jurisdiction over the open space and buildings to different agencies and review bodies. Those government agencies, lacking an updated master plan, have been making it up as they go, with the Park Service developing its own definitions and approach to public use. If the Mall is to preserve its historical integrity and still remain a lively place for recreation and public celebration, it needs an updated, coherent, and all-inclusive master plan, in the tradition of the McMillan Plan, and a modern vision that acknowledges its modern public function as a people's park.

Who's in Charge? A Collection of Government Fiefdoms

Unified stewardship will be crucial to the future of the National Mall and the successful implementation of a new master plan. Today, management and oversight of the National Mall is fractured among six or more federal and local government agencies (including the Architect of the Capitol, the Smithsonian Institution, the National Gallery of Art, the National Park Service, the Department of Agriculture, and the District of Columbia government), seven review agencies, and at least eight committees in Congress. The Mall's chaotic growth in recent years is in many ways a manifestation of government turf

wars that pit agency against agency and preservation against politics, with the public watching from the sidelines. The agencies and committees have their separate missions, mandates, and priorities, often at odds with one another. They generally do not speak to one another or plan or make policy in any coordinated fashion because no one agency or committee has jurisdiction over the Mall as a whole. Nothing better illustrates the effects of fractured oversight than the unhappy compromise legislation that created the moratorium (sponsored by the Senate Energy Committee) and exempted the Vietnam visitor center from it (House Resources Committee). In the case of the World War II Memorial, the President's Advisory Council on Historic Preservation ruling that rejected the memorial design was overturned by a Congress impatient to expedite a politically popular project. Lacking unified management and oversight, political expediency trumps historical preservation.

Congress gave control of the Mall in 1898 to the Chief of Engineers of the United States Army. It transferred authority in 1925 to the office of Public Buildings and Public Parks of the National Capital and, in a reorganization of the executive branch in 1933, transferred control once again, this time to the Department of the Interior and the National Park Service. But Congress also over time gave authority to a number of other agencies including the Smithsonian, as its collection of museums and buildings grew; the U.S. Park Police; the D.C. government for the Mall's streets; and the National Gallery of Art, a semi-independent entity. (When the Congressional Research Service researched National

Mall jurisdiction in 2005, it came to the confusing and contradictory conclusion that the National Park Service is in charge except for the areas where other agencies have jurisdiction.)[19]

To oversee design changes to the Mall and ensure protection of the historic L'Enfant and McMillan plans, Congress created the Commission of Fine Arts in 1910, the precursor to the National Capital Planning Commission in 1924, the Advisory Council and Council on Environmental Quality in the 1960s, and the National Capital Memorials Commission in 1986. By the end of the twentieth century, the authorities Congress created to protect and manage the Mall had grown into fiefdoms, each with its own bureaucracy dedicated to its own priority and approach to the Mall. The public was excluded from any meaningful involvement.

Furthermore, Congress set up the oversight or review commissions in such a way that their membership is dominated not only by the agencies that manage the Mall but also by members of the other review commissions. In effect, the agencies police their own decisions. The extent of the agencies' interdependence seems almost incestuous. The National Capital Memorials Commission, the agency that advises potential memorial sponsors, is chaired by the National Park Service (represented by a regional administrator), which also acts, as we have seen, as co-sponsor of all memorial projects. The NCMC includes representatives from the American Battle Monuments Commission (which built the Korean War and World War II memorials), the office of the Architect of the Capitol, the Secretary of Defense, the Mayor of the District of Columbia, and the two federal review agencies, the National Capital Planning Commission and the Commission of Fine Arts. This commission makes judgments about whether a memorial belongs in Washington and whether it marks an event of "preeminent historical and lasting significance to the Nation" and so is permitted a site on or near the Mall. While these decisions should ideally engage also historians and cultural leaders, the commission includes no such representation.

The National Capital Planning Commission, the federal planning agency for the city and region, includes ex-officio members representing the federal government (Defense, Interior/National Park Service, GSA), congressional oversight committees (Senate, Energy; House, Resources), and the city (mayor and city council), as well as five citizen members, three of them appointed by the president of the United States (at least one from adjoining states Virginia and Maryland) and two by the mayor. The federal agencies and congressional representatives, who outnumber citizens seven to five, tend to vote as a bloc, assuring almost certain approval of just about any government project. They frequently defer to one another instead of questioning projects on their individual merits. Professional staffers are under pressure to evaluate favorably projects sponsored by commissioners' agencies.

Private, behind-closed-doors decision making by the government is built into the approval process, especially with projects governed by the Commemorative Works Act, over which the National Park Service wields all-powerful authority (as described earlier). In recent years Congress has undermined even the limited review process provided by the act. By exempting the World War II Memorial and the Vietnam visitor center from the act, Congress has removed any semblance of public process and taken direct control over the Mall for the benefit of special interests, at the expense of the Mall's historical and cultural integrity.

Fractured planning and management can result in conflicting approaches to planning and design. The Smithsonian seeks to attract more people to its museums and large festivals, such as the Folklife Festival, while the National Park Service, expressing concern over the wear and tear from twenty-five million visitors and three thousand events each year, proposes measures to restrict use. Each agency is working on its own security plan, and there are notable differences between them. For example, the Smithsonian's efforts to balance security needs with designs that complement the museum architecture and retain open access to pedestrians have won general acclaim from the review agencies and private citizens. The Park Service, in contrast, has put physical protection of the monuments above all other factors in response to the Secretary of the Interior's call to secure national icons. Thus, park officials rejected outright concerns that the location of barrier walls on the Washington Monument's open landscape would impede free pedestrian movement.

This maximum-security approach has resulted in long delays as the NCPC and CFA balk at obtrusive design solutions proposed at the Lincoln Memorial (now finally under construction) and at the Jefferson Memorial (still unresolved

after five years). Although the NCPC endeavored to encourage a unified design approach to security in the nation's capital, with its 2002 Urban Design and Security Plan, these guidelines may or may not be followed by the various agencies; in any case, the NCPC lacks authority to enforce its policies. The differences between agencies, documented in a 2005 report by the Government Accountability Office ("National Mall: Steps Identified by Stakeholders Facilitate Design and Approval of Security Enhancements," GAO-05-518, June 14, 2005), virtually assure that there will be no comprehensive and unified design approach to security on the Mall, or to other design issues, unless Mall management and oversight can be coordinated under a new entity.

One solution to the problem of fractured planning and management is to create an updated master plan. A forward-looking, all-inclusive plan for the Mall as a whole would provide a holistic context within which each jurisdiction could carry out its own, limited plans. The review agencies would have a standard against which to judge projects coming before them for evaluation. Congress, if fully invested in the new vision for the twenty-first century, may be less prone to accede to the demands of special interests.

But another critical part of the solution has to be increased public participation. With the Mall governed today as a collection of government fiefs, the public is shut out. The city of Washington, particularly local citizens directly affected by what happens on the Mall, has suffered through decades of its decline and neglect; the Mall has become a physical and psychological barrier in the heart of the community and an impediment to city efforts to reconnect downtown to the southwest waterfront. The Mall master planning process should include a strong public role, since the twenty-first century Mall, more than ever before, will be about accommodating the myriad public uses it has taken on over the past century.

Reform of Mall oversight can begin by reevaluating the make-up of the commissions to reduce the dominance by the federal bureaucracy and to include citizen members. The public also will need to buy into the new vision and, in an era of tight budgets, help fund its implementation. That calls for creation of a new entity, a permanent independent commission or conservancy, that can consolidate and coordinate a partnership between the federal interest, the city of Washington, and the public at large. Successful conservancies across the country provide models.

The Next Hundred Years

Mall planning is broken, after more than a century of growth, change, increasing public use, and the accumulation of jurisdictions, authorities, and oversight committees. Modern public use, commemoration, and security overwhelm and continue to chip away at the integrity of the Mall's majestic public open space. The multiple managing and review agencies protect their fiefs while the public's needs are neglected. The National Park Service treats the Mall as a collection of memorial parks combined into a giant theme park, a vision that ignores the Mall's unique purpose as civic stage and living expression of ever-evolving American democ-

FIG. 59
The Washington Monument with Fourth of July celebrants
Tom Wachs

racy. Congress turns the Mall into a political football, ignoring or overturning protection laws and the public review process to benefit special interests. The nation deserves better.

It needs a forward-looking vision and master plan for the twenty-first century that recognizes the Mall's modern function as grand stage for our democracy (fig. 59), that expands the Mall onto contiguous areas to boost its historical and cultural meaning and reconnect it with the surrounding city, that coordinates planning and management into a unified system that includes strong public participation. The McMillan Plan did not lose its power to "stir men's blood," but its finite design and century-old concept were "completed" several decades ago; how do we get from there to the future? Planning for the Mall of the twenty-first century gives us an opportunity to rejuvenate the L'Enfant and McMillan plan concepts that have lost integrity in recent years. And it invites us to imagine an inspiring, exciting, and welcoming future for the Mall-to-be. In its day, the McMillan Plan was the latest thing, a vision of a proud, gleaming city for the United States at the turn of what was to become the American Century. The Mall of the twenty-first century can in its own way presage a hopeful future for American democracy.

This is not a job for the agencies or the entrenched system now in place.[20] It will be up to Congress to take leadership and create an independent commission to develop an all-inclusive master plan and a coordinated means of implementing it. The commission must include nationally esteemed designers, planners, historians, engineers, and cultural leaders across a broad spectrum. No doubt there will be resistance to change from the Mall's current managing agencies and congressional oversight committees. But this can be overcome. Unlike in 1901, when Congress faced the task of removing industrial buildings and a railroad station and tracks—and the considerable costs for building a new Union Station as well as public buildings and museums—today the Mall is public land managed by government entities. The immediate needs are less about costly removal and building campaigns and more about rejuvenating the existing landscape and creating new, inviting public spaces. Congress owes it to the Mall and to the nation to put aside politics and take the lead in championing what should become a national dialogue about what it means to be an American, who we are as a people, and where we hope to be a century from now.

Public involvement, a critical component missing in all three case studies and in the past century of Mall development, will be essential to achieving success. It is the public, after all, that gave the Mall a unifying concept and purpose in the twentieth century and whose support will be needed to bring the future Mall into being. The American people through their actions—whether marching for civil rights, celebrating the Fourth of July, or simply strolling amid its open expanses—have made the Mall above all the "people's place," their common ground. The people's vision of the Mall is a good place to start imagining the future.

Planning beyond the Monumental Core
Patricia E. Gallagher

❧ THE TWO-HUNDRED-YEAR evolution of the National Mall reflects the course of American civic life. Pierre Charles L'Enfant's original concept of the Mall as iconic open space proclaimed and defined the fledgling democracy. The nineteenth-century encroachment of railroad tracks and commercial enterprise demonstrated that era's embrace of unbridled capitalism. By the early twentieth century, the nation's longing for an idealized and ordered public realm manifested itself in the stately city beautiful vision advanced by the Senate Park Commission, also known as the McMillan Commission (see the essays by Cynthia Field and Richard Guy Wilson).

Today, the National Mall and the surrounding monumental core of the city of Washington are again the focus of national discussion about American aspirations and civic values. The decades since the adoption of the McMillan Plan brought not only increased use of the Mall as a national gathering place, during the civil rights movement for example, but also home rule for the District of Columbia, middle-class flight from Washington, new economic pressures, and a growing division between the local, living city and the federal, national capital. Washington policy makers and planners are once again seeking a new formula to balance the national desire for a beautiful, symbolic capital city with the social and economic needs of its residents.[1]

From 1970 to 2000, as Washington's middle class fled to the suburbs, the city's population dropped from 757,000 to 572,000, its tax base eroded, and its finances faltered.[2] At the same time, federal Washington was also facing formidable problems. The city's symbolic heart, known as the monumental core, developed and grew as an almost exclusively governmental precinct, stretching along two great axes from the Capitol to the Lincoln Memorial and from the White House to the Jefferson Memorial. Apart from tourists in the Mall museums, the central city was populated by commuting workers during weekdays, but abandoned and sterile outside of office hours. An endless stream of proposals for new museums and memorials threatened the historic open space of the Mall and adjacent ceremonial corridors. The city's road and transit systems struggled to meet the needs of a fast-growing tourist population. There was an increasing sense that the federal establishment had failed to meet its responsibilities to the larger city. Although many exciting changes have taken place over the last several years, particularly in the downtown area, federal and city planners still confront the challenge of preserving and enlivening Washington's monumental legacy while distributing its benefits more equitably throughout the city.

Planning for the Mall and the Monumental Core

Today, planning in the nation's capital is a complex dance of local and national interests with an ever-changing ensemble of federal, congressional, city, regional, and citizen partners. Through its planning initiatives and review of federal development proposals, the National Capital Planning Commission seeks to bring coherence and a professional perspective to this process.

Established in 1924 by Congress as the central planning agency for the federal government in Washington and the surrounding region, the National Capital Planning Commission (NCPC) is mandated "to plan the appropriate and orderly development of the National Capital and the conservation of the important natural historical features."[3] As part of its mission to preserve and enhance the capital city's unique beauty and historic urban design, the commission provides overall planning guidance for federal land and buildings in the region. It also reviews the design of federal construction projects, oversees long-range planning for future development, and monitors capital investment by federal agencies. By law, no new development on federal land in Washington, D.C., including the National Mall, can proceed without commission approval. The twelve-member commission considers sometimes competing local and national interests in planning for the nation's capital. The commission includes appointees of the president of the United States and the mayor of the District of Columbia. The heads of the federal land-owning agencies and the chairmen of the House and Senate committees responsible for district affairs are members, as are the mayor of the District of Columbia and the chairman of the city council.

The National Capital Planning Commission is not, however, the city's planning agency. The District of Columbia has its own office of planning and plans for its own social, economic, and physical needs. Because almost half of the land in the city is under federal jurisdiction, city and federal agencies have developed a variety of ways to work together. For example, the NCPC and the district government jointly publish the *Comprehensive Plan for the National Capital,* which is the key planning document that establishes goals and policies for future development.[4] The plan is composed of two parts: the Federal Elements, formulated by NCPC, which guide development of the federal establishment in the district and the region, and the District Elements, which are prepared by the District of Columbia government and direct city planning.

The Commission of Fine Arts (CFA) is yet another player in Washington's complex planning establishment. Created in 1910, the CFA is made up of presidential appointees who advise on the design of federal and municipal government projects and memorials, on private development in Georgetown, in Rock Creek Park, and on land abutting the monumental core of downtown Washington. The Commission of Fine Arts reviews proposals within the District of Columbia only, whereas the National Capital Planning Commission has a review role in both the city and surrounding region. Within the city, federal projects must receive NCPC approval in order to go forward; in most instances, the CFA's review is advisory.

In addition to the city and federal governments, the third key partner in Washington planning is the public: private citizens, civic and business organizations, and the professional design and planning community. The city and federal planning organizations all have elaborate procedures to ensure that the public has an opportunity to comment on proposed development. Balancing the desire of citizens to participate in shaping their own communities with the need of government agencies to meet civic and institutional responsibilities is essential to the planning process in the nation's capital.

The Legacy Plan

In the 1990s, amid growing concerns about the threat of overbuilding on the National Mall, the NCPC undertook a major long-range planning effort for Washington's monumental core. This planning initiative was subject to congressional review and direction as part of the annual appropriations process, and it reflected the commission's commitment to preserve the Mall's historic open space. The result, *Extending the Legacy: Planning America's Capital for the 21st Century* (fig. 60), is bold and ambitious in the tradition of the L'Enfant and McMillan plans, and, like its predecessors, it expresses many of the civic and national values of contemporary American society.

In tracking earlier development trends to predict future needs, federal planners documented the relentless tide of proposals for new museums and memorials. Since the turn of the last century, an average of one new memorial has been built in the nation's capital each year. Since 1980, nearly twenty memorials have been completed in the vicinity of the monumental core, eight of them in the traditional Mall and West Potomac Park area (fig. 61), and Congress has authorized a dozen more. At

this rate, planners will have to find space for fifty new memorials by the middle of this century. Similarly, past trends indicated that sites for the equivalent of ten new Air and Space Museums would have to be found. Clearly a victim of its own success, the Mall and surrounding ceremonial area were being threatened with museum and memorial overload. The great gifts of Pierre Charles L'Enfant and of Daniel Burnham and the McMillan Commission risked being smothered in marble and steel. The Legacy Plan called on planners, policy makers, and the public to think about how these attractions could be placed in neighborhoods and commercial areas beyond the traditional core in ways that contribute to the cultural and economic life of the city while protecting the open space of the Mall.

The defining urban design concept of the Legacy Plan is expressed in an axial diagram placing the U.S. Capitol at the center with bold lines radiating north, south, east, and west. Today, most of the federal government's memorials, museums, and great public buildings are located west of the Capitol, and the Washington Monument feels like the focal point of this official precinct. By using the Capitol as the center, however, the Legacy Plan extends the traditional core north, south, and east, creating extraordinary opportunities for new development and investment in these other, often neglected, parts of Washington.

The Legacy Plan also establishes some underlying principles for future growth of the monumental core. These principles include building on the legacy of the L'Enfant and McMillan plans; protecting the Mall and its historic landscape from

future building; using new memorials, museums, and other public buildings to stimulate economic development; integrating the Potomac and Anacostia Rivers into the city's public life; and developing a comprehensive, flexible, and convenient transportation system that eliminates barriers and eases movement throughout the city.

The Legacy Plan represents a dramatic departure from years of government planning that had directed federal facilities and investment to the Mall and adjacent areas. In very specific ways, its new approach builds upon L'Enfant's idea of distributing the federal presence throughout the city. The L'Enfant framework for distributing open space and civic features was designed both to beautify the capital city and to encourage nearby development. In a report to George Washington in 1791, L'Enfant recommended that development "be begun at various points equidistant as possible from the center; not merely because settlements of this sort are likely to diffuse an equality of advantages over the whole territory allotted, and consequently to reflect benefit from an increase of the value of property, but because each of these settlements by a natural jealousy will most tend to stimulate establishments on each of the opposed extremes."[5] The new federal approach to Washington planning shares L'Enfant's premise that civic beautification can and should contribute to economic development and be used as a catalyst to encourage private investment.

Expanding the monumental core and driving development into other parts of the city will stoke the twin engines of Washington's economy—the federal gov-

FIG. 60
The Legacy Plan, 1997: Capitol and development north, south, and east of the Mall
National Capital Planning Commission

FIG. 61
West Potomac Park near the Lincoln Memorial and Memorial Bridge
National Capital Planning Commission

ernment and tourism. The Legacy Plan's proposals locate museums, memorials, and public buildings in areas of the city beyond the traditional core, attracting tourists to interesting and culturally rich neighborhoods where they might not otherwise go. And because the plan encourages a mix of federal offices, housing, open civic spaces, and retail and commercial activities, both tourists and residents will be drawn to these development areas. By using federal resources to encourage private investment, planners hope to offer real opportunities for jobs, economic expansion, and community renewal. These changes, it is hoped, will reunite the federal, monumental national capital of policymakers, bureaucrats, and tourists with the real, working city of neighborhoods and residents.

One example of this approach can be seen in the vision for transforming North and South Capitol Streets (fig. 62). City and federal planners imagine these two now-neglected thoroughfares as great urban boulevards lined with a bustling mix of shops, federal and private offices, hotels, apartments, national memorials, and open space. The improvement of these key axial roadways is commensurate with the prominence L'Enfant gave them in his plan. By mixing both commercial, private, and government uses along these streets and strengthening views of the Capitol from them, the new plan reconnects the national capital and the local city in a way L'Enfant would have appreciated and at the same time asserts contemporary notions of urban diversity.

Environmental stewardship is a critical concern in modern city planning, and federal and city planners offer bold proposals to renew the city's waterfront. The notion of Washington as a river city may seem

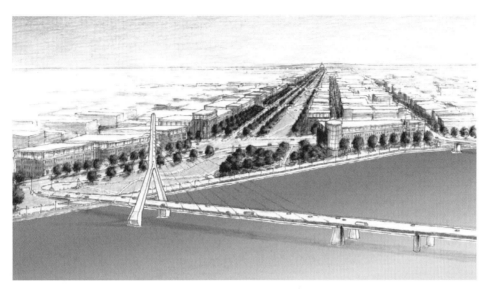

FIG. 63
The future South Capitol Street
riverfront
*National Capital Planning
Commission*

odd to many. The founders' vision of a
busy port, lined with wharves and cargo
ships and interlaced with canals, faded
before the Civil War. Nearly all of Washington's twenty-two miles of waterfront
along the Potomac and Anacostia Rivers is
publicly owned, but much of it is inaccessible to residents and visitors. Freeways
divide the city from its rivers; abandoned
lots and surface parking dot its shores.
Washington planners are calling for a
continuous river walk, parks, plazas, and
scenic overlooks along the entire length
of the waterfront. They envision some
quiet and pastoral stretches for walks and
picnics; other areas would be urban waterfront with restaurants, concerts, and festival areas for residents and visitors alike.
Where South Capitol Street meets the
river, planners propose a major civic feature such as a museum, monument, or
festival park (fig. 63). The area around
what is now Robert F. Kennedy Memorial
Stadium is seen as a new eastern gateway
for Washington, featuring a major memorial site, recreational fields and open

space, and housing and commercial development. By emphasizing views of the Capitol, the Legacy Plan strives to strengthen
visual connections between the long-
neglected east side of the Anacostia River
and the city's monumental core to the
west (fig. 64). The underlying concept in
all of these proposals is that well-planned
and strategically located federal development in neglected parts of the city can help
attract private and municipal resources
and contribute to the renewal of the
capital.

Mobility is essential in successful
twenty-first-century cities. While Washington's Metrorail system does an excellent job of getting commuters and visitors
from the suburbs *into* the city, it is less successful moving them *around* downtown
and the monumental core. Metrorail
skirts many of the city's most important
tourist points, such as the Washington
Monument and the Lincoln, Jefferson,
and World War II Memorials, and it does
not link enough of these attractions with
the shops, restaurants, and hotels of

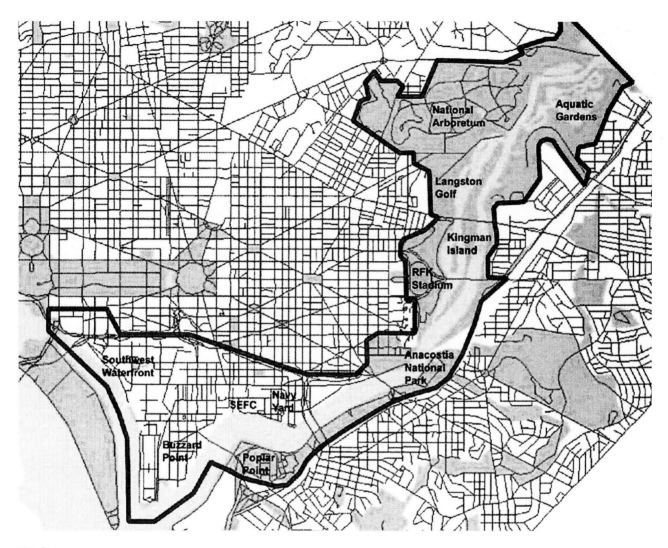

FIG. 64
Map of waterfront boundaries,
representing the partnership of
the Office of Planning, U.S.
General Services Administra-
tion, and National Park Service
*National Capital Planning
Commission*

downtown Washington. Anticipating a
doubling of tourism by the year 2050, the
Legacy Plan proposes a surface transit system to link the Metro to major attractions
within the monumental core. It also calls
for convenient transit centers where commuters can switch quickly from cars to
trains and buses. With a rejuvenation of
the city's waterfront, the plan envisions
water taxis serving dozens of locations
along the Potomac and Anacostia Rivers.
It also calls for improvements to bridges,
highways, and tunnels.

When the commission released the Legacy Plan in 1997, it characterized the work
as a fifty- to one-hundred-year vision, but
in only ten years, contrary to most expectations, many proposals have already come
to life. The commission took pains to refer
to the Legacy Plan as a flexible framework
that would be realized over time and that
would not usurp the planning preroga-
tives of future generations. Public support
for the plan has been so widespread that
today, not only does the Legacy Plan
remain a source of inspiration to planners

and designers, but it is also the single most important touchstone for shaping the future development of the nation's capital.

A New Geography of Commemoration

Almost immediately following adoption of the Legacy Plan, the NCPC established a task force to examine location policies for memorials and museums and invited the Commission of Fine Arts and the National Capital Memorials Advisory Commission to take part. These are the three federal bodies responsible for approving the location and design of memorials on federal land in the nation's capital.[6]

The Joint Memorials Task Force first considered the character of the Mall and its meaning for the nation, issuing a January 2000 policy statement:

The great cross-axis of the Mall forms one of the world's premier examples of civic art, which itself is a monument to democracy. Here the nation commemorates its history, and citizens can join in celebration, congregation, contemplation, and the exercise of their rights of free speech and assembly. . . . The Mall is a historic, monumental open space and a substantially completed work of public urban design. . . . This vast open space enhances public and individual gatherings and recreation. The Mall's sweeping vistas and reciprocal views contribute greatly to the power and beauty of the Nation's Capital.[7]

With public controversies over the placement and design of recent memorials as the backdrop, especially the World War II Memorial, the Joint Memorials Task Force moved quickly to establish a reserve in the central cross axis of the Mall and agreed to approve no new memorial or museum sites in this area: "The Reserve is a unique national space, an embodiment of our democratic ideals and achievements, and must be preserved as an indispensable, nationally significant cultural resource. This setting has matured as the nation has matured. The cross-axis, framed by monuments and museums, constitutes the historic urban design framework of the capital established by the L'Enfant and McMillan plans—open spaces, long axes, and dramatic vistas. It must be rigorously protected. No new memorial sites will be approved in this area."[8] In the same policy, the commissions designated the area immediately adjacent to the reserve for a very limited number of memorials of preeminent national significance. It was in the rest of the city, they agreed, where they would encourage future memorial locations.

Assisted by a blue-ribbon group of architects, designers, and planners, the Joint Memorials Task Force developed an urban design framework for the placement of future memorials and museums. The most important element of the framework is the "Waterfront Crescent," encompassing the public lands and open space along the Potomac and Anacostia Rivers. These sites have spectacular water views and potentially strong visual connections to the Capitol, the Washington Monument, and other major landmarks. The "Monumental Corridors" of the framework are the broad streets and avenues that are part of the original L'Enfant city and that, together with square, circles, and triangles, form an internal network of urban spaces with strong commemorative possibilities. Three "Commemorative Focus Areas" mark the intersections of the Waterfront Crescent and major streets and corridors, such as the juncture of South Capitol Street and the Anacostia River. These areas are sufficiently large and prominent to accommodate national memorials and museums. The framework is completed by "Special Sites"—some in neighborhoods, others near parks and scenic areas—that will help distribute the nation's rich historic and cultural resources beyond the traditional tourist orbit.

The Memorials and Museums Master Plan (2001) identifies one hundred new sites for cultural and commemorative facilities and sets out broad design parameters and development policies that will guide the federal commissions in their review of these future facilities. The master plan encourages community leaders and designers to think of commemorative works not as *objects,* but rather as *place makers.* Memorials and monuments in the form of civic plazas, gardens, water features, and rehabilitated historic buildings can support urban revitalization efforts, define the city's identity, and create new urban destinations. Successful alternatives to the traditional neoclassical forms that have long defined monumental civic art can satisfy both artistic and urban-design aspirations. For example, the U.S. Navy Memorial, dedicated in 1987 near the National Archives, was designed as the centerpiece of a new mixed-use development. In addition to its commemorative function, the memorial is a lively city plaza surrounded by shops, apartments, galleries, and restaurants. Tourists, office work-

ers, and residents enjoy open-air concerts, lunch in the seating areas around the fountains, and after-work drinks on the café terraces. While the memorial may not have launched the redevelopment of the surrounding city neighborhood, it clearly has reinforced it.

The Memorials and Museums Master Plan offers a pragmatic response to a daunting problem: balancing the desires of memorial sponsors to be in the heart of the city with the need to protect the beauty and openness of the McMillan Plan's vision for the Mall. It gives the public a greater voice while reserving final decisions for the government review agencies. It reaffirms L'Enfant's intention that the local and federal city coexist to the benefit of both. The master plan ensures that future generations of Americans will have an abundant supply of sites for their own needs and, because it was developed from its earliest stages with significant input from the community, it reflects public consensus on where those sites should be.

Thanks in large part to the publication of the Memorials and Museums Master Plan, Congress amended the Commemorative Works Act of 1986 in 2003, declaring the National Mall "a substantially completed work of civic art." Congress adopted the plan's concept of the "reserve," and with the exception of three projects—a memorial to Martin Luther King Jr., the Museum of African American History and Culture, and an underground museum and visitors' center for the Vietnam Veterans Memorial—no other museums or memorials can be built on the Mall.

The Memorials and Museums Master Plan has also guided the placement of new commemorative works, such as memorials to American Disabled Veterans, the U.S. Air Force, President John Adams, President Dwight D. Eisenhower, and Tomas Masaryk, the first president of Czechoslovakia. All have either been constructed or are in development on sites identified in the master plan. Veterans of Washington's "memorial wars" may one day find that new proposals will not spark the epic battles that often marred the establishment of national commemorative works in the past.

Much work remains, however, to secure a lasting peace. Many of these monuments occupy sites that required very few changes to become appealing locations. Other potential sites identified in the master plan are less attractive at the moment because they suffer from neglect, inaccessibility, or inadequate connections to the most visited areas of the city. Few museum or memorial sponsors currently want to consider these locations despite their enormous untapped assets. Some sites, like those in the Southwest Federal Center, have good connections to public transportation, but they lack visitor amenities and continuous pedestrian traffic, which makes them feel isolated and unwelcoming. Other sites, like East Potomac Park, possess inspiring vistas and magnificent open spaces, but they are difficult to access by public transportation.

To facilitate the ongoing reorientation of the city's monumental core to the north, south, and east, NCPC will release the National Capital Framework Plan in 2008. This plan will provide detailed concept designs for improving seven pivotal off-the-Mall locations for major new cultural and commemorative works. By illustrating the necessary changes to the sites and the infrastructure that serves them, the Framework Plan will extend the Legacy Plan's vision of redefining the geography of commemoration and generating opportunities for development in all quadrants of the city.

The Anacostia Waterfront Initiative

As federal and city planners seek strategies to relieve development pressure on the National Mall, they have turned their attention to one of Washington's great underused treasures: its waterfront. The city's southeast waterfront on the Anacostia River offers special opportunities for environmental reclamation, recreation, and new civic attractions. From the earliest days of Washington, the Navy Yard on the Anacostia River south of the Capitol and the nearby federal arsenal employed blue-collar workers and served as a residential center. The nation's primary navy yard until 1815, the Washington yard's shipping activities, industrial facilities, and wharves attracted craftsmen and laborers as well as midshipmen attending the Navy's training school. In recent decades, however, the southeast waterfront neighborhood immediately surrounding the Navy Yard deteriorated significantly. Dilapidated housing, abandoned commercial establishments, and vacant lots testified to the area's neglect. The Anacostia River has become increasingly polluted, and its shoreline is largely inaccessible to Washington visitors and residents.

An ambitious effort is now under way to transform the southeast waterfront. The Anacostia Waterfront Initiative is a partnership of the District of Columbia government, federal agencies, and citizen stakeholders committed to cleaning up the river and reviving its shores. The initiative focuses on the full range of development issues, from water quality and traffic to economic development and affordable housing. Tangible signs of renewal are evident. After a significant expansion of its workforce, the Washington Navy Yard now has a daily population of more than ten thousand civilian and military workers. The Navy has invested more than $200 million in a sensitive rehabilitation of its historic structures. The Navy Yard's expansion has helped generate considerable private-sector development.

Next to the Navy Yard is the Southeast Federal Center, a previously underused fifty-five-acre government facility. The federal government completed more than $30 million of environmental improvements, and congressional action permitted joint development by the federal government and the private sector. The new headquarters building of the U.S. Department of Transportation on an eleven-acre parcel within the Southeast Federal Center nears completion and will serve as an anchor to help spur mixed-use public and private development in the area. Planners have identified numerous sites along the river for future memorials and museums, and a river walk and trail will provide continuous waterfront access on both sides of the river.

South Capitol Street

As part of the effort to preserve the open space of the National Mall and direct the siting of public buildings and attractions to areas beyond the monumental core, planners are designing a new South Capitol Street that will accommodate future memorials and museums. South Capitol Street should be one of the great urban boulevards of the world. Like the Champs-Elysées in Paris or Commonwealth Avenue in Boston, South Capitol Street can be a place that defines and animates its city. This one-mile stretch from the Capitol to what will be a magnificent waterfront terminus on the Anacostia River has the potential to rival the world's great urban places and can become a vibrant city street for Washington residents and a national capital destination for all Americans.

Included in L'Enfant's plan, anchored by the Capitol, and marking the southern axis of the four-part city, South Capitol Street is envisioned as a symbolic gateway to the original L'Enfant city. In keeping with contemporary urban-design principles that value diversity, community, and economic opportunity, proposals call for a high-density, mixed-use precinct and a lively mix of shops, offices, housing, hotels, museums, restaurants, public buildings, and civic open spaces.

Construction is under way along South Capitol Street for a new major league baseball stadium to house the Washington Nationals. NCPC reviewed the initial design for the ballpark and recommended several changes to integrate the stadium into the emergent neighborhood, encourage the inclusion of street-level stores and restaurants to attract pedestrian traffic when the stadium is not in use, and to enhance pedestrian views along the adjacent monumental avenues. It is hoped that the thoughtful design principles advocated by NCPC planners will ensure

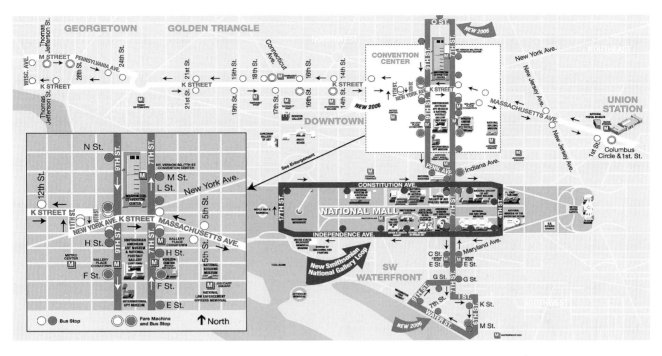

FIG. 65
The planned Circulator outlined in the NCPC's 2001 Legacy Plan
National Capital Planning Commission

that the stadium is a catalyst for the long-envisioned redevelopment of the South Capitol Street Corridor.

South Capitol Street meets the river at one of the most symbolic locations in the city, which is being designed to accommodate a major civic feature, such as a national memorial or museum, as well as gathering areas for waterfront entertainment and activities. Planners have proposed a linear park along the length of the street that connects the monumental core with the river and that provides sites for commemorative works and civic art.

Getting around Town

With the proliferation of memorials and museums on the Mall in recent years and their attraction for an increasing number of tourists, transit in and around the monumental core has become inadequate. Pri-

vate vehicles and private tour buses vie for space on congested downtown streets, and visitors on the Mall have difficulty making their way to the shops, restaurants, and hotels in the city's central business district. In this environment, public transit must seek to provide beautiful and orderly public spaces while creating environments conducive to economic vitality and growth.

The Circulator (fig. 65), a new transit system launched in July 2005, supplements the existing subway and bus services with an east-west route connecting Georgetown to Union Station and a north-south route linking the Convention Center to the Southwest Waterfront. Designed as a convenient, hop-on/hop-off shuttle, the Circulator makes downtown Washington more accessible to more people. Office workers, residents, and visitors are able to leave their cars behind and get around on the Circulator without having to find on-street parking, thus easing downtown traffic congestion.

Just in time for the 2006 National Cherry Blossom Festival, the Circulator introduced a third route. The Smithsonian–National Gallery loop runs along Constitution and Independence Avenues, serving major tourist destinations along the National Mall between Fourth and Seventeenth Streets. Service is offered daily during the peak tourist season from March to October and on weekends throughout the rest of the year. Tourists can now move more easily between the Mall and adjacent locations downtown, which enhances the economic and social vitality of the city. Ridership has grown dramatically since the introduction of the service, and in April 2006, the millionth passenger stepped aboard the distinctive buses.

Designing for Security

Perhaps the greatest threat to the McMillan Commission's vision in recent years has been the alarming proliferation of makeshift security barriers on the Mall and throughout the monumental core. Even before the 1995 bombing in Oklahoma City, Washington's streets and public spaces had become a jumble of fences, Jersey barriers, and concrete pots. After September 11, 2001, the situation has only become worse. On the Mall, Jersey barriers ringed the major memorials, and even the Washington Monument was not spared the indignity of an unsightly guard hut appended to its base (fig. 66). The preeminent icons of our national heritage were under siege and we looked like a country in fear.

Working with a partnership of the federal and District of Columbia governments, the professional planning and design community, security agencies, and civic, business, and community groups, the NCPC released the National Capital Urban Design and Security Plan in October 2002. The plan proposes solutions to integrate building-perimeter security seamlessly into the historic urban fabric of the monumental core. While enhancing security installations, the plan creates a more welcoming and beautiful public realm and demonstrates that good security and good urban design can coexist. The plan proposes concepts for special streets and areas within the core and offers a variety of security solutions such as hardened street furniture, low retaining walls, bollards, decorative fences, and landscaped plantings concealing security elements. The plan approaches security in a districtwide context, rather than building by building, and its goal is better city streets rather than conspicuously fortified buildings.

Pennsylvania Avenue in front of the White House is one of the most symbolic and visible places in the nation. Its closure to traffic in 1995 significantly affected downtown Washington and has been the topic of intense debate among Washington residents. Because overriding security concerns require the continued closure of this portion of the avenue, the NCPC successfully initiated its redesign as a civic space. The commission selected the New York–based Michael Van Valkenburgh Associates to develop a design that preserves the existing street pattern while creating an environment that is welcoming and dignified. The vision came to life

FIG. 66
Washington Monument with
security barriers, 2006
*National Capital Planning
Commission*

in 2004 with a beautiful pedestrian promenade that secures the president's house
while respecting the historical character
of Pennsylvania Avenue and the surrounding landmarks. The plaza accommodates
presidential inauguration parades, and it
can be reopened in the future if the security environment changes.

On the Mall, the Washington Monument and the Jefferson and Lincoln
Memorials are three of the most widely
recognized icons in America, and they
therefore have special security needs.
All three are surrounded by sweeping
expanses of lawn that provide opportunities for adding low stone walls, planters,

and landscape elements as needed, while
respecting their historic setting. Working
with the National Park Service, landscape
architect Laurie Olin redesigned the
grounds of the Washington Monument.
The design, completed in July 2005, has
met with public approval and serves as a
testament that security elements can be
attractive and effective. Low, overlapping
granite walls placed along gently curved
pathways serve as vehicle barriers and
provide visitor seating. At the base of the
monument, white granite benches and a
new lighting system create a more appealing space, and hundreds of new shade and
flowering trees in the lawns around the

monument complement the landscape.

Today, the nation's capital is challenged to find acceptable ways to protect itself from unprecedented terrorist threats. We are in uncharted waters, seeking innovative technology and design solutions to safeguard citizens, public buildings, monuments, and civic spaces. But our security must not be gained at the expense of the values that we seek to protect—accessibility, openness, and civic beauty—the very values asserted by the L'Enfant and McMillan plans.

Like the L'Enfant and McMillan plans, the Legacy Plan reflects the national values of its time. Among the values that define American society and reflect its collective aspirations at the beginning of the twenty-first century, one can mention community, diversity, opportunity, environmental stewardship, and mobility. These are the values that underlie the Legacy Plan's vision. Now, at the beginning of Washington's third century, there is a wide range of opinions among Americans about what they want from urban planning. The Legacy Plan embraces that diversity while building on the fundamental principles that unite us as a nation. Americans expect the design of their cities to benefit all citizens, promote social and economic equity, restore the urban environment, and anticipate emerging technologies. They expect the new plan for their nation's capital, like the McMillan Plan, to reflect the country's history, showcase its national icons, and still serve as a worthy model of America's urban future.

CHARLES BULFINCH (1763–1844). Architect. In Boston, designed townhouses of Tontine Crescent (1793–95), Park Row (1803–5), and Colonnade (1810–12). Designed the Massachusetts State House (1795–97) and the enlargement of Faneuil Hall (1806) also in Boston. Appointed Architect of the Capitol by President James Monroe (1817). Continued work on the Capitol begun by Benjamin Henry Latrobe and brought it to completion, designing the old Library of Congress dome (destroyed 1851) in the north wing, the Capitol dome (later replaced), and the west front. Proposed a landscape design for the Capitol grounds (1822), which was not implemented.

DANIEL HUDSON BURNHAM (1846–1912). Architect and planner. First became known for several early skyscrapers in Chicago. His firm of Burnham & Root was appointed consulting architect to the World's Columbian Exposition in Chicago (1893); after John Root's death, Burnham continued as the exposition's Director of Construction, collaborating with Richard Morris Hunt and the firm of McKim, Mead & White, among others; is credited with establishing that the buildings would all be white in coloring (the "White City") and their exteriors artificially lit at night. The exposition had an enormous impact on urban design and the city beautiful movement over the next half-century. Burnham's firm produced six additional urban plans along with office buildings and department stores after 1893 as well as the Flatiron Building (1903) in New York and Union Station (1907) in Washington. Served as chairman of the McMillan Commission (1901–2). In 1910, he became the first chairman of the Commission of Fine Arts, overseeing public building in Washington.

ANDREW JACKSON DOWNING (1815–1852). Horticulturalist and writer; sometimes considered America's first landscape designer. Wrote *Treatise on the Theory and Practice of Landscape Gardening, Adapted to North America* (1841). Advocated large public parks in city centers. Asked by President Millard Fillmore in 1850 to create a landscape design for the Mall; proposed a series of naturalistic parks. After William Cullen Bryant called for the creation of a large public park in New York, joined in the effort; as New York City began to set aside land for Central Park, undertook preliminary plans for the park with his partner, Calvert Vaux; died unexpectedly while the two were at work.

BENJAMIN HENRY LATROBE (1764–1820). Architect and engineer; born in England; to America 1796. Designed Hammerwood Lodge (1792) and Ashdown House (1793–95) in England. Built the Bank of Pennsylvania (1798–1801, destroyed 1867) in Philadelphia

Biographical Notes

as well as the city's waterworks. Became Surveyor of Public Buildings in Washington, D.C. (1803–17), and continued work on the U.S. Capitol, in progress since 1793; redesigned the south wing, for the House of Representatives and created a design for the main entrance and central dome. After British troops burned the building during the War of 1812, rebuilt the north and south wings (1815–17). Resigned from direction of the Capitol in 1817. Designed the Basilica of the Assumption of the Blessed Virgin (1804–20) in Baltimore.

PIERRE CHARLES L'ENFANT (1754–1825). Urban planner and architect; born in France; to America 1777. Volunteered for service in the American War of Independence; served at Valley Forge. Practiced architecture in New York from 1784, including addition to Saint Paul's Chapel (1787) and a redesign of Federal Hall for George Washington's inauguration (1788–89). Invited by President Washington to create a plan for the new U.S. capital city on the Potomac River (1791); although he was dismissed in 1792, his plan became the basis for the development of Washington, D.C. Designed the Robert Morris residence (1794–96) in Philadelphia. After the War of 1812, designed the reconstruction of Fort Washington, south of the capital.

CHARLES FOLLEN MCKIM (1847–1909). Architect. After studying at Harvard (1866–67) and the École des Beaux-Arts in Paris (1867–70), worked in the office of H. H. Richardson for two years. Became associated with William Mead in 1877 and Stanford White in 1879; partner in the firm of McKim, Mead & White from 1879. Proponent of the "American Renaissance" aesthetic. Designed the Casino (1879–81) in Newport; the Henry G. Villard houses (1882–85) in New York; the Boston Public Library (1887–95); the Agriculture Building for the World's Columbian Exposition (1893) in Chicago; Columbia University Library (1893) in New York; Pennsylvania Station (1902–11; destroyed 1963–65) in New York; and the renovation of the White House (1902–3), among many other projects. Member of the McMillan Commission (1901–2); president of the American Institute of Architects (1902–3).

JAMES MCMILLAN (1838–1902). Businessman and railroad executive; born in Canada; to Detroit 1855. Elected to the U.S. Senate (Republican, Michigan) in 1888; reelected 1894, 1900. Chairman of the Senate Committee on the District of Columbia, Fifty-fourth through Fifty-seventh Congresses. In 1901, established the Senate Park Commission, commonly called the McMillan Commission, to make a comprehensive plan for the further development of Washington. The McMillan Commission's report was published in 1902 and, implemented in stages over several decades, largely determined the present-day character of the Mall.

ROBERT MILLS (1781–1855). Architect and engineer. Recommended by Thomas Jefferson to Benjamin Henry Latrobe; remained Latrobe's assistant until 1808. Designed Monumental Church (1812–17) in Richmond, Virginia. Designed a Washington Monument (1813–42) in Baltimore, a Doric column surmounted by a statue. Moved to Washington in 1830 and contributed to renovations and restorations at the White House and the Capitol. Appointed Architect of Federal Buildings. Designed the south wing of U.S. Patent Office and directed the building's construction (1836–40) and expansion (1849–52); designed the General Post Office (1839–42). In 1833 began design of the Washington Monument (constructed

1848–84); the monument's intended temple base was not built. In conjunction with a landscape plan for the nascent Smithsonian Institution, in 1841, proposed a new landscape design for the Mall, which was not carried out. Proposed a design for the Smithsonian Institution's building; did not obtain the commission but supervised the construction of James Renwick's design for the Smithsonian "Castle" (1847–55).

FREDERICK LAW OLMSTED (1822–1903). Landscape architect and urban planner. With various partners including Calvert Vaux and subsequently members of his firm, designed Central Park (1858–77) in New York; Prospect Park (1865–71) in Brooklyn; and the Buffalo Park System (1870). Designed the grounds and terraces of the Capitol (1874) in Washington; the "Emerald Necklace" of public spaces in Boston (1880s); the campus of Stanford University (1886); and the landscape design for the Biltmore estate (1889–95) in Asheville, North Carolina. Oversaw landscape and transportation planning of the World's Columbian Exposition (1893) in Chicago.

FREDERICK LAW OLMSTED JR. (1870–1957). Landscape architect and planner. Assisted his father in the landscape design of the Biltmore estate (1889–95) in Asheville, North Carolina, and in many other projects. A partner in the firm of Olmsted Brothers from 1898 to 1950. Planned Forest Hills Gardens (1909–31) and Fort Tryon Park (1927–35) in New York. As a member of the McMillan Commission (1901–2) was influential in determining the character of the National Mall as an open greensward. Served on the Commission of Fine Arts (1910–18) and the National Capital and Park Planning Commission (1926–32).

AUGUSTUS SAINT-GAUDENS (1848–1907). Sculptor. With Stanford White, designed the Admiral Farragut Monument (1881) for Madison Square Park in New York. Major works include the Shaw Memorial (1884–97) for the Boston Common; the Adams Memorial (1886–91) for Rock Creek Cemetery in Washington, D.C.; *Diana* (1886–91), originally for the top of Madison Square Tower in New York; and the Sherman Monument (1892–1903) for Grand Army Plaza in Manhattan. Selected sculptures for the World's Columbian Exposition (1893) in Chicago. Worked with the McMillan Commission (1901–2). Designed several U.S. coins (1905–7).

1790

July 16: The Federal District is established by the Residence Act of 1790 as the future site of the national capital.

1791

Pierre Charles L'Enfant is commissioned by George Washington to draw up a plan for the capital city. In L'Enfant's design the main axis of the Mall—conceived as a four-hundred-foot-wide "Grand Avenue"—runs from the Capitol to the designated site of the Washington Monument. L'Enfant completes his design but is dismissed in 1792 and replaced by Andrew Ellicott, his assistant.

1792

October 13: The cornerstone of the White House (then called the President's House or Executive Mansion) is set.

1793

Andrew Ellicott submits a revised plan of the city, based on L'Enfant's.

September 18: The cornerstone of the U.S. Capitol is set and construction begins that will continue through the first decade of the new century.

1800

December: The national government, previously located in New York and then Philadelphia, moves to Washington.

John and Abigail Adams move into the still-unfinished White House.

1802

Mathew Carey's map of Washington is the first to name the stretch of land west of the Capitol as "The Mall."

1804

President Thomas Jefferson sets a marker at a point directly south of the White House and directly west of the Capitol that is intended as the nation's official meridian. It is near the site of the Washington Monument.

1814

August 4: The White House and the Capitol are burned by British troops during the War of 1812.

1815

Tiber Creek is converted into the Washington City Canal.

Benjamin Henry Latrobe creates a design for the Capitol grounds and, the next year, for a national university on the Mall. Neither project is carried out.

1820

Congress appropriates funds for the construction of a botanic garden west of the Capitol grounds along Pennsylvania Avenue between First and Third Streets.

Administered by the Columbian Institute, it functions until 1837.

1822
Charles Bulfinch proposes a landscape design for the eastern end of the Mall, but it is not implemented.

1829
Initial reconstruction of the Capitol is substantially completed.

1838
The will of James Smithson, an Englishman who died in 1829, is settled in England. He bequeaths funds to the United States for the establishment of an institution "for the increase and diffusion of knowledge among men." It is known as the Smithsonian Institution.

1840
Joel R. Poinsett, overseeing the effort to plan the Smithsonian, commissions Robert Mills to design a building for the Institution and landscape its grounds, to be located on the south side of the Mall. Mills uses the opportunity to lay out a revised plan for the entire Mall, incorporating a number of separate landscape vignettes. His ambitious landscape design is not carried out.

1847
May 1: The cornerstone of Smithsonian Institution Building (the "Castle") is set.

1848
July 4: The cornerstone of the Washington Monument is set.

1850
President Millard Fillmore asks the landscape designer and horticulturist Andrew Jackson Downing to draw up a landscape plan for the Mall's future development, including the Smithsonian grounds.

Downing's plan, begun in 1851, calls for a series of naturalistic parks, departing from L'Enfant's idea of a "Grand Avenue." Downing's death in 1852 largely ends the implementation of his landscape plans. Nonetheless, by the end of the century, seven gardens are completed on the Mall, each the responsibility of a different government bureau or institution.

Work begins on the expansion of the Capitol.

Construction of the Washington Monument is halted owing to lack of funds.

1855
The Smithsonian Institution Building (the "Castle") is completed.

A national armory is built on the south side of the Mall; it is later demolished.

1856
A memorial by the Pomological Society is dedicated to Andrew Jackson Downing, the first memorial built on the Mall. This memorial urn remains today on the Smithsonian grounds.

The United States Botanic Garden is constructed on the former site of the Columbian Institute garden.

1861–65
During the Civil War, Union troops train on the Mall and cattle graze on the grounds of the uncompleted Washington Monument.

1863
Construction of the new dome of the Capitol is completed.

1867
The extensions of the Capitol are completed.

1871
Washington Canal (the site of present-day Constitution Avenue) is filled in.

1874
The Corcoran Gallery of Art opens in its original building (now the Renwick Gallery).

1878
Construction of the Washington Monument resumes.

1881
October 18: The National Museum building opens to the public (renamed the Arts and Industries Building in 1910).

A major flood inundates the Mall and the White House grounds.

1882
Dredging of the Potomac River begins, eventually reclaiming hundreds of acres of new land for East and West Potomac Parks, creating the sites of the Lincoln Memorial and the Tidal Basin, and increasing the western expanse of the Mall.

1885
February 21: The capstone is installed on the completed Washington Monument.

1888
October 9: The Washington Monument opens to the public. Visitors are able to ride a steam-powered elevator to the observation post at the top.

1894
March 25–May 1: Jacob Coxey leads his "army" of the unemployed in a march from Ohio to Washington, culminating in a protest rally on Pennsylvania Avenue.

1897
More than seven hundred acres of new parkland, resulting from the land-reclamation project begun in 1882, are officially designated Potomac Park.

The Library of Congress building opens on Capitol Hill (renamed the Jefferson Building in 1980).

The Corcoran Gallery of Art moves into its new building.

1900
The centennial of the relocation of the capital from Philadelphia to Washington is observed.

1901
Senator James McMillan, chairman of the Senate Committee on the District of Columbia, appoints a commission to extend the park system of the district. Daniel H. Burnham is head of the Senate Park Commission (also known as the McMillan Commission); other members include the architect Charles Follen McKim, the landscape designer Frederick Law Olmsted Jr., and the sculptor Augustus Saint-Gaudens.

1902
Designs for the McMillan Plan are exhibited at the Corcoran Gallery of Art on January 15, and the commission's official report is published. The plan extends the Mall westward, greatly increasing its length, and incorporates West Potomac Park. The commission's report also proposes a Reflecting Pool west of the Washington Monument, a memorial to Abraham Lincoln, another new memorial to be located in West Potomac Park, a memorial to the nation's founders, a bridge from the Lincoln Memorial to Arlington National Cemetery, the creation of classical-style government buildings in the area now known as the Federal Triangle, and in general the restoration of the openness and geometric clarity of L'Enfant's original design. It also

removes the naturalistic gardens from the Mall. Acknowledging the Washington Monument as the centerpiece, the plan conceives the monument grounds, the Mall, and West Potomac Park as a unified landscape symbolizing a "Pageant to American History."

1905
Controversy over the proposed Department of Agriculture building is resolved in favor of the McMillan Plan.

1907
October 27: The new Union Station indicated in the McMillan Plan opens, replacing the Baltimore and Ohio Railroad depot located on the Mall.

1908
The east and west laboratory wings, components of the Department of Agriculture's proposed Administration Building, are built on the south side of the Mall.

1910
May 17: The Commission of Fine Arts, an outgrowth of the McMillan Commission, is created to help oversee the implementation of the McMillan Plan.

Congress limits the height of future buildings in the city so that none will exceed the U.S. Capitol.

1911
The National Museum of Natural History is completed.

1912
The city of Tokyo donates three thousand Japanese cherry trees to the United States as a token of friendship. Most of the trees will be planted along what will become the Cherry Walk at the Tidal Basin.

1914
Construction of the Tidal Basin is completed by the Army Corps of Engineers.

1915
February 12 (Lincoln's birthday): The cornerstone is set for the Lincoln Memorial, marking the westernmost point of the Mall as envisioned by the McMillan Plan.

1917
During World War I, "temporary" structures are erected in West Potomac Park and on the Mall for military and civilian staff. The last of the structures will not be demolished until 1971.

1922
April 27: The Ulysses S. Grant Memorial is dedicated, just west of the Capitol.

May 30: The completed Lincoln Memorial is dedicated.

December: The Lincoln Memorial Reflecting Pool, between the memorial and the Washington Monument, is completed.

1923
The Freer Gallery of Art opens.

1924
Congress creates the National Capital Park Commission, with responsibility to acquire lands to complete a park, a parkway, and a playground system for the national capital.

1926
Congress reestablishes the Park Commission as the National Capital Park and Planning Commission to oversee the long-term development of the McMillan Plan and the city (renamed the National Capital Planning Commission in 1952).

1928
January: Congress allocates funds and authorizes the acquisition of land for several new government buildings within the Federal Triangle, the wedge-shaped area bounded by the Mall, Pennsylvania Avenue, and Fifteenth Street. Most of the buildings

are completed during the 1930s: the Internal Revenue Service (1930); the Department of Commerce Herbert C. Hoover Building (1932); the Treasury Department Auditorium, now the Andrew W. Mellon Auditorium (1934); the Department of Justice (1935); the New Post Office, now the Ariel Rios Federal Building (1935); and the Federal Trade Commission (1938).

1930
The central structure of the Department of Agriculture's Administration Building is completed (renamed the Whitten Building in 1995).

1932
June 17: Ten thousand members of the so-called Bonus Army gather on the grounds of the Capitol as the Bonus bill, granting relief bonuses to veterans during the Great Depression, is considered by Congress. The bill is not passed. Many of the marchers remain in the city in makeshift housing and are eventually routed by the military (on July 28).

Arlington Memorial Bridge is completed.

1933
The National Park Service assumes administration of the Mall.

The United States Botanic Garden is relocated to its present facility on Independence Avenue, which includes the Conservatory and display gardens in Frédéric-Auguste Bartholdi Park.

1935
The National Archives building is substantially completed.

The Supreme Court building is completed.

1936
The Department of Agriculture's South Building is completed, the largest office

building in the world until the opening of the Pentagon.

The Department of the Interior building is completed.

1938
The Smithsonian Institution is granted the right to build on additional sites on the Mall.

1939
President Franklin D. Roosevelt sets the cornerstone of the Jefferson Memorial. This southernmost point of the McMillan Plan area anchors the Mall's north-south axis.

Easter Sunday: Marian Anderson, the distinguished African American opera singer, performs at the Lincoln Memorial before a crowd of 75,000; the event had been denied the use of Constitution Hall by the Daughters of the American Revolution in order to avoid seating an integrated audience.

1941
A. Philip Randolph announces a plan for a march on Washington by fifty thousand African American workers to protest job discrimination. After President Roosevelt signs an executive order banning discrimination in defense industries, plans for the march are cancelled.

The National Gallery of Art opens.

1943
April 13: The Jefferson Memorial is dedicated on the two hundredth anniversary of Thomas Jefferson's birth. President Roosevelt delivers the dedicatory speech.

The Pentagon is completed on the opposite bank of the Potomac River.

Kutz Memorial Bridge, crossing the north side of the Tidal Basin, is completed.

1952
The National Capital Park and Planning Commission is renamed the National Capital Planning Commission and designated as the central planning agency for the federal government in the District of Columbia and the surrounding region.

1957
May 17: Dr. Martin Luther King Jr. speaks at the Prayer Pilgrimage for Freedom at the Lincoln Memorial.

1959
Congress authorizes a memorial to Franklin Delano Roosevelt.

1963
August 28: At the culmination of the March on Washington for Jobs and Freedom, Dr. Martin Luther King Jr. delivers his "I Have a Dream" speech on the steps of the Lincoln Memorial in front of a quarter of a million civil rights supporters.

1964
The National Museum of History and Technology opens. Renamed the National Museum of American History in 1980.

1965
The Renwick Gallery opens. The building had been the home of the Corcoran Gallery of Art from 1874 to 1897.

1965–66
The architectural firm of Skidmore, Owings & Merrill develops a master plan for the Mall and West Potomac Park. The plan calls for the creation of Constitution Gardens in West Potomac Park, a new Reflecting Pool near the Capitol, and the conversion of the Mall's inner roadways (George Washington Drive and John Adams Drive) into walkways.

1967
The first annual Smithsonian Folklife Festival is held on the grounds of the Mall. The festival has continued each year to the present.

1968
May 14: The Poor People's Campaign, organized by the Southern Christian Leadership Conference, sets up its "Resurrection City," a series of shantytowns housing two to three thousand people in fifteen acres of West Potomac Park from the Reflecting Pool to the base of the Lincoln Memorial. Closed down by police on June 24.

The National Collection of Fine Arts (renamed the National Museum of American Art in 1980 and now the Smithsonian American Art Museum) and the National Portrait Gallery open in the Old Patent Office (built 1836–67).

1970
April 22: The first Earth Day is celebrated on the grounds of the Washington Monument and at the adjacent Sylvan Theater.

1971
The last of the wartime "temporary" structures is removed.

The U.S. Capitol Reflecting Pool, at the east end of the Mall, is completed.

April: Vietnam Veterans against the War stages five days of antiwar protests, leading to a demonstration of half a million (on April 24).

1974
The landscape design for Constitution Gardens is approved by the Commission of Fine Arts.

The Hirshhorn Museum and Sculpture Garden is completed.

1976
May 27: Constitution Gardens dedicated.

July 4: The Bicentennial of the nation's independence is celebrated with fireworks on the Mall.

The National Air and Space Museum opens.

The inner drives along the Mall from Fourteenth to First Streets are converted into pedestrian paths.

The Skidmore, Owings & Merrill master plan of 1965–66 is revised.

1978
The East Building of the National Gallery of Art opens.

1982
November 11 (Veterans Day): The Vietnam Veterans Memorial is dedicated.

1984
July 2: The memorial to the signers of the Declaration of Independence is dedicated in Constitution Gardens.

November 11: The *Three Soldiers* statuary group is dedicated near the Vietnam Veterans Memorial.

1985
The National Building Museum opens in the former Pension Bureau building (completed in 1887).

1986
Congress passes the Commemorative Works Act, instituting policies and procedures for memorial building on the Mall and surrounding areas.

1987
The National Museum of Women in the Arts (founded in 1981) opens its permanent headquarters at a site near the White House.

The Quadrangle complex opens, including the Arthur M. Sackler Gallery, the National Museum of African Art, the S. Dillon Ripley Center, and the Enid A. Haupt Garden.

The AIDS Quilt is displayed on the Mall. It will be displayed again in 1988, 1989, 1992, and 1996.

1993
November 11: The Vietnam Women's Memorial is dedicated near the Vietnam Veterans Memorial.

The United States Holocaust Memorial Museum opens.

1995
July 27: The Korean War Veterans Memorial is dedicated in West Potomac Park on the forty-second anniversary of the signing of the armistice in Korea.

October 16: The Million Man March takes place.

The area of Pennsylvania Avenue near the White House is permanently closed to traffic.

1997
May 2: The Franklin Delano Roosevelt Memorial is dedicated in West Potomac Park.

The National Capital Planning Commission publishes the Legacy Plan to guide the urban development of Washington and identify sites for future memorials outside the Mall.

The Promise Keepers rally is held.

1998
The Ronald Reagan Building and International Trade Center opens in the Federal Triangle. After the Pentagon, it is the largest federal building ever constructed.

2001
September 12: A candlelight vigil is held after sunset on the day following the terrorist attacks on New York and Washington.

The National Capital Planning Commission, the Commission of Fine Arts, and the National Capital Memorial Commission adopt the Memorials and Museums Master Plan, which declares a no-build policy on the central cross axis of the Mall and proposes one hundred potential sites throughout the city for future memorials and museums.

2002
October: The National Capital Urban Design and Security Plan is put forward, to integrate building-perimeter security features into the historic urban fabric of the core area.

2003
September 1–4: The National Football League Kickoff Festival occupies much of the Mall during four days of commercially sponsored events.

Passage of the Commemorative Works Clarification and Revision Act imposes a moratorium on future memorials, museums, and visitor centers on a reserve at the center of the Mall.

2004
The World War II Memorial is completed.

The National Museum of the American Indian opens.

2005
The National Capital Memorial Advisory Commission approves a four-acre site on the south side of Independence Avenue for a memorial to Dwight D. Eisenhower. The location is across the street from the National Air and Space Museum and in front of the Department of Education building.

2006
The Smithsonian American Art Museum and the National Portrait Gallery reopen after several years of renovations.

The board of the Smithsonian Institution selects a five-acre site on the Mall, northeast of the Washington Monument, for the National Museum of African American History and Culture.

The National Park Service, working alongside the National Capital Planning Commission, launches a nationwide initiative to rethink the future development and design of the Mall.

November 13: Ground is broken for the Martin Luther King Jr. National Memorial.

Information drawn in part from chronologies compiled by the Architect of the Capitol, the National Capital Planning Commission, the National Coalition to Save Our Mall, the National Park Service, the Smithsonian Institution, and the University of Virginia.

Citations given in full in the Selected Bibliography appear in abbreviated form in these notes.

INTRODUCTION

1. See Benjamin Forgey, "A Giant Step That Could Trample Mall," *Washington Post*, July 12, 2003; Lynette Clenetson, "Smithsonian Picks Notable Spot for Its Museum of Black History," *New York Times*, January 31, 2006.

2. An item in the *Washington Post* (September 24, 2003) reported: "Rep. Xavier Becerra (D-Calif.) said yesterday that he planned to introduce a bill that would create a federal commission to explore the feasibility of a 'National Museum of the American Latino,' which would be part of the Smithsonian Institution. . . . The bill is similar to one that formed the federal committee that drafted a proposal this year for the National Museum of African American History. . . . Becerra said [the museum] . . . should be on or near the Mall."

3. Linda Hales, "NFL's Civic Fumble on Mall Tarnishes Museum's Honor," *Washington Post*, September 13, 2003.

4. "Banning Ads on the Mall," *New York Times*, September 24, 2003.

5. Brody Mullins, "Companies Say Amendments May Curb Mall Events," *Roll Call*, September 24, 2003.

6. Roger K. Lewis, "Park Service Has a Bad Case of Tunnel Vision on Washington Monument Security," *Washington Post*, July 12, 2003.

7. Richard Longstreth, "Introduction: Change and Continuity on the Mall, 1791–1991," in Longstreth, *The Mall in Washington*, p. 16.

THE IDEA OF THE AMERICAN MALL

1. The most reliable and up-to-date history is Scott and Lee, *Buildings of the District of Columbia*, pp. 62–112.

2. Barber, *Marching on Washington*.

3. Reps, *Monumental Washington*, p. 10.

4. Jefferson first mentioned "publick walks" in November 1790, in a memorandum of the items necessary for the new capital city. See *Jefferson and the National Capitol* (Washington, D.C.: Government Printing Office, 1946), p. 30.

5. Quoted in Pamela Scott, "'The Vast Empire': The Iconography of the Mall," in Longstreth, *The Mall in Washington*, p. 55.

6. L'Enfant to George Washington, August 19, 1791, reproduced in Caemmerer, *Pierre Charles L'Enfant*, p. 158.

7. Reps, *Monumental Washington*, p. 16.

8. Caemmerer, *Pierre Charles L'Enfant*, p. 156.

9. Ibid., p. 125.

10. "Plan of the City," published in the *Gazette of the United States*, January 4, 1792,

reproduced in Caemmerer, *Pierre Charles L'Enfant*, p. 165.

11. Scott, "The Vast Empire," p. 46.

12. Reps, *Monumental Washington*, pp. 35–37.

13. Therese O'Malley, "'*A Public Museum of Trees*': Mid-Nineteenth Century Plans for the Mall," in Longstreth, *The Mall in Washington*, pp. 60–76.

14. Pamela J. Scott, "Design for the Mall, Washington, D.C." in J. F. O'Gorman, ed., *Drawing toward Building: Philadelphia Architectural Graphics* (Philadelphia: University of Pennsylvania Press, 1986), pp. 87–88. Also see Rhodri Windsor Liscombe, *Altogether American: Robert Mills, Architect and Engineer, 1781–1855* (New York and Oxford: Oxford University Press, 1994), pp. 224–25.

15. Francis R. Kowsky, *Country, Park, and City: The Architecture and Life of Calvert Vaux* (New York and Oxford: Oxford University Press, 1998), pp. 47–48.

16. A. J. Downing, "Explanatory Notes to Accompany the Plan for Improving the Public Grounds at Washington," March 3, 1851, cited in Reps, *Monumental Washington*, p. 53.

17. Ibid., p. 51.

18. Frederick Law Olmsted, "To the Chairman of the Committee on Plans of the Park Commission of Philadelphia," in *The Papers of Frederick Law Olmsted*, series ed. Charles E. Beveridge, ed. in chief Charles Capen McLaughlin, vol. 6: *The Years of Olmsted, Vaux & Company*, ed. David Schuyler and Jane Turner Censer (Baltimore: Johns Hopkins University Press, 1992), p. 233.

19. Among other protests, see Michael J. Lewis, "Pedantry Spoils the World War II Memorial," *Weekly Standard* 2, no. 22 (February 17, 1997): 34–35, and "Mumbling Monuments," *Commentary* 111, no. 2 (February 2001): 50–54.

AMERICAN RENAISSANCE

1. On Burnham, see Moore, *Daniel H. Burnham*; Hines, *Burnham of Chicago;* and Cynthia Field "The City Planning of Daniel Hudson Burnham" (Ph.D. diss., Columbia University, 1974).

2. There is no adequate biography of Frederick Law Olmsted Jr. See Susan L. Klaus, *A Modern Arcadia: Frederick Law Olmsted Jr. and the Plan for Forest Hills Gardens* (Amherst: University of Massachusetts Press, 2002). See also Susan L. Klaus, "'Intelligent and Comprehensive Planning of a Common Sense Kind': Frederick Law Olmsted Jr.'s, Contributions to Comprehensive Planning, 1900–1916" (M.A. thesis, George Washington University, 1988).

3. U.S. Congress, *Improvement of the Park System*, pp. 51–52. This is the official report of the Senate Park Commission. Considerations can be found in Reps, *Monumental Washington;* Thomas Walton, "The 1901 McMillan Commission: Beaux-Arts Plan for the Nation's Capital" (Ph.D. diss., Catholic University, 1980); Longstreth, *The Mall in Washington.* See also Richard Guy Wilson, "Renaissance in the Prairie," *Inland Architect* 24 (April 1980): 5–8.

4. U.S. Congress, *Improvement of the Park System*, p. 51.

5. Ibid., p. 42.

6. Ibid., p. 45.

7. Moore, *Charles Follen McKim*, p. 184.

8. The standard source for McKim is Moore, *Charles Follen McKim*.

9. Richard Guy Wilson, *McKim, Mead & White, Architects* (New York: Rizzoli, 1983); Leland Roth, *McKim, Mead & White, Architects* (New York: Harper & Row, 1983).

10. See the exhibition catalogue *The American Renaissance, 1876–1917* (Brooklyn: Brooklyn Museum, 1979), with essays by Richard Guy Wilson, Dianne H. Pilgrim, and Richard N. Murray; see also Richard Guy

Wilson, "Architecture and Reinterpretation of the Past in the American Renaissance," *Winterthur Portfolio* 18 (spring 1983): 69–91.

11. H. Van Buren Magonigle, "A Half-Century of Architecture, 3," *Pencil Points* 15 (March 1934): 116–17; and Moore, *Charles Follen McKim*, p. 57.

12. A. J. Bloor, quoted in Harry W. Desmond, *Stately Homes in America* (New York: D. Appleton, 1903), p. 251.

13. Henry Adams, quoted in Harold D. Cater, *Henry Adams and His Friends* (Boston: Little, Brown, 1947), p. 404.

14. Saint-Gaudens, quoted in Moore, *Daniel H. Burnham*, vol. 1, p. 47.

15. Joy Wheeler Dow, *American Renaissance: A Review of Domestic Architecture* (New York: W. T. Comstock, 1904), p. 167.

16. The first apparent usage of the term American Renaissance was in *The Californian* 1 (June 1880), pp. 1–2. The term continued to be used in Talbot Faulkner Hamlin, *The American Spirit in Architecture*, vol. 13 of *The Pagent of America*, ed. Ralph Henry Gabriel (New Haven: Yale University Press, 1926).

17. See Lawrence W. Levine, *Highbrow/Lowbrow: The Emergence of Cultural Hierarchy in America* (Cambridge, Mass.: Harvard University Press, 1990).

18. Francis Millet, "The American Academy in Rome," *Review of Reviews* 31 (June 1905): 713–14.

19. Kenyon Cox, *The Classic Point of View* (New York: Scribner's, 1911), pp. 3–5.

20. John Ruskin, *The Seven Lamps of Architecture* (1849; reprint, London: Everyman's Library, 1907), p. 203.

21. Dixon Wecter, *The Saga of American Society* (New York: Scribner's, 1937), chap. 10; Edith Wharton, *The House of Mirth* (New York: Scribner's, 1905).

22. *Oxford English Dictionary*, s.v. "Renaissance"; see also Howard Mumford Jones, "The Renaissance and American Origins,"

in *Ideas in America* (Cambridge, Mass.: Harvard University Press, 1945), pp. 140–51.

23. *New York Herald*, October 18, 1880.

24. *The Art Interchange* 2 (May 14, 1879): 81.

25. Bernard Berenson, *The Venetian Painters* (1894), reprinted in *The Italian Painters of the Renaissance* (Cleveland: Meridian, 1957), p. iii.

26. Charles F. McKim, "Address of the President," 36th Annual Convention of the American Institute of Architects (1902), Washington, D.C., ts., McKim Collection, New York Public Library.

27. McKim's Royal Institute of British Architects speech is printed in Moore, *Charles Follen McKim*, pp. 236–40.

28. *Old Newport Houses* ([Newport]: privately printed, [1874]). Copies are in the Society for the Preservation of New England Antiquities and the Newport Historical Society.

29. *New York Sketch Book of Architecture* 1 (January 1874), introductory page. The Bishop Berkley house, Middletown, R.I., was published as "Old House in Newport" in the December 1874 issue.

30. *New York Sketch Book of Architecture* 3 (July 1876).

31. Moore, *Charles Follen McKim*, p. 237.

32. McKim to Hunt, March 3, 1893, cited in ibid., pp. 122–23.

33. McKim to Burnham and to Charles B. Atwood, n.d., cited in ibid., p. 122.

34. Samuel A. B. Abbott to McKim, November 28, 1889, McKim Collection, Library of Congress.

35. McKim, ca. 1899, quoted in Moore, *Charles Follen McKim*, pp. 167–68.

36. Quoted in ibid., p. 260; originally appeared in Herbert F. Sherwood, ed., *H. Siddons Mowbray, Mural Painter (1858–1928)* (n.p.: privately printed by Florence Millard Mowbray), p. 28.

37. Henry W. Desmond and Herbert

Croly, "The Work of Messrs. McKim, Mead & White," *The Architectural Record* 20 (September 1906): 217. This was probably Jefferson's letter to L'Enfant: "I should prefer the adoption of some one of the models of antiquity which have had the approbation of thousands of years"; quoted from Jefferson to L'Enfant, April 10, 1791, in Saul K. Padover, *Thomas Jefferson and the National Capital* (Washington, D.C.: Government Printing Office, 1946), p. 59.

38. McKim, "Address of the President."

39. Quoted in Moore, *Charles Follen McKim*, pp. 188–89.

40. McKim, "Memoranda to Mrs. Wharton," ca. February 5, 1897, McKim Collection, Library of Congress. See also Richard Guy Wilson, "Edith and Ogden: Writing, Decoration, and Architecture," in Pauline Metcalf, ed., *Ogden Codman and the Decoration of Houses* (Boston: David R. Godine, 1988), pp. 133–84.

41. Moore, *Charles Follen McKim*, p. 192.

42. Ibid., p. 198.

43. See Moore, *Daniel H. Burnham*, vol. 1, p. 144, and *Charles Follen McKim*, p. 187. On the trip, see also Cynthia R. Field, "The McMillan Commission's Trip to Europe," Occasional Papers No. 1, Center for Washington Area Studies; proceedings of the symposium *Historical Perspectives on Urban Design: Washington, D.C., 1890–1910*, October 7, 1983.

44. Moore, *Charles Follen McKim*, p. 187.

45. Ibid., p. 188.

46. Ibid., pp. 188, 190.

47. Ibid., p. 189.

48. McKim, "Address of the President."

WHEN DIGNITY AND BEAUTY WERE
THE ORDER OF THE DAY

1. For example, Arthur B. Goodno, "Burnham's Manila," *Planning*, December 2004, p. 30, appears under the headline

"A century later, the master planner's City Beautiful ideas still have meaning" and asserts that "for much of the 20th century, pockets of reality matched Burnham's vision."

2. U.S. Congress, *Improvement of the Park System*, pp. 7–8.

3. U.S. Congress, *The Mall Parkway*, p. 13.

4. U.S. Congress, *Improvement of the Park System*, p. 65.

5. Moore, *Daniel H. Burnham*, vol. 1, p. 206, reprinting a statement made by Burnham to Secretary of the Treasury Leslie Shaw in 1903.

6. Burnham, "A City of the Future under a Democratic Government," in "The Conference and the International Town Planning Exhibition Transactions," issue of *Journal of the Royal Institute of British Architects* 17, no. 19 (September 24, 1910): 378 (issue hereafter cited as "Transactions").

7. It has been reported on more than one occasion that Daniel Burnham did not actually create the phrase "Make no little plans."

In 1912, the San Francisco architect Willis Polk sent out a Christmas card honoring his friend Daniel Burnham, who had died in that year. The card read: "Make no little plans; they have no magic to stir men's blood and probably themselves will never be realized. Make big plans, aim high in hope and work, remembering that a noble, logical diagram once recorded will never die, but long after we are gone will be a living thing, asserting itself with ever-growing insistency. Remember that our sons and grandsons are going to do things that would stagger us. Let your watchword be order and your beacon, beauty." The message purported to be taken from Burnham's speech to the London Town Planning conference of 1910. The lines in the middle section of this passage are essentially as given by Burnham in London (see "Transactions," p. 378). However, the famous first line ("Make no little plans; they have no magic to stir men's blood") and the last line ("Let your watchword be order and your beacon, beauty") are not in the published transcript of the conference.

An undated letter in the files of the Chicago Historical Society from reference librarian Elizabeth Baughman to the *Encyclopaedia Britannica* says that Moore's quotation is exactly the same as Polk's Christmas card of 1912 and that each sentence could be found in some place in the 1910 London report. However, she had not consulted the text of the London speech herself but depended on the correspondence of Daniel Burnham Jr. We know what Daniel Burnham Jr., had to say on the subject. Hans Paul Caemmerer, who was secretary of the Fine Arts Commission from 1922 to 1954, wrote to Daniel Burnham Jr., to get the source of the quotation in 1940. Burnham Jr. replied: "What my father said is all contained in the report of the London City Planning Conference of 1910. As I remember it, Willis Polk, an architect who was my father's resident partner in San Francisco, assembled the quotation by picking out sentences from the 1910 London City Planning Conference published report and sent out Christmas cards about 1912, after my father's death on June 1, 1912 in the form as quoted in Moore's books, Vol. 2, p. 147. In other words, I believe that my father never used the words in the sequence quoted by Mr. Moore." This correspondence was published in an unsigned note in the *Journal of the Society of Architectural Historians* 4, no. 1 (January 1944): 3. More extensive coverage to the same effect was given in Henry Saylor, "Make No Little Plans," *American Institute of Architects Journal* 27, no. 3 (March 1957): 95–96. Citing the Saylor article, the 16th edition of *Bartlett's Familiar Quotations*

(p. 555) informs the reader that the attribution of the quotation to Burnham is now doubted. Burnham may have said it aloud, or a reporter might have created the phrase for a newspaper article, as Wolfgang Sonne has pointed out to me. However, all those people who were close to Burnham referred this motto back to the 1910 meeting, the transcript of which contains no such phrase.

8. See J. Theodore Klein, *The Power of Service: A Swedenborgian Approach to Social Issues in the Twenty-First Century* (San Francisco: J. Appleseed & Co., 1998), p. 30. Klein explained the vital importance of the relation between the whole and its parts, saying: "To Swedenborg, the whole—whether heaven, the human body; or all of God's creation—is present in each part."

9. Moore, *Daniel H. Burnham*, vol. 2, p. 147.

10. Ibid., p. 174.

11. Daniel Burnham to Richard Watson Gilder, September 27, 1909, Burnham Papers, Burnham and Ryerson Library, Art Institute of Chicago.

12. Thomas Macaulay's *History of England* (published 1848–61) begins with a statement that "the history of our country during the last hundred and sixty years is eminently the history of physical, of moral, and of intellectual improvement."

13. "Transactions," p. 372.

14. Ibid., p. 378.

15. Moore, *Daniel H. Burnham*, vol. 1, p. 95.

16. Daniel Burnham to the Honorable James McMillan, March 23, 1901, Burnham Papers: "I enclose a copy of correspondence between Mr. Olmsted and myself. Is it your wish that I be Chairman of the Commission? I presumed it was your intention. . . ."

17. Daniel Burnham to Frederick Law Olmsted Jr., April 10, 1901, Burnham Papers.

18. Moore, *Daniel H. Burnham*, vol. 1, p. 143.

19. Henry Adams, *The Education of Henry Adams* (1907; reprint, New York: Random House, 1931), p. 343.

20. Alice Freeman Palmer, "Some Lasting Results of the World's Fair," *Forum* 16, no. 4 (December 1893): 519.

21. "Washington: Past and Present," ms. 0447G, Charles Moore Papers, Manuscripts Division, Library of Congress, Washington, D.C.

22. Paul Bourget, "A Farewell to the White City," *Cosmopolitan* 16, no. 2 (December 1893): 133–40.

23. Daniel Burnham, "White City and Capital City," *The Century Illustrated Monthly Magazine* 63, no. 2 (February 1902): 620.

24. Moore, *Daniel H. Burnham*, vol. 1, pp. 73–74; vol. 2, p. 139.

25. In Cleveland and Chicago, Burnham's work remains a guide to development. As for Baguio and Manila, according to the official website for Baguio (*www.baguio.gov .ph*), "The American Governor Luke E. Wright commissioned Architect Daniel H. Burnham, a prominent Urban Planner, to develop a plan for a health resort where the American soldiers and civilian employees can find respite from the sweltering lowland heat. The plan better known as the Burnham Plan greatly altered the original mountain settlement and provided the first physical framework plan for the City. It paved the way for a very rapid physical development, the undertones of which are still visible up [to] this date. The physical framework as embodied in the Burnham Plan integrates a road and park system into one. It envisioned evolving a compact garden city for 25,000 to 30,000 people. Supporting this development plan was the enactment of a charter approved on September 1, 1909 that provided administrative as well as managerial autonomy for the city."

26. Daniel Burnham to Lorado Taft, July 12, 1911, Burnham Papers.

27. Daniel Burnham to Frederick Law Olmsted Jr., April 28, 1904, Burnham Papers.

28. Daniel Burnham, "The Commercial Value of Beauty," *Architect's and Builder's Journal* 3, no. 8 (March 1902): 20–21.

29. Burnham, "White City and Capital City," pp. 619–20.

30. Moore, *Daniel H. Burnham*, vol. 1, p. 221.

31. Ibid., vol. 1, chap. 15: "The Struggle to Preserve the Mall in Washington, 1903–4," pp. 205–29.

32. Ibid., vol. 1, p. 73.

33. Daniel Burnham to Charles McKim, May 24, 1904, Burnham Papers.

34. "Transactions," p. 378.

35. Ibid., p. 769.

36. Ibid., pp. 9–10.

37. Ibid., pp. 368–78.

38. Ibid., p. 369.

39. Ibid., p. 371.

40. See Cass Gilbert, "Daniel Hudson Burnham: An Appreciation," *Architectural Record* 32, no. 167 (August 1912): 175.

41. Peterson, *Birth of City Planning in the United States*, p. 127.

42. See Daniel Burnham to Augustus Saint-Gaudens, n.d. [ca. 1903–4], Burnham Papers.

A SIMPLE SPACE OF TURF

1. L'Enfant's plan is reproduced in Reps, *Making of Urban America*, 251, 255.

2. In Caemmerer, *Pierre Charles L'Enfant*, p. 153.

3. Spiro Kostof, *The City Shaped: Urban Patterns and Meanings through History* (Boston: Bulfinch Press, 1991), p. 249.

4. Moore and Jones, ca. 1804, reproduced in Longstreth, *The Mall in Washington*, plates XV, XVI.

5. Schuyler, *New Urban Landscape*, p. 68.

6. Frederick Law Olmsted to Edward Clark, October 1, 1881, *Annual Report of the Architect of the United States Capitol* (Washington, D.C.: Government Printing Office, 1882), pp. 14–15.

7. The paper was later reproduced in its entirety in *The American Architect and Building News*, January 19, 1901, pp. 19–21.

8. Frederick Law Olmsted Jr., "Landscape in Connection with Public Buildings in Washington," in Brown, *Papers Relating to the Improvement of the City of Washington*, p. 26.

9. Ibid., p. 28.

10. Ibid., p. 29.

11. Ibid., p. 30.

12. Jon A. Peterson, "The Nation's First Comprehensive Plan," *Journal of the Architectural Planning Association* 51, no. 2 (1985): 141.

13. "Introduction" to Brown, *Papers Relating to the Improvement of the City of Washington*, p. 9.

14. Quoted in Charles Moore, "Memoirs," ms., Charles Moore Papers, Manuscript Division, Library of Congress, p. 76.

15. Quoted in Susan L. Klaus, "'Intelligent and Comprehensive Planning of a Common Sense Kind': Frederick Law Olmsted Jr.'s, Contributions to Comprehensive Planning, 1900–1916" (M.A. thesis, George Washington University, 1988), p. 111.

16. For example, see Brown, *Memories*, p. 268, and Reps, *Making of Urban America*, p. 508.

17. See Susan L. Klaus, *A Modern Arcadia: Frederick Law Olmsted Jr. and the Plan for Forest Hills Gardens* (Amherst, Mass.: University of Massachusetts Press, 2002), p. 26.

18. See John J. Pittari Jr., "Potential Idealism: Frederick Law Olmsted Jr. and the Modern American City Planning Movement" (Ph.D. dissertation, University of Washington, 1997), p. 90; Klaus, "Intelligent and Comprehensive Planning," pp. 93–94.

19. Pittari, "Potential Idealism," p. 99.

20. Norma Evanson, "Monumental Spaces," in Longstreth, *The Mall in Washington*, p. 33.

21. Lewis Mumford, *The City in History: Its Origins, Its Transformations, and Its Prospects* (New York: Harcourt, Brace & World, 1961), p. 406.

22. Longstreth, *The Mall in Washington*, plate LXXI.

23. Olmsted, "Landscape in Connection with Public Buildings in Washington," p. 34.

THE PEOPLE'S HOME GROUND

I am grateful to the Center for the Study of World Religions for the time afforded by their Senior Fellowship in the fall of 2001. Amy Brogna provided able and creative assistance to the research needs of the article. Much of the inspiration for the article derived from the enthusiasm of Ralph Rinzler, head of the Smithsonian Folklife Program in the 1980s, when Victor Turner and I worked with Ralph on the festivals and museums on the Mall.

1. See, e.g., A. K. Ramanujan, *Speaking of Śiva* (Baltimore: Penguin, 1973).

2. See Merrill D. Peterson, *Lincoln in American Memory* (New York: Oxford University Press, 1994).

3. Quoted in James R. Carroll, "King's Dream, Legacy Set in Stone: Marker Honors the Civil-Rights Leader's Speech," *Louisville Courier-Journal*, August 23, 2003.

4. See Raymond Michalowski and Jill Dubisch, *Run for the Wall: Remembering Vietnam on a Motorcycle Pilgrimage* (New Brunswick, N.J.: Rutgers University Press, 2001).

5. "AIDS Quilt Draws Huge Crowds to Nation's Capital," CNN report datelined Washington, D.C., October 12, 1996.

6. *Native American:* In the Aztec calendar of 360 days, the people used the remaining five days of the year as empty days, sacred and unpredictable.

Aborigines: The walkabout was the "absent" time.

New Ireland Barok people, New Guinea: At the end of all sequences of the "opening-up" of ritual mysteries, there is always a hidden mystery, a *pidik,* beyond that.

Indigenous Indonesia: Their patterns of ritual leave an empty center.

CULTURE OF, BY, AND FOR THE PEOPLE

1. Quoted in Ken Ringle, "Of Lawyers and Other Folk: Even Barristers Join the Blend at the Smithsonian's Festival of Diversity," *Washington Post,* June 25, 1986.

2. William Seale, *The President's House: A History* (Washington, D.C.: White House Historical Association, 1986), pp. 108–9.

3. Curtis M. Hinsley, "The World as Marketplace: Commodification of the Exotic at the World's Columbian Exposition," in Ivan Karp and Steven D. Lavine, eds., *Exhibiting Cultures: The Poetics and Politics of Museum Display* (Washington, D.C.: Smithsonian Institution Press, 1991), pp. 344–65.

4. James Conaway, *The Smithsonian: 150 Years of Adventure, Discovery, and Wonder* (Washington, D.C.: Smithsonian Institution Books; New York: Knopf, 1995), p. 340.

5. S. Dillon Ripley, *The Sacred Grove: Essays on Museums* (New York: Simon & Schuster, 1969), pp. 52–53; Conaway, *The Smithsonian,* pp. 18–36.

6. Cheryl Brauner, "A Study of the Newport Folk Festival and Newport Folk Foundation" (M.A. thesis, Memorial University of Newfoundland, 1985).

7. From an oral history interview of Ralph C. Rinzler with Roger Abrahams by Marc Pachter, July 9, 1993, Smithsonian Institution Archives.

8. Report on the 1967 Festival of American Folklife, ms., Ralph Rinzler Folklife Archives and Collections, Smithsonian Center for Folklife and Cultural Heritage.

9. Paul Richard, "Folk Art Show Opens at Mall," *Washington Post,* July 2, 1967.

10. For a history of the festival, see Richard Kurin, *Smithsonian Folklife Festival: Culture of, by, and for the People* (Washington, D.C.: Smithsonian Institution, 1998), and *Reflections of a Culture Broker: A View from the Smithsonian* (Washington, D.C.: Smithsonian Institution Press, 1997), pp. 109–238.

11. Barbara Dubivsky, "Some Fresh Air for the Nation's Attic," *New York Times,* April 9, 1967.

12. Conaway, *The Smithsonian,* p. 340.

13. Dean Anderson, Festival of American Folklife opening ceremony, June 25, 1986, Ralph Rinzler Folklife Archives and Collections FP-1986-RR-0024, Smithsonian Center for Folklife and Cultural Heritage.

14. Bernice Johnson Reagon, quoted by Gerald B. Jordan, "Philadelphians Break Out Beat of Urban America," *Philadelphia Inquirer,* June 29, 1984.

15. See the annual program books *Festival of American Folklife* (Washington, D.C.: Smithsonian Institution, 1968–97) and *Smithsonian Folklife Festival* (Washington, D.C.: Smithsonian Institution, 1998).

16. Survey results have been presented internally to festival staff and excerpts occasionally published in *Talk Story,* the newsletter of the Smithsonian Center for Folklife and Cultural Heritage. See, for

example, Richard Kurin, "Friends of the Festival Survey Results," *Talk Story* 10 (fall 1996), p. 14; "Festival Visitor Survey," *Talk Story* 14 (fall 1998), p. 8; "Festival Visitor Survey Summary," *Talk Story* 16 (fall 1999), p. 9; "Director's Talk Story," *Talk Story* 20 (fall 2001), p. 2. Press coverage has also been examined to gauge public perception and knowledge; see Richard Kurin and Carey Cauthen, "The Promotional Value and Public Image of Cultural Display: Press Coverage of Tennessee at the Smithsonian's Festival of American Folklife," in *Preserving and Promoting Cultural Resources*, a special issue of *Tennessee Business*, vol. 6, no. 1 (1995): 45–55.

17. Senator Mark Hatfield, Festival of American Folklife opening ceremony, October 6, 1978, Ralph Rinzler Folklife Archives and Collections, FP-1978-RR-0002, Smithsonian Center for Folklife and Cultural Heritage.

18. According to Smithsonian staff folklorist Peter Seitel (personal communication), the term "low-resolution media" was applied to the festival by Robert Byington, a former member of the staff.

19. The Smithsonian Center for Folklife and Cultural Heritage does periodic surveys of festival participants to determine the quality of their experience. Student fellows from Emory University participating in a joint project with the Center with support from the Rockefeller Foundation, have conducted additional research. Published studies include, among others, Richard Bauman, Patricia Sawin, and Gale Carpenter, *Reflections on the Folklife Festival: An Ethnography of Participant Experience*, Special Publications no. 2 (Bloomington: Indiana University Folklore Institute, 1992); Robert Cantwell, *Ethnomimesis: Folklife and the Representation of Culture* (Chapel Hill: Univer-

sity of North Carolina Press, 1993); Juan Gallo, *Mis Ojos Vieron* (Chiapas: Gobierno del Estado de Chiapas, 1992); Barbara Kirshenblatt-Gimblett, "Objects of Ethnography," in Karp and Lavine, *Exhibiting Cultures*, pp. 423–30; Richard Price and Sally Price, *On the Mall: Presenting Maroon Tradition-Bearers at the 1992 Festival of American Folklife*, Special Publications no. 4 (Bloomington: Indiana University Folklore Institute, 1994); Laurie K. Sommers, ed., *Folklore and Use: Applications in the Real World*, special issue of *Michigan on the Mall*, vol. 2, no. 2 (1994).

20. Margaret Mead, "Our 200th Birthday: What We Have to Celebrate," *Redbook*, July 1975, pp. 38–40.

21. James Boon, "Why Museums Make Me Sad," in Karp and Lavine, *Exhibiting Cultures*, pp. 259–60.

22. Victor Turner, ed., *Celebration: Studies in Festivity and Ritual* (Washington, D.C.: Smithsonian Institution Press, 1982), pp. 11–30.

23. See Bert Feintuch, "Introduction: Folklorists and the Public Sector," in Feintuch, ed., *The Conservation of Culture: Folklorists and the Public Sector* (Lexington: University of Kentucky Press, 1987), pp. 1–16.

24. This extended Rinzler's work, begun with Nancy Sweezy and John Kenneth Galbraith with Country Roads, to the Smithsonian museum shops; see oral history interview of Ralph C. Rinzler with Roger Abrahams by Marc Pachter, July 9, 1993, Smithsonian Institution Archives.

25. Bernice Johnson Reagon and Linn Shapiro, eds., *Black People and Their Culture: Selected Writings from the African Diaspora* (Washington, D.C.: Smithsonian Institution Press, 1976); Bernice Johnson Reagon, ed., *We'll Understand It Better By and By: Pioneering African American Gospel Composers*

(Washington, D.C.: Smithsonian Institution Press, 1992), pp. 7–9.

26. Robert H. Byington, ed., *Working Americans: Contemporary Approaches to Occupational Folklife*, Smithsonian Folklife Studies, no. 3 (Washington, D.C.: Smithsonian Institution Office of Folklife Programs, 1978), reprinted from *Western Folklore* 37, no. 3 (July 1978).

27. Edward Samarin to the Smithsonian, August 9, 1995, Ralph Rinzler Folklife Archives and Collections, Smithsonian Center for Folklife and Cultural Heritage.

28. How the festival serves this representative function is critically discussed in a number of studies and assessments, including Susan Roach, "The Journey of David Allen, Cane Carver: Transformations through Public Folklore," in Robert Baron and Nicholas Spitzer, eds., *Public Folklore* (Washington, D.C.: Smithsonian Institution Press, 1992); Charles Camp and Timothy Lloyd, "Six Reasons Not to Produce Folklife Festivals," *Kentucky Folklife Record* 26 (1982): 67–74; Daniel Mato, "The Transnational Making of Representations of Gender, Ethnicity, and Culture: Indigenous Peoples' Organizations at the Smithsonian Institution's Festival," *Cultural Studies* 12, no. 2 (1998): 193–209; Diana Baird N'Diaye, "Between the Rock of Applied and the Hard Place of Public: A Chronicle of Community Collaboration in Public Sector Folklore Practice at the Smithsonian," *Journal of Applied Folklore*, 2, no. 1 (1999): 91–114; Jack Santino, "The Tendency to Ritualize: The 'Living Celebrations' Series as a Model for Cultural Presentation and Validation," in Feintuch, *Conservation of Culture*, pp. 118–31; and Sam Schrager, *Trial Lawyer's Art* (Philadelphia: Temple University Press, 2000).

29. Kurin, *Reflections of a Culture Broker*, pp. 29–56, 204–11, 239–64; Richard Kurin,

"We Are Very Much Still Here!," *Smithsonian Folklife Festival* (Washington, D.C.: Smithsonian Institution, 2006), pp. 10–23.

30. Alan Lomax, Festival of American Folklife evening concert, July 7, 1968, Ralph Rinzler Folklife Archives and Collections FP-1968-RR-003X, Smithsonian Center for Folklife and Cultural Heritage.

31. Senator William Fulbright, 1970, cited in Tom O'Brien, "Country Folk and the City," *Washington Post*, July 3, 1970.

32. Marsha Mercer, "In Celebration of American Folk Life," *Richmond Times-Dispatch*, July 2, 1989.

33. Henry Allen, quoted in *Life*, July 1995, p. 21.

34. Steven R. Weisman, "A Global Gathering on the Mall," *New York Times*, July 6, 2002.

35. *USA Today* on the 1987 festival, quoted in Kurin, *Smithsonian Folklife Festival*, p. 26.

36. Diana McLellan of the *Washington Star* on the 1973 festival, quoted in ibid., p. 25.

37. *Washington Post* on the 1974 festival, quoted in ibid., p. 27.

38. Richard Kurin, briefing to State Department advance team, June 20, 2002.

39. For the text of the letter, see Kurin, *Reflections of a Culture Broker*, pp. 68–69.

40. Mei-Mei Chan, "Once a Year, USA Diversity Center Stage," *USA Today*, June 27, 1986, pp. 1–2.

41. Diana Parker, "Festival of American Folklife," in Conaway, *The Smithsonian*, p. 372.

42. G. B. Runion, H. H. Rogers, C. W. Wood, S. A. Prior, and R. J. Mitchell, "Effects of Traffic on Soil Physical Characteristics and Vegetative Resources of the National Mall," *Journal of Soil and Water Conservation* 48, no. 5 (September–October 1993): 389–393.

43. The terms of the Smithsonian's use

of the Mall for the festival have been governed by a letter of agreement (Wes Wolfe to James Morris, March 22, 1973); a cooperative agreement between the Smithsonian and the National Park Service (June 14, 1976); 36 CFR 7.96 as revised and designating the festival as a "National Celebration Event"; another cooperative agreement (March 16, 2000); annual permits issued by the National Park Service, National Capital Region; and the attendant "National Park Service Requirements for Special Events Held on Parkland" guidelines as updated.

44. *ISKCON v. Ridenour*, Civil Action 92-1092, was filed in the District of Columbia on August 6, 1993, wherein the Hare Krishna organization disputed the National Park Service effort to limit the sales of beads and audiotapes on the Mall. This was followed with *ISKCON v. Kennedy*, 61 F 3d 949, 952 (1995), which held that the National Park Service could restrict such sales. The National Park Service then sought to restrict T-shirt sales on the Mall by Vietnam Veterans organizations and vendors. The U.S. District Court for the District of Columbia (95cv00808) held for the Vietnam Veterans, who claimed the T-shirts were a matter of free speech. In *Friends of the Vietnam Veterans Memorial v. Kennedy*, 95-5393, the U.S. Court of Appeals for the District of Columbia Circuit then, on June 6, 1997, reversed the District Court ruling, and upheld the National Park Service ban on T-shirt sales.

45. This sentiment is captured in a widely reprinted 1992 cartoon from South Carolina's *Index-Journal* composed by Sitarz and showing the Washington Monument and an elm tree on the Mall with two signs. The first, issued by the National Park Service, reads "keep off"; the second, by the Smithsonian, reads "keep on."

46. Ralph Rinzler, 1971, quoted in Kurin, *Smithsonian Folklife Festival*, p. 7.

MONUMENTS, MODERNISM, AND THE MALL

1. Bedford, *John Russell Pope*, pp. 220, 222.

2. Richard Guy Wilson, "High Noon on the Mall: Modernism versus Traditionalism, 1910–1970," in Longstreth, *The Mall in Washington*, pp. 143–67.

3. All quoted in Kohler, *Commission of Fine Arts*, pp. 71–72.

4. Lewis Mumford, *The Culture of Cities* (New York: Harcourt, Brace, 1938), all quotations from pp. 433–40.

5. The quotations in this paragraph are from Sigfried Giedion, *Architecture, You, and Me* (Cambridge, Mass.: Harvard University Press, 1958), pp. 48–49, 50–51.

6. James E. Young, *The Texture of Memory* (New Haven: Yale University Press, 1993), p. 168.

7. Harriet Senie, *Contemporary Public Sculpture: Tradition, Transformation, and Controversy* (New York: Oxford University Press, 1992), p. 3.

8. For the story of the Franklin Delano Roosevelt Memorial, see Isabelle Hyman, "Marcel Breuer and the Franklin Delano Roosevelt Memorial," *Journal of the Society of Architectural Historians* 54, no. 4 (December 1995): 446–57. I am indebted to the anonymous reviewer of the Johns Hopkins University Press for this reference.

9. Quoted in Bedford, *John Russell Pope*, p. 200.

10. J. Carter Brown, "The Designing of the National Gallery of Art's East Building," in Longstreth, *The Mall in Washington*, p. 283.

11. See, for a possible modern memorial, the illustrations in Nicolaus Mills, *Their Last Battle: The Fight for the National World*

War II Memorial (New York: Basic Books, 2004), illustrations after p. 108. This book also gives a full account of the conflicts over the World War II Memorial, and the Vietnam Veterans Memorial.

TURNING POINT

In moving from the academic world to the realm of public policy and politics, I depended on the expertise and good sense of many colleagues who have helped me understand the history and processes outlined in this essay. Above all, to fellow members of the National Coalition to Save Our Mall and the Committee of 100 on the Federal City, and especially to W. Kent Cooper, FAIA, and George Oberlander, AICP. Experience is a great teacher, and I learned much in frequent conversations, debates, and sometimes disputes with the government agencies involved day to day with Mall issues: the National Park Service, the National Capital Planning Commission, the Commission of Fine Arts, and the Advisory Council on Historic Preservation.

1. For a graphic report on the numerous construction projects at that time, see Monte Reel, "Sightseeing on the Mall Not Exactly Picture-Perfect," *Washington Post*, March 27, 2004. The website of the National Coalition to Save Our Mall, www.savethemall.org, archives the numerous news stories, editorials, and essays that in recent years have noted with increasing alarm the degradation of the Mall and the visitor experience of it. One particularly trenchant essay by the journalist Andrew Ferguson, "The Mess on the Mall: Confusion Reigns Supreme on America's Promenade," *Weekly Standard* 10, no. 45 (August 15–22, 2005): 20–27, also discusses the coalition's ideas for a new master plan for the Mall, including Mall expansion in its "third century."

2. See Longstreth, *The Mall in Washington*. The essay by Richard Guy Wilson, "High Noon on the Mall: Modernism versus Traditionalism, 1910–1970," pp. 134–67, provides a discussion of various competing attitudes toward the McMillan Plan that characterize change in the twentieth century through 1970 and concludes on the positive note of the Mall's enduring democratic values. Robert A. M. Stern and Raymond W. Gastil's "A Temenos for Democracy: The Mall in Washington and Its Influence," pp. 263–78, sees change in the Mall as still "a fundamentally optimistic vision of democracy." That 1991 collection of essays (reprinted in 2002 with a new introduction) predates many more recent changes, including construction of the Korean Veterans Memorial, the FDR Memorial, and the World War II Memorial. Older, indispensable studies of the Mall include Reps, *Monumental Washington*; Gutheim and Lee, *Worthy of the Nation*; and Kohler, *Commission of Fine Arts*. Also valuable are the Park Service's official historical studies of various parts of the Mall. These include the National Register nomination for the Mall's western part, *East and West Potomac Parks Historic District, Revised National Register of Historic Places Nomination*, July 16, 1999, and *Cultural Landscape Report, West Potomac Park, Lincoln Memorial Grounds* (National Capital Parks Central), August 1999, Part 1: *Site History, Analysis and Evaluation and Design Guidelines*, published by the Department of the Interior as part of the Park Service's Cultural Landscapes Program. More complex, mixed, and even pessimistic assessments of the realization of the Mall's democratic potential appear in recent studies of social, political, and cultural forces. See, for example, Gillette, *Between Justice and Beauty*; and Barber, *Marching on Washington*. Two recent

studies analyze the Mall's multifaceted, changing meaning: Thomas, *Lincoln Memorial and American Life*, and Meyer, *Myths in Stone*.

3. Over ninety articles, editorials, cartoons, and essays about the World War II Memorial controversy are archived at www.savethemall.org/wwii/controversy.html. Senator Jeff Bingaman of New Mexico made his comments condemning the NFL event on the Senate floor on September 15, 2003, and entered into the *Congressional Record* three articles: "Desecration of The Mall," by Albert Eisele in his "On the Record" column of *The Hill* (September 10, 2003); a *Washington Post* editorial titled "Marketing the Mall" (September 3, 2003); and an article by columnist Tom Shales of the *Post* titled "America, Brought to You by . . ." (September 5, 2003). Christopher Knight, "America's Maul," *Los Angeles Times*, April 20, 2003, was aware of the work of the National Coalition to Save Our Mall, a grassroots citizens group founded in 2000 during the World War II Memorial controversy and dedicated to the protection of the Mall. In late 2003, the coalition began a new project called the "National Mall Third Century Initiative" (www.nationalmall.net) to seek solutions to the Mall's many problems.

4. The environmental assessment for the project provides most of the history of the earlier plans, as well as details of the security design. See "Washington Monument Permanent Security Improvements Environmental Assessment," produced by the National Park Service in cooperation with the National Capital Planning Commission, April 2002, pp. 29–31, Sections 2.2–2.3.

5. Deborah K. Dietsch, "New Bunker Mentality Will Mar Washington," *USA Today*, July 29, 2002; Catesby Leigh, "Sub-terranean Blues: Washington Digs Itself into a Hole," *Weekly Standard* 8, no. 17 (January 13, 2003): 29–34; Roger K. Lewis, "Shaping the City: Park Service Has a Bad Case of Tunnel Vision on Washington Monument Security," *Washington Post*, July 12, 2003; Benjamin Forgey, "Tunnel Visions of the Dim Future," *Washington Post*, August 9, 2003. Testimony before the NCPC and CFA by citizens questioning the effects of the walls on public use of the monument grounds is archived at www.savethemall.org/washmon/index.html.

6. In his October 4, 2002, letter to the Park Service, then commission chairman Harry G. Robinson III stated: "From its initial exposure nine months ago to these proposals, the Commission has expressed serious concerns about the underground schemes for admitting visitors to the monument. Without exception, all the proposals reviewed, to date, have resulted in major interventions in the historic landscape, diminishing the Monument's precinct." He concluded that the commission "looks forward to reviewing alternative proposals." That was not to be, as the Park Service never returned for commission review. The NCPC—whose commissioners include a Park Service representative—was more deferential to the plans. While the NCPC initially balked at the size and architectural style of the lodge addition, eventually its differences with the Park Service were resolved, as is generally the case with projects involving government agencies with representation on the commission. NCPC staff members produce detailed evaluations of the projects and executive director recommendations (EDRs). For the report recommending approval of the landscape plan, "Washington Monument Grounds: Revised Development Concept Plan and Preliminary Site and Building Plans for

Visitor and Security Improvements" (January 2, 2003), see NCPC file no. 1303/6152.

7. See the transcript of the NCPC meeting, June 5, 2003, for Mr. Olin's extensive remarks about the desirability of a naturalistic design for the monument grounds. A 1981 "Development Concept Plan and Alternatives" report, produced by the Park Service for an earlier version of the visitor center plan, evaluated potential effects of that plan on the L'Enfant and McMillan concepts of the Mall as a whole. Its conclusions, if applied to the current scheme for walls erected in a curvilinear pattern on the open grass, would probably condemn it. The report reviewed the various historical design schemes for the monument since 1791 and criticized the nineteenth-century Downing plan's "curvilinear walks" on the monument grounds as having "obliterated the formal east-west axis of the L'Enfant plan." If simple walkways violated the L'Enfant plan, then presumably adding walls in a large oval formation around the monument does too.

8. See Knight, "America's Maul." See also Anna Palmer, "Visitors Center Revisited: Legislation for Vietnam Facility on the Mall Reintroduced," *Roll Call*, April 3, 2003, p. 27; Abraham Genauer, "Monumental Endeavor, Uphill Climb: Group Strives to Preserve Historic Vision of National Mall," *The Hill*, June 3, 2003, pp. 19–20. After the NCPC approved a Mall site for the center in August 2006, Knight wrote "The Continued Mauling of the National Mall" (*Los Angeles Times*, September 9, 2006), in which he concluded, "The Mall's planning and oversight process is irreparably broken." In testimony before the NCPC and CFA, speakers pointed out that even an underground facility would need aboveground components—an entry pavilion, skylights, and airshafts—and that underground con-

struction at the memorial site, which is composed of fill over former riverbeds, faces serious engineering challenges.

9. The original legislation for the visitor center was introduced in the Senate by Chuck Hagel of Nebraska and in the House by John Murtha of Pennsylvania and reintroduced in 2003 by Richard Pombo in the House and by Hagel, John Kerry, and John McCain in the Senate. Its list of supporters reads like a who's who of powerful members of Congress. As late as July 2003 the legislation used the words "education center," but the final version signed by President Bush in November 2003 (PL 108-126) called it a "visitor center." The history of the project is outlined in "Vietnam Veterans Memorial Center Site Selection Environmental Assessment," produced by the National Park Service in association with the Vietnam Veterans Memorial Fund and the National Capital Planning Commission, May 2006, pp. 9–12, Sections 1.1–1.2. The size of the visitor center is described at Section 2.2.1.

10. A history of the memorial is provided on its official website, www.wwiimemorial.com. Another source, which provides greater detail, is www.savethemall.org/wwii/history.html. Already in 1995, at the time the site was selected, there had been some media coverage of the controversy over site selection, and in 1996 more voices raised alarm over the memorial project. See, for example, the editorial by Deborah K. Dietsch, "Memorial Madness: A War Memorial Competition Threatens to Diminish a Precious National Site," *Architecture* 85, no. 7 (July 1996): 15. Major media coverage grew in 1997. Over the next three years, editorials criticizing the site and design appeared in the *New York Times, Wall Street Journal, New Yorker,* and *Los Angeles Times.* Commentary in dozens of publica-

tions represented a broad spectrum of political opinion around the country. See, for example, Charles Krauthammer, "Don't Build It Here! A WWII Memorial: Great Idea, Wrong Spot," *Time* 149, no. 16 (April 21, 1997): 126. In Washington, D.C., both the *Washington Post* and the *Washington Times* editorialized in favor of the memorial, probably in part convinced by influential memorial champions former senator Robert Dole and Commission of Fine Arts chairman J. Carter Brown. A sampling of the numerous critical commentaries can be read at www.savethemall.org/wwii/controversy.html.

My own involvement with the World War II Memorial opposition dates to 1997, when, on reading an op-ed piece by Senator Bob Kerrey in the *Washington Post* opposing the Rainbow Pool location (he later testified that "My objection to this particular site is that there is something already there . . . the Rainbow Pool"), I contacted his office to offer my professional assistance. At the time, I was teaching Washington architecture at American University. At the invitation of Senator Kerrey's staff, I joined a group of congressional and local citizens groups, known as Friends of the Mall, united in opposition to the project, which was rejected in 1997. In 1998, however, in response to the new, less obtrusive design, Kerrey dropped his opposition. The leadership vacuum resulted in the dissolution of the group. As a new board member of the citizens planning group, the Committee of 100 on the Federal City, I continued to help lead opposition to the siting of the memorial. Eventually, in 2000, I was among a small group of Committee of 100 trustees who founded the National Coalition to Save Our Mall. The coalition, together with the Committee of 100 and the D.C. Preservation League, then brought

legal action against the approved memorial site and design.

11. The council had acted amid growing controversy in late summer 2000, as the World War II Memorial moved toward final design approvals. The council held a public hearing on August 28 to review all sides, and it issued a formal finding in a September 5 letter to Secretary of the Interior Bruce Babbitt signed by Cathryn B. Slater, chairman, Advisory Council on History Preservation.

12. In its September 5, 2000, letter to Secretary Babbitt rejecting the memorial design, the Advisory Council on Historic Preservation stated: "At the heart of our procedural concern is how the NPS conducts its Section 106 [public consultation] responsibilities. . . . Regrettably, such consultation on the World War II Memorial did not occur. The NPS did not consult with the Council on either site selection or the design competition. When the NPS did bring the Council into the process in July 1997, the most critical aspects of the memorial proposal were firmly set."

13. The act was signed into law by President Reagan. A representative of the National Park Service described as "monumental chaos" the situation that led to passage of the Commemorative Works Act during testimony before Congress opposing a bill that would authorize a memorial to President Reagan on the Mall, before the House Committee on Resources on March 8, 2001.

14. In a report dated November 20, 2003, the Congressional Research Service concluded, "existing federal statutes and regulations do not provide a definition or a description of the term 'the Mall.' When a specific description/definition of the term is needed, the NPS makes reference/citation to a description and a map con-

tained in the 1902 'MacMillan Plan' [*sic*] of the District of Columbia."

15. Such statements were made in several public meetings in 2003 and 2004 during discussion of National Park Service projects involving the Lincoln Memorial and Washington Monument. NPS official and NCPC commissioner John Parsons made a point of stating for the record that the NPS considers the Mall to end at Fourteenth Street but, surprisingly, went on to say that the "National Mall" extends all the way to the Lincoln Memorial. Transcript of National Capital Planning Commission, February 5, 2004.

16. East and West Potomac Park, National Register of Historic Places nomination, section 7, p. 2. This interpretation appears in a footnote that goes to great lengths to distinguish the common perception of the Mall from the official Park Service definition. The NCPC, incorrectly cited in the footnote, actually defines the Mall, in its Memorials and Museums Master Plan, as the great cross axis from the Capitol to the Lincoln Memorial and from the White House to the Jefferson Memorial. The definition cited above is more accurately derived from the Park Service's park system map.

17. The confusion over boundaries is evident in the materials and statements that accompanied the announcement in November 2006 of the National Park Service's new management plan, the National Mall Plan; see www.nps.gov/nationalmall-plan/. It showed up as well in background information the Park Service provided to design competition architects in October 2001 for the Washington Monument security project. The materials imply that the Mall ends not at Fourteenth Street but at Fifteenth: "The Washington Monument Grounds are bounded by Independence and Constitution Avenues and 15th and 17th Streets" (from the "Program Requirements For Washington Monument Permanent Security Improvement," November 2001). In his introductory essay to *The Mall in Washington* (p. 16, n. 2), Richard Longstreth appears to adopt the narrow Park Service definition: "Properly speaking, the Mall extends from the Capitol grounds to Fourteenth Street between Constitution and Independence avenues." He then points out that this area is only a portion of the larger entity, and so for the purposes of the book the Mall would be considered to extend to the Potomac River. The National Register of Historic Places, established in 1966 as the nation's official list of cultural resources worthy of preservation and administered by the National Park Service, provides a physical description of the place and information about its history and significance. Some of the National Register's resources, including nominations for the Mall areas, are available on the Park Service website: www.cr.nps.gov/nr/research/.

18. Susan Levine, "Trampling the Nation's Front Lawn: Mall Is Worn Down by Causes and Feet," *Washington Post*, November 13, 2000. Parsons states the same desire to get visitors into shuttle buses and invokes the Disney model—"Nobody drives around Disney World"—in a profile by Elaine Sciolino, "Public Lives: Guardian Honors Mall by Curbing Number of Memorials," *New York Times*, July 16, 2001.

19. Congressional Research Service report on National Mall Jurisdiction, March 18, 2005.

20. Two new planning initiatives by the NPC and NCPC can be usefully incorporated into the larger master planning effort. The NCPC's Capital City Framework Plan aims to improve federal areas around and near the Mall to make them more Mall-

like. The NPS's new management plan, which the agency calls its National Mall Plan, will look at ways to improve maintenance of turf grass and trees and improve visitor amenities for the open spaces under NPS jurisdiction.

PLANNING BEYOND THE MONUMENTAL CORE

1. A short list of recommended reading on the planning of Washington's monumental core and related issues might include the following: Gillette, *Between Justice and Beauty;* Gutheim and Lee, *Worthy of the Nation;* Thomas S. Hines, "The Imperial Mall: The City Beautiful Movement and the Washington Plan of 1901–1902," in Longstreth, *The Mall in Washington;* Jane Jacobs, *The Death and Life of Great American Cities* (New York: Random House, 1961); Kolson, *Big Plans;* Denise Liebowitz and Tony Simon, "Plans in Time," *Journal of the American Planning Association* 68, no. 2 (2002): 128–31; Jon A. Peterson, "The Mall, the McMillan Plan, and the Origins of American City Planning," in Longstreth, *The Mall in Washington;* Reps, *Washington on View;* Witold Rybczynski, *City Life: Urban Expectations in a New World* (New York: Simon & Schuster, 1995). See also National Capital Planning Commission, *Extending the Legacy* (1997), *Commemorative Zone Policy* (2000), *Memorials and Museums Master Plan* (2001), and *National Capital Urban Design and Security Plan* (2002); and the District of Columbia Office of Planning's *Anacostia Waterfront Initiative: Draft Framework Recommendations* (2001). Of great historical interest is the published report of the McMillan Commission: U.S. Congress, *Improvement of the Park System.*

2. See the U.S. Department of Commerce, Bureau of the Census, *Statistical Abstract of the United States: 1990, 110th edition* (Washington, D.C.: Government Printing Office, [1990]), p. 36; and U.S. Department of Commerce, Economics and Statistics Administration, U.S. Census Bureau, *Country and City Data Book: 2000, 13th edition* (Washington, D.C.: Government Printing Office, 2001), p. 648.

3. National Capital Planning Act of 1952, U.S. Code 40 (1952) §§ 8701 et seq.

4. *Comprehensive Plan for the National Capital: Federal Elements* (Washington, D.C.: National Capital Planning Commission, 2004).

5. Elizabeth S. Kite, *L'Enfant and Washington, 1791–1792* (Baltimore: Johns Hopkins University Press, 1929), pp. 54–55.

6. The 1986 Commemorative Works Act guides the location and development of new memorials on federal land in Washington administered by the National Park Service and the General Services Administration. The act requires that (1) all memorials must be authorized by Congress; (2) for any memorial to be located in the immediate vicinity of the National Mall (Area 1), additional special legislation is required; and (3) memorial sites and designs must be approved by the National Capital Planning Commission, the Commission of Fine Arts, and either the secretary of the interior, in the case of National Park Service land, or the administrator of general services, in the case of General Services Administration land. Established by the 1986 legislation, the National Capital Memorial Commission advises Congress, the secretary of the interior, and the administrators of the General Services Administration on the appropriateness of subjects for commemoration and on the location and design of memorials on land under their jurisdiction. The commission is an advisory board comprised of repre-

sentatives from federal agencies with either jurisdiction over land in the monumental core or review responsibilities for memorials, the mayor of the District of Columbia, the architect of the Capitol, and the American Battle Monuments Commission.

7. NCPC, *Commemorative Zone Policy*, n.p.

8. Ibid. The commission first adopted the Commemorative Zone Policy on January 6, 2000, in an internally produced staff report that was available to the public. The policy later appeared in an August 2001 "Report of the Joint Task Force on Memorials," an internally produced document that was also available to the public.

Abbott, Carl. *Political Terrain: Washington, D.C., from Tidewater Town to Global Metropolis.* Chapel Hill: University of North Carolina Press, 1999.

Barber, Lucy G. *Marching on Washington: The Forging of an American Political Tradition.* Berkeley and Los Angeles: University of California Press, 2002.

Bedford, Steven McLeod. *John Russell Pope, Architect of Empire.* New York: Rizzoli, 1998.

Bednar, Michael J. *L'Enfant's Legacy: Public Open Spaces in Washington, D.C.* Baltimore: Johns Hopkins University Press, 2006.

Brown, Glenn. *Memories: 1860–1930; A Winning Crusade to Revive George Washington's Vision of a Capital City.* Washington, D.C.: [Press of W.F. Roberts Co.,] 1931.

———, ed. *Papers Relating to the Improvement of the City of Washington, District of Columbia.* Washington, D.C.: Government Printing Office, 1901.

Bushong, William. *A Centennial History of the Washington Chapter, The American Institute of Architects, 1887–1987.* Washington, D.C.: Washington Architectural Foundation Press, 1987.

Caemmerer, Hans Paul. *The Life of Pierre Charles L'Enfant.* Washington, D.C.: National Republic Co., 1950; reprint, New York: Da Capo Press, 1970.

Cary, Francine Curro, ed. *Urban Odyssey: A Multicultural History of Washington, D.C.* Washington, D.C.: Smithsonian Institution Press, 1996.

Fallen, Anne Catherine, William C. Allen, and Karen D. Solit. *A Botanic Garden for the Nation: The United States Botanic Garden.* Washington, D.C.: Government Printing Office, 2007.

Field, Cynthia, and Jeffrey Tilman. "Creating a Model for the National Mall: The Design of the National Museum of Natural History." *Journal of the Society of Architectural Historians* 63, no. 1 (March 2004): 52–73.

Gillette, Howard, Jr. *Between Justice and Beauty: Race, Planning, and the Failure of Urban Policy in Washington, D.C.* Baltimore: Johns Hopkins University Press, 1995.

Goode, James M. *Capital Losses: A Cultural History of Washington's Destroyed Buildings.* 2nd ed. Washington, D.C.: Smithsonian Books, 2006.

The Grand Design: An Exhibition Tracing the Evolution of the L'Enfant Plan and Subsequent Plans for the Development of Pennsylvania Avenue and the Mall Area. Washington, D.C.: Library of Congress, 1967.

Green, Constance McLaughlin. *Washington: A History of the Capital, 1800–1950.* 2 vols. Princeton: Princeton University Press, 1976.

Gutheim, Frederick. *The Potomac.* Rev. ed.

New York: Holt, Rinehart & Winston, 1974.

Gutheim, Frederick, and Antoinette J. Lee. *Worthy of the Nation: Washington, D.C., from L'Enfant to the National Capital Planning Commission*. Baltimore: Johns Hopkins University Press, 2006.

Gutheim, Frederick, and Wilcomb E. Washburn. *The Federal City: Plans and Realities*, Washington, D.C.: Smithsonian Institution Press, 1976.

Hegemann, Werner, and Elbert Peets. *The American Vitruvius: An Architect's Handbook of Civic Art*. Edited and with an introduction by Alan J. Plattus, preface by Leon Krier, and introductory essay by Christiane Crasemann Collins. New York: Princeton Architectural Press, 1988.

Hines, Thomas S. *Burnham of Chicago, Architect and Planner*. New York: Oxford University Press, 1974.

Jacobs, Kathryn Allamong. *Capital Elites: High Society in Washington, D.C., after the Civil War*. Washington, D.C.: Smithsonian Institution Press, 1995.

Kohler, Sue A. *The Commission of Fine Arts: A Brief History, 1910–1995*. Washington, D.C.: Commission of Fine Arts, 1996.

Kolson, Kenneth L. *Big Plans: The Allure and Folly of Urban Design*. Baltimore: Johns Hopkins University Press, 2003.

Lee, Antoinette J., ed., *Historical Perspectives on Urban Design: Washington, D.C., 1890–1910*. Washington, D.C.: George Washington University, 1983.

Lessoff, Alan. *The Nation and Its City: Politics, "Corruption," and Progress in Washington, D.C., 1861–1902*. Baltimore: Johns Hopkins University Press, 1994.

Longstreth, Richard. "A Historical Bibliography of Built Environment in the Washington, D.C., Metropolitan Area." Society of Architectural Historians. www.sah.org.

———, ed. *The Mall in Washington, 1791–1991*. Washington, D.C.: National Gallery of Art, 1991; 2d ed., 2002.

———. "Washington and the Landscape of Fear." *City and Society* 18, no. 1 (2006): 7–30.

Melder, Keith, with Melinda Young Stuart. *City of Magnificent Intentions: A History of Washington, District of Columbia*. Rev. ed. Washington, D.C.: Intac, 1997.

Meyer, Jeffrey F. *Myths in Stone: Religious Dimensions of Washington, D.C.* Berkeley and Los Angeles: University of California Press, 2001.

Miller, Iris. *Washington in Maps, 1606–2000*. New York: Rizzoli, 2002.

Mills, Nicolaus. *Their Last Battle: The Fight for a National World War II Memorial*. New York: Basic Books, 2004.

Moeller, G. Martin, Jr. *AIA Guide to the Architecture of Washington, D.C.* Baltimore: Johns Hopkins University Press, 2006.

Moore, Charles. *Daniel H. Burnham, Architect, Planner of Cities*. Boston: Houghton Mifflin, 1921; reprint, New York: Da Capo Press, 1968.

———. *The Life and Times of Charles Follen McKim*. Boston: Houghton Mifflin, 1929; reprint, New York: Da Capo Press, 1970.

———, ed. *The Promise of American Architecture: Addresses at the Annual Dinner of the American Institute of Architects, 1905*. Washington, D.C.: American Institute of Architects, 1905.

National Capital Planning Commission (NCPC). *Extending the Legacy: Planning America's Capital for the 21st Century* (1997). *Memorials and Museums Master Plan* (2001). *National Capital Urban Design and Security Plan* (2001). *Comprehensive Plan for the National Capital: Federal Elements* (2004). (Full texts of these and other planning documents are posted at www.ncpc.gov.)

Passonneau, Joseph R. *Washington through Two Centuries: A History in Maps and Images.* New York: Monacelli Press, 2004.

Peterson, Jon A. *The Birth of City Planning in the United States, 1840–1917.* Baltimore: Johns Hopkins University Press, 2003.

Reps, John W. *Monumental Washington: The Planning and Development of the Capital Center.* Princeton: Princeton University Press, 1967.

———. *Washington on View: The Nation's Capital since 1790.* Chapel Hill: University of North Carolina Press, 1991.

Schuyler, David. *The New Urban Landscape: The Redefinition of City Form in Nineteenth-Century America.* Baltimore: Johns Hopkins University Press, 1986.

———. "The Washington Park and Downing's Legacy to Public Landscape Design." In George B. Tatum, ed., *Prophet with Honor: The Career of Andrew Jackson Downing, 1815–1852.* Washington, D.C.: Dumbarton Oaks Research Library and Collection; Philadelphia: Athenaeum of Philadelphia, 1989.

Scott, Pamela. *Capital Engineers: The United States Army Corps of Engineers in the Development of Washington, D.C., 1790–2004.* Alexandria, Va.: Office of History, U.S. Army Corps of Engineers, 2005.

Scott, Pamela, and Antoinette J. Lee. *Buildings of the District of Columbia.* New York: Oxford University Press, 1993.

Sonne, Wolfgang. *Representing the State: Capital City Planning in the Early Twentieth Century.* Translated from the German by Elizabeth Schwaiger. Munich and New York: Prestel, 2003.

Spreiregen, Paul D., ed. *On the Art of Designing Cities: Selected Essays of Elbert Peets.* Cambridge, Mass.: MIT Press, 1968.

Thomas, Christopher A. *The Architecture of the West Building of the National Gallery.* Washington, D.C.: National Gallery of Art, 1992.

———. *The Lincoln Memorial and American Life.* Princeton: Princeton University Press, 2002.

Tompkins, Sally Kress. *A Quest for Grandeur: Charles Moore and the Federal Triangle.* Washington, D.C.: Smithsonian Institution Press, 1992.

Turner, Victor Witter, and Edith L. B. Turner. *Image and Pilgrimage in Christian Culture: Anthropological Perspectives.* New York: Columbia University Press, 1978; reprint, 1995.

U.S. Congress, Senate Committee on the District of Columbia. *The Improvement of the Park System of the District of Columbia.* Senate Report no. 166. Edited by Charles Moore. Washington, D.C.: Government Printing Office, 1902.

———. *The Mall Parkway: Hearing before the Committee on the District of Columbia of the United States Senate, Saturday, March 12, 1904, on the bill (S. 4845) regulating the erection of buildings on the Mall, in the District of Columbia.* Washington, D.C.: Government Printing Office, 1904.

U.S. Congress, Senate Committee on Energy and Natural Resources, Subcommittee on National Parks. *National Mall: Hearing before the Subcommittee on National Parks of the Committee on Energy and Natural Resources, United States Senate, One Hundred Ninth Congress, first session . . . April 12, 2005.* Washington, D.C.: Government Printing Office, 2005.

Vale, Lawrence J. *Architecture, Power, and National Identity.* New Haven: Yale University Press, 1992.

JUDY SCOTT FELDMAN, president and founding member of the National Coalition to Save Our Mall and a native Washingtonian, is an art and architectural historian specializing in the medieval period and in Washington architecture.

CYNTHIA R. FIELD teaches at the Corcoran College of Art and Design. She is architectural historian emeritus, Smithsonian Institution, and coauthor of *The Castle: An Illustrated History of the Smithsonian Building.*

PATRICIA E. GALLAGHER is executive director of the National Capital Planning Commission. Her writings on urban design and the planning of open spaces have appeared in more than a dozen professional publications.

NATHAN GLAZER is professor of education and sociology emeritus at Harvard University. His books include *The Limits of Social Policy* and *We Are All Multiculturalists Now.*

RICHARD KURIN is director of the Smithsonian Institution Center for Folklife and Cultural Heritage and the author of *Reflections of a Culture Broker: A View from the Smithsonian.*

MICHAEL J. LEWIS teaches American art at Williams College. His books include *Frank Furness: Architecture and the Violent Mind* and *The Gothic Revival.*

WITOLD RYBCZYNSKI is Martin and Margy Meyerson Professor of Urbanism

at the University of Pennsylvania and has written the prizewinning *A Clearing in the Distance: Frederick Law Olmsted and America in the Nineteenth Century,* as well as *City Life: Urban Expectations in a New World* and *The Look of Architecture,* among other books. He currently serves on the U.S. Commission of Fine Arts.

EDITH L. B. TURNER is lecturer in the Department of Anthropology at the University of Virginia, coauthor of *Image and Pilgrimage in Christian Culture: An Anthropological Perspective,* author of *Among the Healers: Studies of Spiritual and Ritual Healing around the World,* and editor of the journal *Anthropology and Humanism.* She wrote the present essay while a senior fellow at the Center for the Study of World Religions, Harvard Divinity School.

FREDERICK TURNER is an internationally known poet and Founders Professor of Arts and Humanities at the University of Texas, Dallas. He has written *The Culture of Hope: A New Birth of the Classical Spirit,* among many other books.

RICHARD GUY WILSON is Commonwealth Professor of Architectural History at the University of Virginia, the author of *McKim, Mead & White, Architects,* and the editor of *Thomas Jefferson's Academical Village: The Creation of an Architectural Masterpiece.*

Contributors

Page numbers in *italics* refer to figures.